HAUNTED MAN'S REPORT

Courtesy of Charles M. Portis Estate LLC, All Rights Reserved.

HAUNTED MAN'S REPORT

READING CHARLES PORTIS

ROBERT COCHRAN

THE UNIVERSITY OF ARKANSAS PRESS
FAYETTEVILLE
2024

Copyright © 2024 by The University of Arkansas Press. All rights reserved. No part of this book should be used or reproduced in any manner without prior permission in writing from The University of Arkansas Press or as expressly permitted by law.

978-1-68226-246-7 (cloth)
978-1-68226-247-4 (paperback)
978-1-61075-816-1 (electronic)

28 27 26 25 24   5 4 3 2 1

Manufactured in the United States of America

Designed by Daniel Bertalotto

∞ The paper used in this publication meets the minimum requirements of the American National Standard for Permanence of Paper for Printed Library Materials Z39.48–1984.

Library of Congress Cataloging-in-Publication Data

Names: Cochran, Robert, 1943– author.
Title: Haunted man's report : reading Charles Portis / Robert Cochran.
Description: Fayetteville : The University of Arkansas Press, 2024. | Includes bibliographical references and index. | Summary: "Robert Cochran's Haunted Man's Report is a pioneering study of the novels and other writings of Charles Portis (1933–2020), best known for True Grit and its film adaptations. Hailed by one critic as 'the author of classics on the order of a twentieth-century Mark Twain' and as America's 'least-known great novelist,' Portis has garnered a devoted fan base with his inventive westerns, picaresque characters, and singular talent for injecting comedy into even the smallest turn of phrase"— Provided by publisher.
Identifiers: LCCN 2023033985 (print) | LCCN 2023033986 (ebook) | ISBN 9781682262467 (cloth) | ISBN 9781682262474 (paperback) | ISBN 9781610758161 (ebook)
Subjects: LCSH: Portis, Charles—Criticism and interpretation. | American literature—20th century—History and criticism. | Authors, American—20th century—Biography. | LCGFT: Literary criticism.
Classification: LCC PS3566.O663 Z66 2024 (print) | LCC PS3566.O663 (ebook) | DDC 813/.54—dc23/eng/20231114
LC record available at https://lccn.loc.gov/2023033985
LC ebook record available at https://lccn.loc.gov/2023033986

CONTENTS

Preface **VII**

—

1 —
"Words Failed Her": Journalism **1**

2 —
"Charity Endureth All Things": *Norwood* **21**

3 —
"Hard, Isolate, Stoic": *True Grit* **45**

4 —
"Horde Control" and "The Ancient Fear": *The Dog of the South* **65**

5 —
"American Pythagoras": *Masters of Atlantis* **95**

6 —
The Haunted Man's Report: *Gringos* **125**

7 —
"A Brief Reprieve": *Delray's New Moon* **147**

—

Acknowledgments **165**

Notes **167**

Suggested Articles, Profiles, Reviews **207**

Index **211**

PREFACE

"VIRTUALLY CLINICALLY *INSANE*"

Terrible injustices, according to sporadic but persistent report, had been visited upon, were yet being visited upon, an Arkansas author of transcendent merit. Charles McColl Portis, it was alleged, had produced at least one Great American Novel (claims were advanced for up to three, an amazing feat given he'd written just five) but was conspicuously lacking due recognition for such spectacular achievement. Comparisons to canonical heavyweights in "the quality lit game" were freely offered. Twain was a favorite from the outset, but over time the list grew increasingly lengthy, ranging from contemporaries close to home (Don DeLillo, Thomas Pynchon, Marilynne Robinson) to luminaries from more distant places and times—Gabriel García Márquez, Melville, Gogol, even Cervantes. One scholar went berserk on the comparisons front, listing thirty-one heavyweight names in an eleven-page survey.

The earliest protests concentrated fire not only on Mr. Portis's insufficient recognition but also on the unavailability of his works. "It is a crime and a scandal, it's virtually clinically *insane*," according to Ron Rosenbaum's 1998 *Esquire* article, "Our Least-Known Great Novelist," that only two of the master's novels were then in print. Before he finished, Rosenbaum called his least-known great novelist "the author of classics on the order of a twentieth-century Mark Twain" and cited Nora Ephron as comparing Portis "in scope, sophistication, and originality to Gabriel García Márquez."

Roy Blount Jr.'s celebration, published a year after Rosenbaum's, eschews comparisons to other writers to center on the pleasures associated with sustained attention to what seem at first glance throwaway lines. A Mexican hotel operator interrupts a conversation with *The Dog of the South* narrator Ray Midge to investigate a "disturbance" in his kitchen. Returning, he reports without elaboration, "It was nothing, the mop caught fire." Buried in a list of scams perpetrated by the same novel's quack doctor, Reo Symes, is the sale of "ranchettes in Colorado." Other items on the list are more immediately hilarious ("hail-damaged pears"), but tarry a moment with "ranchettes." (More soon on the burning mop.) A "ranch" is, first of all, *big*, right? A sprawling tract, hundreds, even thousands of acres, outbuildings and livestock monitored on horseback. But attempt to situate a "ranchette" in an actual landscape, and the term reveals itself as a realtor's clever appeal to a threadbare fantasy. A bleakness breaks the comic surface, highlighting the fundamental mendacity of marketing, the diminutive "-ette" now carrying a taint of huckster fraud, deprivation via ridiculous miniature. The Marlboro Man surveys his spread on a driveway Shriner trike. Speed right past the inconspicuous word, still chuckling over the hail-smooshed pears, and you miss such delayed-release gags.

And the flaming mop? It's "nothing"—really? In fact, it's Cleveland writ small and moved south. Up north, big red trucks, sirens wailing, roll down to douse the Cuyahoga; south of the border a single business owner addresses a blaze in a bucket—two conflagrations linked by a shared fuel source. But the kitchen fire itself should give us pause, the proprietor's "nothing" understood as reflexively protective of his establishment. Combustible solvents sloshing around in the *cocina* where they're grilling your fajitas? Check out pronto, before the whole place blows! Number such musings among your reading pleasures, and Portis's meandering narratives at once triple the laughs and darken the mood by shifting your thinking into his madcap grooves.

Ed Park's piece opens, like Rosenbaum's, with registration of grievance over his subject's lack of due recognition—"A GUY YOU'VE NEVER HEARD OF. BUT SHOULD," all in caps, forms the close of his extended subtitle. But he, like Blount, soon turns to the prose, generally opting for more extended samples. Here's Midge again, describing the workplace behavior of Guy Dupree, a former friend and colleague now run off to Mexico with Midge's wife and Ford Torino: "He hardly spoke at all except to mutter 'Crap' or 'What crap' as he processed news matter." It takes another pause to appreciate the economy of this, its deft capture of both Dupree's oafish misanthropy and Midge's prim rectitude in a single stroke. The copy editor who sees his own task as processing "news matter" is the same husband who sees the connubial bed as a site for "weekly embraces." As the story gets underway, he has just quit his job "to return to school," still swaddled in Dad's money at twenty-six. That his Norma has fled, even with the likes of Dupree, is already less of a surprise. Cormac McCarthy is cited in Park's title, though the essay thereafter steers clear of comparative claims, the better to focus on sampling Portis's achievements.

Yet another fan of the underappreciated author is Donna Tartt, the most successful in opening an apparently welcome communication channel with the allegedly reclusive author. She cold-called in search of permission to record a *True Grit* audiobook and (though initially mistaken for a persistent crank) won him over by the simple expedient of introducing herself not as a prying journalist but as a fellow human, southern to boot and, as it developed in conversation, sharing a familiarity with Memphis. "A long, relaxed conversation ensued," Tartt reports, many of its topics notable for their "lack of any reference whatsoever beyond the Reconstruction South." Portis "might as well have been . . . a veteran of the Civil War," she says, so studded was their talk with detailed reference to "the line of Lee's retreat" in Virginia or "General William 'Billy' Mahone and his lively counterattack in the late-war siege of Petersburg." By demonstrating her own conversational grace, Tartt secured her permission without even reading her prepared audition—"Naw," Portis said, "you're a good Mattie." Other conversations and letters followed, ended only by Portis's declining health. Tartt also makes flattering comparisons, her mention of Buster Keaton contending for the most insightful observation of the whole list. More about Keaton later.

All these, and many others, made powerful cases. By means ranging from vociferous claims to copious citations, they hammered home their point: this man Portis had created a strikingly varied cast of memorable characters endowed with unmistakable voices. His body of work deserved wider distribution, more sustained attention, enhanced appreciation. The labors of these articulate and well-connected supporters have long since paid off. Not only is every Portis novel back in print, but a wide-ranging "miscellany," *Escape Velocity*, diligently assembled and ably edited by Portis's leading Arkansas celebrant, Jay Jennings, appeared in 2012. It included generous portions of Portis's journalism and (in a revised paperback edition) all his short fiction, a play, and an article-length memoir. Jennings followed this up with a yet more solid achievement, editing a 2023 reissue of all five novels in a single volume plus a "Stories and Other Writings" selection for the gold-standard Library of America imprint.

If anything like a coherent quality lit canon survives, it's here. With this edition, the labors of Portis's supporters, sustained over a quarter century, would seem to have carried the day.

BUT IS IT DEEP TOO?

So how might one best set out to give this now-ascendant notion a boost, however modest? Or expose it to more searching doubt? We're not shills, after all, but rigorously trained, fair-minded assessors of fictional matter. A biography, perhaps? It's a plausible, even obvious idea. It's a familiar genre—I've turned out two and a half. (The third had a coauthor; the subject was not abandoned in midlife.)

But there is a problem. Portis fled interviews, refused book tours, did not pick up extra change by holding forth at aspirant writers' workshops. He was a private man. No Philip Roth he, holding audiences with prospective hagiographers, not even a coy Sam Beckett, providing his initial chronicler with "neither help nor hinder." Portis's aversion to the whole biographical enterprise appears clearly if obliquely expressed. Besides, the genre itself, however popular, carries with it a general air of unseemly intrusion. Janet Malcolm put her distaste in print—the biographer is a "professional burglar," the eager subject a megalomaniac fool. Joyce was more succinct—the avid would-be chronicler is a satanic figure, a "biografiend." It's also on closer inspection a comic genre if ever there was one—every week brings to the groaning shelf its hefty brick. Hear ye, hear ye—Ozymandias arrives with his herald.

Elvis got two volumes, more than thirteen hundred pages, from his best biographer, and even these doorstops are mere feuilletons when compared to the heroic evacuations of the genre's heavyweights—Freeman's four-volume veneration of Lee, Malone's six-volume prostration before Jefferson, both now widely regarded as the work of learned toadies. Our man fled this scene in his well-serviced pickup, all cylinders firing. The company of fools he might have found entertaining, but sycophants would have held little appeal. (There's a dark anecdote out there in the internet ozone on this topic: Portis is sitting at a bar minding his drink. An admirer intrudes, spouts superlatives, departs. A silence follows. "I'm not even the best writer in this bar," Portis mutters.)

So, no bio, but how else put a geriatric shoulder to the wheel? How about a closer look at the prose, the source at last of every attention, start to finish, the 1950s pieces for a student newspaper to a play and short story from 1996? A sustained examination, allegedly long overdue—how about this? With biographical detail only as needed and within strict boundaries. No hounding of relatives and friends for interviews, no *New York Review of Books* notice requesting correspondence, zero inquiry into details of private life. Straight-up lit crit.

But this subgenre, too, like biography, has its detractors. "Critics are the words without the music," said Jascha Heifetz. This canard no doubt inheres in part to the term itself, negative at the core, prompting images of a carping emphasis on flaw at the expense of appreciation. "Analysis" isn't measurably better, with its root in breakdown, a tedious atomizing, and the recent fashion for "interrogation" in academic circles only makes things worse, the nerdy prof promoted from library carrel to bare-bulb police station, the hapless artist subjected to third-degree grilling.

None of this here. As "Portishead" a volume as possible—this is the aim. Appreciation, a fan's notes. Of a wiseacre sort. The published scholarship on Portis is still pretty slim, often sludgy, and concentrated on *True Grit*. But there's a rich lode of sharply written article-length pieces from the popular press (see "Suggested Articles, Profiles, Reviews") aimed at boosting his readership and keeping his work in print. We'll take this job as accomplished, the better to preach to the choir. If you've read no Portis, you bought this volume too soon—better you should shelve it, read two novels first. *Norwood* and *True Grit* would start you at the beginning. The fan's notes can wait.

For years I foisted *The Dog of the South* on sophomore classes, billing it as "the funniest if not the finest thing on the syllabus," picking out paragraph-length riffs more or less at random and challenging anyone present to read them aloud with a straight face. Later, this volume newly in view, I scheduled a graduate seminar in the spring of 2022 devoted to the whole Portis list, *Escape Velocity* included. Hilarity is guaranteed, I told the cohort at the start. A Berryman "Dream Song" eulogy would have managed "he mutter funny" where the recently deceased Stevens got "spiffy." But they were all going pro in the lit or lit-crit business (they were a mix of MA, PhD, and MFA candidates), and our task there was to find out if it's deep too. You

XII   PREFACE

ENGL 5803/6803: Portis Seminar (Spring 2022) at the
University of Arkansas. *Photo by Leigh Pryor Sparks.*

know, the best that has been thought and said in the world. High seriousness. We devoted a sixteen-week semester to looking; here's a snap of our group. Names are listed in the acknowledgments.

TELLURIC CURRENTS

Truth is, I've had decades of haphazard prep for this task—journalism BA, like the author and for similar reasons; longtime quality-lit teacher; Arkansan not by birth but by half a century's residence; indulged for thirty-plus years as director of a center for the study of the region's culture; author of a dissertation on Beckett's plays. Portis's journalism, fiction, memoir, even the drama—these should be wheelhouse topics.

But here, right at the start, things threaten to get weird. Take even one step down the "I'm destined to do this" slope, and straightaway you're loony as any Gnomon. You'll open your email one soon morning and find yourself joined with Lamar Jimmerson on some "Odd Birds of Arkansas and Oklahoma" list. Speaking of Gnomons, however, summons Indiana, as the fictional Burnette, "most fashionable suburb" of factual Gary, is home to *Masters of Atlantis*'s Gnomon Temple. And then, yet more unsettling, just twenty-five pages past the Gary temple, at the Naval Observatory in Washington, DC, a Professor Cezar Golescu is introduced, in residence as subordinate "custodian of almanacs and star catalogues." He's Romanian. Still later, in *Gringos*, a lawyer named Nardo talks incessantly about his football career at (fictional) Bonar College in Illinois. All this is wholly coincidental, of course, but I attended high school and taught college in Indiana, attended college in Illinois, and spent the 1985–86 academic year as a Fulbright lecturer in Cluj-Napoca, Romania. The clincher: I also edited and wrote the introduction for a book about Arkansas botanical illustrator and naturalist Kent Bonar.

Before a single page is produced, then, occupational and biographical alignments add up, words like "destiny" surface in the cerebral word feed, and the slippery slope returns at steeper pitch. Telluric Currents flow ever faster underfoot, and right off you've got seated at the keyboard a nutjob brother in delusion of Maurice Babcock exhilarated as he senses his destiny as "Master of the New Cycle." A bizarre sense of mission speeds the pacemaker-monitored pulse of the codger assessor. We'll fight this pull, batten the hatches against the folly of an ordinary turd indulging himself as a cosmically authorized exegete, but we're going in expecting fun.

1 —

"WORDS FAILED HER"

JOURNALISM

FEATURE EDITOR

The belated arrival of due recognition of Portis the novelist stands in stark contrast to the applause that greeted his earliest bylined efforts as a journalist. In September 1957, incensed at a *Time* magazine cover story correctly understood as insulting to Arkansas, he produced "Of *TIME* and the River and Greasy Creek, Etc." for the University of Arkansas student newspaper, the *Arkansas Traveler*. It was only his second column, but it made quite a splash. "Wide Acclaim Given *Traveler* Feature Writer Portis" crowed a front-page *Traveler* story on October 23, ten days after the column had been reprinted in the Sunday *Arkansas Democrat Magazine.* Letters had come in from across the state, a Springdale attorney reported mailing the column to the *Time* offices and receiving a cordial if predictable reply (also printed), and in December a substantial excerpt from the column was reprinted in the Davidson College student newspaper in North Carolina. Heady stuff for a student writer in his first weeks on the job.

The piece itself, along with the other "Feature Editor" columns, holds up poorly today. The *Time* essay was feeble stuff, "The Sahara of the Bozart" reprised for the thousandth time without Mencken's punchy invective. But instead of focusing on the *Time* story's egregious lapses into yokel stereotype Portis launched a scattershot assault on the magazine's owner/editor Henry Luce—the man himself, his spouse, and all his works. Luce is "ugly," his spouse is "about as feminine as a meat-axe" (this attributed to the playwright Irwin Shaw), and his publication empire's flagship journals, *Time* and *Life*, are "for people who can't think" and "for people who can't read." The sustained critique of Clare Boothe Luce would now be read as sharply misogynist, and both husband and wife are scolded for simply being old. It's puerile stuff, despite the literary window dressing of the references to Wolfe (in the title) and Steinbeck (in the body), though the final paragraph does feature a now-signature lowbrow panache: "A source not at all close to the President summed up the situation in New York this way: The whole damned place ought to be plowed up and planted in turnip greens."

Portis was right, forty years later, when he dismissed it as "my smartass response" to the *Time* story's stale hillbilly caricature. He also told fellow journalist Roy Reed he wasn't sure he "ever worked for the *Traveler*, in any formal way," though in fact he's bylined as "Traveler Feature Editor" on all but the first column. The "smartass" tone of the "Of *TIME* and the River" piece is typical of the other columns as well, with the follow-up "Imaginary Poll Divulges Opinions on Integration," published on October 1, an especially cringeworthy number.

The author clearly thinks his imaginary segregationists are loathsome bigots ("Cretin P. Slime" is their featured spokesperson), but N-word formulations, standard for the day, flow easily and unselfconsciously, and a final respondent, identified as "Booker T. Thurgood," puts himself on record as favoring "utter, immediate, and complete mongrelization."

The initial piece, where Portis's name (he's "Buddy Portis" for the whole run) is followed by "of the Traveler Staff," may hold the most durable interest. Appearing on September 17, a week before the assault on the Luce empire, "Who, What, When, Where" is described in an editorial prefatory note as "a parody on an editor's column such as might be seen in a back, back woods weekly newspaper." What follows is a hilarious if slapdash send-up of the very columns Portis was editing for the *Northwest Arkansas Times* in his first paying job as a journalist. The "parody" is action packed. Five elderly women suffer hip fractures (two in motor vehicle accidents involving sons-in-law); three are "reported to be doing nicely," though one is "reported to be dead." Members of "Busy Bee Circle No. 3" hear a talk on "Red China and Church Work," their hostess going all in for the theme by serving her guests "fig newtons cut in the shape of China." A local soldier musters out, returning home to his mother with a "beautiful satin-covered pillow from Fort Chaffee with a picture of a tank on it." A "golden wedding anniversary" is celebrated by "Mr. and Mrs. J. E. B. Stuart."

"Mr. and Mrs. J. E. B. Stuart," "Red China and Church Work," even the Busy Bees—all recur as staples of Portis's comedy. Not quite a decade later, in the first chapter of *Norwood*, moved from the Busy Bees meeting to the Nipper Junior High Essay Contests via the repellent voice of Grady Fring the Kredit King, the political note resurfaces: "Their theme was 'Communism in the National Council of Churches.' They laid it right on the line. Wrote their hearts out. I was proud to be a part of it." Civil War references are even more recurrent. Explaining to Norwood his ruptured friendship with Nipper, Fring claims he outmaneuvered the Houston oilman on a deal involving rental properties and a registered bull "like Stonewall Jackson took Nathaniel P. Banks in the Valley of the Shenandoah." Ray Midge and Dr. Reo Symes bring sustained analyses of Civil War campaigns to their *The Dog of the South* conversations. *True Grit*'s Mattie Ross is explicitly proud of her father's service, while Cogburn and LaBoeuf exchange intermittent attacks on the other's wartime record. The Busy Bees themselves, transported to Indiana, undergo gender reassignment to reappear as a "very exclusive lawyers' club" in *Masters of Atlantis*, gathered for seminars on "Systematic Estate Looting" at their annual retreat.

"I edited the country correspondence from these lady stringers in Goshen and Elkins," Portis told Reed in 2001. "My job was to edit out all the life and charm from these homely reports. Some fine old country expression, or a nice turn of phrase—out they went." His "relaxed conversation" with Donna Tartt revisited these columns when she mentioned a grandmother, an "indefatigable writer" for the local newspaper, who would "be writing about Grover Cleveland and go off on some rant about the danger of water fluoridization." Great stuff, Portis told her. "Those are just the kind of lively asides I enjoy." Back in Fayetteville in 1957, finishing up his BA in journalism, Portis was paid to take out such liveliness at the downtown offices of the *Northwest Arkansas Times*. Up on campus he put them back in the *Arkansas Traveler* for a comic spoof. Over the following decades he spun them into fictional gold.

MEMPHIS AND LITTLE ROCK

Portis followed the big splash of his stint as a college newspaper's feature editor with an astonishingly rapid ascent up journalism's career ladder. Beginning in the second half of 1958 as a general assignment reporter for the Memphis *Commercial Appeal*, he rose by 1964 to London bureau chief for the *New York Herald Tribune*, one of the most coveted positions in the profession.

This interval was filled with both opportunities and challenges. In his six months in Memphis, Portis covered the illness and death of Elvis Presley's mother, his stories skillfully walking the rhetorical fine line between respect for the son's and husband's grief and skeptical regard for the tawdry public circus surrounding it on all sides. Interviewed in a hospital corridor, the singer explains his widely reported generosity toward his family with understated force: "I like to do what I can for my folks. We didn't have nothin' before, nothin' but a hard way to go." Two days later, the funeral report opens with Presley "shaken and limp with grief," leaning on his mother's casket, but three paragraphs down the reportorial eye, shifting to the gathered spectators, turns colder: "Most of the crowd at the service, and later at the cemetery, appeared more interested in the singer than the funeral."

Portis's next stop was Little Rock, early in 1959 at the *Arkansas Gazette*. "I came over to Little Rock one weekend and asked Mr. Nelson about a job," he told Reed. He started on the police beat, already familiar from his time in Fayetteville for the *Northwest Arkansas Times*—"Judge Ptak's municipal court. A weird judge, to say the least. Justice was swift there"—but soon moved to general reporting and sometime in midyear was asked to take over the Our Town column, published five days each week with a longer feature on Sundays. "Clumsy, half-baked stuff," he remembered. "It was a grind." He did recall one Sunday piece on a big cockfighting meet in Garland County (from March 20, 1960)—"high-rollers in dusty Cadillacs" with their "fighting chickens," shouting out bets with "their thick wads of cash." Here his disregard for the scene is as evident as his sympathy for the animals (the "drag pit" where wounded birds were dispatched is described at gruesome length—"It may go on for hours there"). There was also "Rare Specimen" earlier the same year (on February 3), a column devoted to Arkansas novelist Francis Irby Gwaltney, who was asked about the challenges of "writing about a people, a state, with almost no literary traditions." No hint here of the columnist imagining a future.

The grind lasted a year and a bit more—Portis's final piece for the *Arkansas Gazette* on Sunday, October 9, 1960, profiled Homer and Jethro after their successful run of grandstand performances at the Arkansas Livestock Show—but ended without an explicit sign-off by the columnist, headed east for a job with the *New York Herald Tribune*. This one would last longer, a four-year run, and would center on a return to general assignment reporting, where the violent crucible of the 1960s civil rights movement would elicit from the still-young ex-Marine his most distinguished journalistic writing. The so-called New Journalism was just getting started, and the worst of the Vietnam debacle was still to come, but Portis and his colleagues in Birmingham and Tuscaloosa and Jackson in the early 1960s were in a very real sense reporting from a war zone, where Old South officialdom's version of events was every bit as mendacious as any "five o'clock follies" press briefing from Saigon. "Californian Is Charged with Murder of Evers" was the now-infamous Jackson *Clarion-Ledger* headline for the story of the arrest of Greenwood fertilizer salesman and Klansman Byron De La Beckwith for the murder of Mississippi civil rights activist Medgar Evers in 1963. Portis covered that story for the *Herald Tribune*, producing what may be the best of a series of remarkable essays.

NEW YORK

At first the work for the *Herald Tribune* was similar in basic content to the stories featured in the Our Town column in Little Rock. A trainload of women journeys to Washington for a peace march to the White House. A Brooklyn longshoreman loses custody of his pet lion. A four-part series describes the trials and triumphs of a "Five-Day Plan to Stop Smoking." The reporter does not surface as a participant in the account of the lion but makes seriocomic appearances in the peace march and smoking stories. In the latter, he writes, "I was the only one in our class of 12 who failed." There were hard news stories too—*Escape Velocity*, the "miscellany" of Portis's work issued in 2021, includes his 1962 account of a horrific boiler explosion at the New York Telephone Company that killed twenty-three people and injured nearly one hundred, most of them women on their lunch break in the company cafeteria. Here Portis's piece is an eyewitness account, though he moves to the first person only in his final sentence: a telephone, knocked to the floor, is still ringing, "its little red extension light winking. I wondered who was calling but I did not answer it." (Unanswered phones also struck other reporters at the scene—*New York Times* reporter David Anderson filed a story with a "Phones in Back Ring Unanswered" in the subhead.)

These stories are already more than a half century old and sometimes come across as dated at the most basic phrasal level. Female office workers in their twenties and older are no longer referred to as "girls," and only a very foolish reporter would today lead off a story on a women's peace march with a reference to "tweedy, well-shod matrons." The basic tone, however, in story after story, shows a deft talent for suggesting authorial approval or disapproval with the subtlety necessary for getting his copy into print. Even the story about the longshoreman with the pet lion goes out of its way to mention his "exemplary" care for the animal, and the marching women soon take over as the stars of their story.

One key is the naming and quoting of three of the women, including "Mrs. Ruth Gage-Colby of New York," described as "one of the powers in the movement," while the president himself, who does not "come out to greet them" at the White House, remains nameless (it would have been JFK). His later press-conference remarks, quoted at length, only make things worse: "I recognized why they were here," he opens, already flailing. "There were a great number of them. It was in the rain." The close is a lofty fatuity: "I understood what they were attempting to say and therefore I consider that their message was received." Pathetic—Camelot's prince as tongue-tied stuffed shirt! The heart of the story, however obliquely presented, is unmistakable: seventeen hundred women charter a train at their own expense for a seven-hour round trip to the nation's capital for an hour's march in the rain at the White House, only to have the biggest suit in the land, lout of the story, stiff them with no greeting and a hash of belated gobbledygook. The student columnist of 1957, flinging muck at Henry Luce and all his works, has seriously upped his game.

There's also a gem of a cameo sketch in the peace march story. Seventy-year-old butcher Abe Stafansky gets only two lines, but they're enough to establish a distinctive character. Asked if he's worried about calling in sick and then showing up in the paper "on a women's peace train to Washington," Abe likes his chances: "My boss, he reads nothing. The stock market maybe. Put my name in the stock market, he might see it." A more sustained look at the story's structure reveals Stafansky as a nicely poised foil to the president too busy to greet the marchers. Abe's self-presentation is modest—"Fifty years I'm an American and I thought I'd like to see the White House"—but he's a blue-collar guy, an immigrant reading a Yiddish newspaper, on a train seven hours, out a day's wages, trudging through the rain. He's also a feminist and a peacenik, a "Four Freedoms" citizen right out of the Rockwell paintings, despite the low profile. No wonder the women "relented under Mr. Stafansky's charm," despite an announced no-men policy. Portis's presentation is a warm, oblique salute. His skill with such sketches—the surface mastery of speech patterns and revealing detail coupled with deft structural alignments—will be a central staple of his fiction. The deadpan tone under it all will be, as here, a signature note.

SALINGER AND MALCOLM X

Portis's time in New York was enlivened by two encounters destined to become staples of later reports about him. He comes off well in both. One, centered on an interview with Malcolm X, has a clear basis in fact; the other, not so solidly anchored, focuses on a chance meeting on an airplane with J. D. Salinger. Roy Reed's *Arkansas Gazette* interview elicited a first-person account of the Malcolm X interview, but Portis apparently left behind not a syllable of comment on the airplane interaction. (More on Salinger later.) Locating the interview at "a studio at some radio station in New York," Portis tells Reed he was "asking him about the 'X' business," why he would reject the assigned surname of "Little" yet retain Malcolm. His mother gave it to him, Malcolm X replied. "Good point," Portis affirms. "A sharp fellow." He goes on to volunteer with some pride that he'd been treated "with a little less contempt" after making a remark about how Marcus Garvey's "back-to-Africa" movement "went nowhere." "He had a presence," Portis concludes. Pressed by Reed about his repeatedly using "Mr. X" as a term of address, Portis replies that he probably did. "But what can you do? To call him 'Malcolm' would have been a little familiar, wouldn't it?" It would have, and in fact the Nation of Islam spokesman may have explicitly forbidden such first-name familiarity at the outset—he at least occasionally reminded his questioners that he was not a dining-car waiter (he'd been one) at their beck and call.

Tom Wolfe's account, in his 1973 anthology, *The New Journalism*, is very different, presenting Portis, labeled as "the original laconic cutup," as deploying the repeated "Mr. X" as a sarcastic send-up. This deliberate needling, Wolfe reports, soon had his formidable interviewee "furious": "He was climbing the goddamned acoustical tiles." Wolfe's vivid story has a surface plausibility, and the "laconic cutup" description seems especially apt, but even a cursory examination registers Portis's account as essentially accurate. Roy Reed's history of the *Arkansas Gazette* includes an account of another "cutup" episode narrated by longtime Arkansas reporter, editorial writer, and columnist Ernest Dumas involving a "middle of the night" prank call to cultural anthropologist Margaret Mead. Portis, however, was having none of it: "Buddy Portis was offended and left." Portis's account also rings true to the general behavior of Malcolm X. A famously self-educated man who continually revised his own thinking, he was a great respecter of education who over time developed relationships with reporters, including white reporters, who wrote about him. Struck by the quality of Peter Goldman's *St. Louis Post-Dispatch* stories on the Nation of Islam, Malcolm X set up an initial interview in 1962, which led eleven years later to Goldman's still-respected biography, *The Death and Life of Malcolm X*.

As it happens, however, Portis's appearance with Malcolm X has been preserved. The "radio station in New York" remembered by Portis in his conversation with Reed was WCBS, and the interview took place on a regular thirty-minute program called *Let's Find Out* aired on Sunday, June 9, 1963, from 12:30 to 1:00 p.m. Four voices are heard—guest Malcolm X; host Joe Dembo, the station's news and public affairs director; and two interviewers, Lou Adler and Portis. Adler worked for WCBS. Both interviewers and the host pose questions, but Malcolm X does most of the talking. He's the guest. He's a very forceful, even fervent speaker, confident in the validity of his position, but there is at no time the slightest audible hint of anger on his part. Portis's memory of having raised questions about the ineffectiveness of prior "back-to-Africa" movements, including Garvey's, is accurate. He does exactly this, eliciting from Malcolm X a deftly humorous response to the effect that if contemporary movements are no better, white folks have nothing to worry about. Malcolm X is throughout painstakingly careful to present himself as a spokesperson for "the honorable Elijah Muhammad." There's absolutely nothing incendiary in the whole program—Portis's "Mr. X" usages certainly do not come off as mocking or baiting. Wolfe, who may or may not have even heard the program, concocted a vivid tale with little to no basis in the day's events.

The real litmus papers for Portis's attitudes toward civil rights efforts by Black Americans are the many reports he produced while covering the civil rights movement in the South. The laconic cutup is present, certainly, but the dominant note, explicit even in the "straight news" pieces, is a steadily mounting sense of outrage at the scenes before him. The observer's admiration for the peace marchers in Washington is clear enough, as is his scorn for the Arkansas cockfighters, but his civil rights reporting would introduce a much wider range. From the end of Georgia's Albany Movement in the summer of 1962, through Alabama's Birmingham violence and George Wallace's shabby schoolhouse-door theatrics in Tuscaloosa, to the cold-blooded assassination of Medgar Evers in his Jackson, Mississippi, driveway in 1963, Portis would be moved to place on view the values that would later, more covertly, serve to both ground and motivate the actions of his fictional worlds. Given all this, one might have guessed, even without hearing the tape, that Portis's retrospective account of his interactions with Malcolm X was fundamentally accurate.

The Salinger tale is less securely rooted in fact and of interest mostly for what it suggests, if true, of Portis's priorities. Portis apparently said nothing of the encounter on record. The source is Wolfe, another cutup, though far from laconic. He's a talking head in *Salinger*, a widely panned 2013 film, though the mystery deepens as later edits often omit the clip with the Portis tale. Here's a bare-bones summary: Portis, boarding a plane, notes a fellow passenger seated just in front of him who bears a strong resemblance to the famously reclusive author. Coincidence morphs into opportunity when a new arrival sits down across the aisle. *Hey, Jerry,* he says, *great to see you. How's it going?* Portis starts scribbling. On leaving the plane, he approaches Salinger and identifies himself as a reporter, provoking a reaction so overwrought, so *vulnerable,* that he on the spot tears up or crumples his notes or perhaps hands them over—in any event makes clear his unwillingness to add to Salinger's distress.

The story might appear on its face improbable. Would any person, let alone Salinger, speak openly in so constricted a public space, even to a friend? Could even the most inconspicuous listener carry out such sustained stenography unnoticed? The final, climactic scene, however, such premises accepted, seems wholly credible. This is the man offended to the point of angry departure by the nocturnal prank call to Margaret Mead, the reporter concerned about coming across as too "familiar" in interviewing Malcolm X. In the fiction ahead Portis would fashion characters who win the affection of readers, despite their obvious flaws, by recurrent acts of consideration for others—Norwood "throttling back on his normal pace" to accommodate the strides of the world's smallest perfect man, Ray Midge unwilling to "embarrass Norma" (despite the fact she's at least abetted Dupree's theft of Midge's Torino) by posting a stolen car notice in the Little Rock newspapers, and Lamar Jimmerson adding sympathy to gullibility in the opening pages of *Masters of Atlantis* by shelling out for dinner and a hotel room for a stranger with at least three fake names (and nationalities).

BACK SOUTH

Portis covered civil rights stories in the South for most of the yearlong period from the summer of 1962, when he covered the final phase of the Albany Movement's pioneering attempts by civil rights activists to dismantle the prevailing segregationist regimes in southwestern Georgia, until the fall of 1963, when he left for England to head the *Herald Tribune*'s London office. Civil rights was not entirely a new topic for him—a 1959 Our Town column for the *Arkansas Gazette* had reported on the national press corps in Little Rock for the reopening of the schools. But there he'd been the local columnist, sending up the "wilted Dacron and damp mustaches" of the outlanders in Arkansas's August heat, oblivious to the available woods they were standing in as they worried about access to restrooms. Now he was that national press, often bitterly resented, covering headline stories in a summer when tensions between long-frustrated civil-rights demands and determined segregationist resistance flared into riot and murder.

The stories he filed, especially those from 1963, carry to new levels the skills already apparent in earlier pieces. When you're a news reporter, focused on events themselves, discouraged by journalistic conventions from indulging your own responses, you quickly learn to let their most repellent bad actors convict themselves with their own tongues. Little Rock segregationist leader Amis Guthridge's willingness to propound his retrograde views—"He would talk freely and at great length"—prepared Portis for his May 10 "Birmingham Bargaining Before Watchful World" dispatch from Birmingham, where the more bellicose if comparably voluble "Bull" Connor spoke enthusiastically of blasting rabbis with fire hoses: " 'If them rabbis get in the way, we'll knock their asses down with the hose like anybody else,' said Mr. Connor." Two days earlier he'd openly rejoiced at the injuries the high-pressure hoses had inflicted on Reverend Fred Shuttlesworth, an aide of Dr. King's: " 'I been waitin' a week to see Shuttlesworth knocked down,' said Commissioner Eugene ('Bull') Connor. 'Too bad it wasn't a hearse.' "

Portis's two-stage portrait of Alabama Highway Patrol director Al Lingo at the riot in Birmingham following the firebombing of the Gaston Motel headquarters of the civil rights leaders is even more scathing. Lingo's very arrival (belated, at 1:10 a.m.) is described as a "frightening development"—he jumps from the car with a twelve-gauge shotgun and heads toward the crowd. " 'I'll stop those——,' he said." Lingo is eventually persuaded back into the car by a city policeman, contenting himself with "jabbing a couple of Negroes with his gun on the way," though the scene ends ominously: "But Col. Lingo would be heard from again before the night was over."

Act 2 occurs two and a half hours later:

> It was pretty much all over at 3:40, when the state troopers began clubbing Negroes sitting on their porches. . . .
> . . . And so the battle ended with the state policemen, who had played only a very minor role in the actual quelling of the riot, rapping old Negro men in rocking chairs.

Col. Lingo and his men had been chafing all week at the moderation and restraint of Chief Moore and his city police. "Moore is a Boy Scout," said Col. Lingo.

Morning breaks with a police loudspeaker "warning individual Negroes to 'get off the God damn streets, get.'" Portis's account, appearing on May 13, closes with thinly veiled ironies: "But someone put a stop to that, evidently because it was Sunday and Mother's Day." The story's final line pulls back to note the ambient scene: "It was a sparkling morning, and around the post office the air was fragrant with the scent of magnolia blossoms." "How the Night Exploded into Terror" is a peak moment in Portis's reporting—the prose is laconic enough, but the cutup note is entirely absent, subordinated to a Swiftian indignation.

But clowns like Connor and Lingo were easy targets; quote them verbatim and they stood revealed. The state cops fared no better—though a hard-nosed reader of the scene on the porches might cavil at the use of "rapping." Rapping is something teachers once did with rulers to the knuckles of little boys caught chewing their fingernails. But "rapping" here is likely the Portis eye for scrupulous accuracy in action—his contempt for the cops' behavior comes through clearly enough, though unlike Connor with his wishes for a hearse the officers were not in this instance bent upon serious injury. Old men of any hue, however, are easily bruised and broken. Here they're a citizen chorus—the reader is on the scene in Birmingham; he or she could get clubbed. It's a terrible scene, peace officers turned B-movie bikers, sowing terror. The "rocking chairs," every traditional resonance violated, are a characteristic Portis detail.

Terrible as it was, the night had its heroes, and Portis's account is careful to record their courage. A "Negro civil defense unit" attempting to restrain the rioters "took just as much abuse and pummelling" as white policemen. Chief Inspector William J. Haley moves "fearlessly from one hot spot to another, taking punches and kicks and rocks, yet never losing his head." He's eventually felled by a brick and taken to the hospital. A photo of the bleeding Haley, described in the caption as "aided and comforted by both whites and Negroes," appears with Portis's story.

It's helpful to remember that Portis was in town for several days, and at least some local readers seem to have read his dispatches with displeasure. When he notes in the Sunday, May 12, story, "Call for a White Boycott Menaces Racial Accord," that reporters were ejected from a meeting the previous Friday, there is a note of pride in his singling out of one for special mention: "A reporter from the *Herald Tribune*, in particular, was booed."

"Klan Rally—Just Talk," a much shorter piece appearing the same day as "How the Night Exploded into Terror," follows a similar approach, though it deploys several comic touches wholly absent from the story about the night of terror (which itself contains a short synopsis of the rally). Bessemer, once a steel town (now an Amazon town) twelve miles southwest of Birmingham, was no place for the fainthearted, but Portis had seen much worse. Just a decade earlier, in 1953, not yet twenty, an infantryman and BAR rifleman with the US Marines, he had celebrated the armistice in a fortified bunker called Camp Ginger. The distance to North Korean and Chinese People's Volunteer Army positions had been measured in meters. He had seen war from Rooster Cogburn's "bullet department." Nothing the kleagles (Klan eagles, get it?) in Birmingham were bringing to the table came anywhere close.

Lacking a voluble Klan counterpart to Connor, Portis summarizes the speeches as "three hours of nothing but Kennedy jokes and invocations of Divine guidance" and describes the event itself as "a much duller affair than one might expect." Two "huge crosses," he reports, were set ablaze, one adorned "with an effigy of Martin Luther King," the Klan chuckleheads apparently blind to the implied elevation of the civil rights leader to messianic status. Your cross, sheet guys—it's a locus of veneration. Mattie Ross, present at this wannabe hanging, would have sent them to Luke's twenty-third chapter. Laugh at them, Father, for they have no clue.

One excerpt from the three hours of blather registers the reporter's contempt via an unusually explicit aside. "If so much as one drop of ****** [N-word] blood gets in your baby's cereal," one speaker claims, "the baby will surely die in one year." "He did not explain," Portis adds, "how he thought a negro would come to bleed in anyone's cereal." His final paragraph opens, "By 10:30 one of the crosses had collapsed and the other was just smoldering." A summary assessment then ends the dismissive account: "Everyone drifted away and the grand dragon of Mississippi disappeared grandly into the Southern night, his car engine hitting on about three cylinders." The laconic cutup, tightly leashed for most of the civil rights assignments, is here let out for a romp.

When he turns from journalism to fiction, Portis often uses carelessness or incompetence in vehicle maintenance (see *The Dog of the South*'s Guy Dupree and the Duvall of *Delray's New Moon*) as reliable indicators of character flaws—and the Mississippi not-so-grand dragon signals his haplessness with his sputtering ride. (There seems to be a decent chance, incidentally, that Portis may have recalled as a model for his account a celebrated Klan story from North Carolina five years earlier, in 1958, when panicked Klan leader James "Catfish" Cole, his rally ambushed and his comrades routed by armed Lumbees, ran his car into a ditch in his haste to escape and by some accounts had to be towed out by jeering tribesmen. *Life* ran a photo spread titled "Bad Medicine for the Klan" with a full-page shot of two smiling Lumbees posing with a captured Klan flag. One was a veteran, according to the caption.)

One month later, Portis was in Tuscaloosa, where his account of the integration of the University of Alabama was closer in tone to the stories he'd filed in Birmingham from the days before the bombings and the riot. The close-up, hour-by-hour reporting of the scenes on the street in "How the Night Exploded into Terror" was preceded by more hopeful pieces from the preceding days of discussion— "Birmingham Bargaining Before Watchful World" headlined his May 10 story—filled with middle-distance, sometimes skeptical analyses of strategies and tactics pursued by demonstrators and city officials. On May 11, under a "Birmingham Peace: An Omen" head, Portis ends his two-sentence lead with overt expression of doubt: "After a month of mass singing, marching, something fairly close to rioting, and 2,000 arrests, Negroes have won the Battle of Birmingham with a four-point settlement. Or so it seems."

No such uncertainty enters the Tuscaloosa story, presented in the language of stagecraft throughout—the events of the historic day (the successful registration for classes at the University of Alabama of James A. Hood and Vivian Juanita Malone, both named in full in Portis's lead) are presented as a tightly scripted "ballet," a "moral drama" with a "final act" and "final moves of the game." At the center of the "pageant" was Alabama governor George Wallace, as talkative in Tuscaloosa as "Bull" Connor had been in Birmingham. His "solemn proclamation" delivered, he "got into his car and drove off in a roar of motorcycle police." The real actions of day then proceeded. Deputy Attorney General Nicholas Katzenbach, having informed Governor Wallace of his disinterest in theater (" 'Governor, I'm not interested in a show,' said Mr. Katzenbach. 'I don't know what the purpose of the show is' "), proceeded to make the only speech that mattered: "They will register today, they will go to school tomorrow and they will attend this summer session. They will remain on the campus."

The ink was barely dry on the successful midafternoon registrations of Mr. Hood and Ms. Malone in Tuscaloosa on June 11 when in the first hours of the next morning NAACP field secretary Medgar Evers was assassinated, shot in the back from ambush in Jackson, Mississippi. Portis arrived later that day for what was surely the most wrenching of his civil rights assignments. He'd been covering the demonstrations for months and seen beatings and bombings, elderly women blasted by high-pressure fire hoses and old men clubbed in rocking chairs on their own porches. But this was straight-up murder, a calculated political assassination carried out in service to a race-based social order. The stories he filed from Jackson perform their journalistic tasks—with who and what smoothly joined to where and when—but if Portis had often been appalled and dismayed by what he'd witnessed in Georgia and Alabama, the scene in Mississippi brought unprecedented outrage and contempt to his reports. "Murder in Mississippi," published on June 13, the day after the killing, stands out for its insistent focus on the victim and his family. Evers's name (with the adjective "respected") is the opening line, and a three-paragraph excerpt from a year-old interview making clear his expectation of and readiness for the attempt on his life occupies the piece's center. A president, a governor, a mayor, and a "man in a beer joint," all speaking boilerplate or worse, are much more briefly cited, and the story closes with Mrs. Evers's tearful hope for continued pursuit of the justice for which her husband had died, a "plea that all of you here will be able to draw some of his strength, some of his courage. Nothing can bring him back," she says, "but this cause can live on."

"Fires of Hate in Jackson," published on June 14, is a remarkable essay that pushes the boundaries of journalistic practice at several points. In particular, the already open critique of police brutality in the Birmingham dispatches appears in Jackson one month later as unreserved sarcasm. The police are "tired and . . . frustrated," Portis reports, "but they seemed to draw some relief yesterday by clubbing a Negro girl on the head." Later, "the crowd scattered," and "there being no one else to threaten, the police turned on a group of newsmen." The reporter's conclusion, stated in its own one-sentence paragraph and attributed to no third party: "The Jackson police do not like to have people taking notes when they are going about their business."

Not all of Portis's attention is focused on the depredations of the police. He is equally contemptuous of their bosses: "Later in the afternoon, 11 Negro ministers called on Mayor Allen Thompson to ask for bread, and he gave them velvet-wrapped stone." Many citizens of a city so richly supplied with churches might presumably pick up on the Sermon on the Mount reference. What they might make of it is another matter.

But "Fires of Hate in Jackson" stands out most of all for a carefully plotted and subtly executed admission of its inevitable failure to capture the full horror of both Medgar Evers's assassination and the city of Jackson's salt-in-the-wounds response. Its lead paragraph's second sentence describes a "Negro woman" who "stood on her front porch yesterday afternoon and simply screamed and cried." It's a shocking image for a report's opening, and it's amplified near the piece's midpoint, after readers have witnessed in detail the bloody scene on her porch: "When the dust had settled, the Negro woman stood on her porch and screamed hysterically at the police. Words failed her."

Portis does his job, produces the words, describes the beatings and the arrests and the velvet-wrapped stone. But he knows from the outset words will fail him too, so he bravely puts the failure in his lead, a woman's wordless scream the emblem of a community ravaged by its paid defenders. "Klan Rally—Just Talk" is a fine piece, appropriately dismissive, worthy of a consideration it never got for the Library of America *Reporting Civil Rights* volumes (which seem, oddly, to lack a single report centered on a Klan rally). But "Fires of Hate in Jackson" is even better, a modest masterpiece, bringing top-drawer parallels to mind. A newspaper story as quality lit? You bet. A 272-word speech?

Check out another instance of the "words must fail" trope: "The world will little note nor long remember, what we say here." *The Federalist Papers* were also newspaper stories.

A vast rhetorical gap exists between the spring and summer high points of "How the Night Exploded into Terror" and "Fires of Hate in Jackson" and Portis's run-up story to the now-iconic March on Washington in August. "The Marchers: Blueprint for Protest" appeared in the Sunday *Herald Tribune* three days before the Wednesday event, with " 'Revolt' and Jamboree" in an italic subhead above the headline and a two-column photo of two smiling marchers at its left. Copy editors did the heads, and both are remarkably opaque, but it turns out they're adroitly chosen, given the text beneath. It's a uniquely dismissive piece, closer in tone to "Klan Rally—Just Talk" than to anything else in Portis's civil rights journalism. There's nothing overtly hostile, but a sustained note of mockery prevails—it's clear the author is not a big fan of marches. The marchers themselves are identified (twice) as "unemployed," and those scheduled to join them are presented in a jumbled, seriocomic list: "Debbie Reynolds will be there Wednesday with the Negro unemployed, and Mayor Wagner, and Malcolm X, Dr. Eugene Carson Blake, the Ladies Garment Workers, Roy Wilkins, Marlon Brando, the New York Association of Elks, and a man from Chicago named Ledger Smith who is said to be roller skating to Washington."

This reads as genuinely bizarre conflation—individual luminaries lost like Waldo in a mob of Elks, garment workers, and unemployed African American citizens. Angry African American citizens, as Portis notes later, in a similarly snarky tone: "Still, the spectre of riot hangs over the march. Some 200,000 angry people in one place on a hot day in August makes for a combustible situation. Throw in Malcolm X, the Black Muslim leader who has been gleefully predicting violence for months from his Harlem soapbox, and Nazi George Lincoln Rockwell, who is trying to rally a master race counter-march for Wednesday, and things look bad indeed."

The "Harlem soapbox" would have been recognized even in 1963 as a striking underestimation of Malcolm X's position. He had access to mainstream microphones, as Portis certainly knew, having interviewed him two months earlier for the WCBS radio show. The implied moral equivalence with Rockwell, now mostly forgotten outside storm trooper dress-up circles, seems even more unsupportable today. Perhaps Portis's distaste for the virtue-signaling "hundred or so Hollywood people who are coming from California by chartered plane" got the best of him, but "The Marchers: Blueprint for Protest" comes across as a puzzling, peevish, even slapdash performance. Martin Luther King Jr., the event's featured speaker and today the indelibly etched center of its remembrance, is unmentioned. "Fires of Hate in Jackson" deserves a lasting renown in the annals of civil rights reporting, along with "Klan Rally—Just Talk," but "The Marchers: Blueprint for Protest" belonged on the cutting-room floor.

TWO YOUNG MEN

Portis spent the better part of four years with the *Herald Tribune*, from 1960 to 1964, as a general assignment reporter, though he spent the final year in London as bureau chief. His New York stint also included the so-called Great Newspaper Strike, which shut down seven city dailies for a three-month period from December 1962 to March 1963. The daily round for much of this period called for copy on the widest imaginable range of stories, from the hard news of the civil rights struggles and local disasters like the New York Telephone Company boiler explosion to seriocomic incidents like the brief piece on the longshoreman and his lion or the longer series on the stop-smoking regimen. Portis filed on, among other topics, droughts and the fires they caused, proposed tax deductions for educational expenditures, a memorial service for victims of Nazi concentration camps, and the reelection for a fifth term of Orval Faubus as Arkansas governor.

Two among these scores of stories stand out as including an obvious if unstated personal component. In July of 1962, the *Herald Tribune* received an invitation from the US Military Academy in West Point, New York, to cover funeral services for First Lieutenant William F. Train III, killed in action in South Vietnam at twenty-four. As an infant he'd been christened in the same chapel that would host his funeral. The paper chose to send Portis, who produced "From West Point to Far East—Taps" for the next day's edition. His account is a detailed narrative of family dignity within heartbreak: Train's father had been in California presiding at Stanford's ROTC commissioning exercises when news arrived of his son's death. The bereft father stayed, spoke, and presented the commissions, including one to a younger son. Portis's tone is as muted as the black-draped drums of the color guard—a solemn, unembellished narration from start to finish. Only the eulogy (channeling Archibald MacLeish's "The Young Dead Soldiers Do Not Speak") is quoted at length: "We were young, we died, remember us; we have done what we could . . . we leave you our deaths; give them their meaning . . . we were young, remember us." Surely this assignment was at the very least a thought-provoking experience for the ex-Marine reporter. He and Train fought in different conflicts, but both men were soldiers, and Train was only four years Portis's junior. Here but for . . .

The second story was written less than a month later. It's not a funeral piece, and it came from rural southwestern Georgia instead of a New York military academy, but it also focuses on a brave young man who put his credo unflinchingly into action. Ralph Waldo Allen was just twenty-one, three years younger than even Train, when Portis, already in Georgia for the Albany Movement stories, drove northwest twenty-five miles to interview him in Dawson, the county seat of Terrell County. Allen wasn't in Vietnam, but he was far from his Massachusetts home, and he had found a battlefield of his own as a white college boy in Georgia working with the activist Student Nonviolent Coordinating Committee (SNCC) seeking to register African American voters in Terrell and neighboring counties as part of SNCC's Southwest Georgia Voter Registration Project. SNCC staffers and local African American communities knew the area as "Terrible Terrell" (and a neighboring county to the south as "Bad Baker"), a place where majority African American populations were politically disenfranchised and socially subordinated by entrenched segregationist regimes that reacted to challenges with murderous violence. Stories of police beatings and church burnings out of Georgia had attracted such notice that just two years earlier, in 1960, the US Department of Justice's first voter-discrimination prosecution under the Civil Rights Act of 1957 had resulted in the Supreme Court ruling in *United States v. Raines* against Terrell County registrar J. G. Raines. "Since he came here in early July," Portis writes in "New Englander on Mission in Georgia," a dispatch published on August 5, Allen had "been threatened almost daily, arrested three times and beaten up twice by angry white citizens." The story also details the de facto suppression of the African American vote: Terrell County had "a population of 8,209 Negroes and 4,533 whites. In 1960 there were 2,894 registered white voters in the county, and only 51 Negro voters."

This piece is markedly less formal than the Train story, but Portis's respect for young Allen's courage is apparent throughout—unlike the assignment at West Point, the profile itself was likely initiated by the reporter. The interview is a lengthy one, with Portis working hard to get at the motivations of an interviewee who is "not a big talker," who spent the previous summer in Quantico, Virginia, "where he attended a Marine Corps officer training camp," and who is "a reader of Sartre, Camus, and Malraux." The reporter keeps pushing and eventually gets his answer: "I'm here because of that one line in *Man's Fate* where Chen says, 'It is necessary to act my ideas.'"

Thirty-nine years later, discussing the severity of an *Arkansas Gazette* editor on "sequence of verb tenses," Portis would quote Lincoln's "nice use of the future perfect" in his second inaugural address: "to care for him who shall have borne the battle." Here, in two short pieces closely associated in time, both with a nearly palpable personal component, he pays pitch-perfect homage to one brave soldier who has borne his battle and brings respectful, searching inquiry to the portrayal of a courageous civilian currently bearing his. Both stories are expressions of the "care" Lincoln called for. In less than a year Portis, already a veteran of battlefields like Train's, would find himself assigned to new ones similar to Allen's, in Birmingham, Tuscaloosa, and Jackson. These battlefields, too, would summon his "care."

2 — "CHARITY ENDURETH ALL THINGS"

NORWOOD

"TO TRY MY HAND AT FICTION"

Sent by the *Herald Tribune* to London as bureau chief in the fall of 1963, Portis soon found his new administrative responsibilities onerous. "I liked it," he told Reed in 2001, "but it was hard staying on top of the job. It was a juggling act. I was bureau chief, meaning administrative duties." One problem was freeloaders scamming free trips and tickets to shows by passing themselves off as travel writers or critics. Another was self-important drunks offended by insufficient deference. A rambling call from a drunken Randolph Churchill and a "pitiful bust" of one freeloader serve as examples, "the point being that I kept getting dragged away from reporting into these management comedies." The London assignment, for all its prestige, was soon a grind similar to the pressures of the Our Town column at the *Gazette*. One year was enough. He was eager to "try my hand at fiction," so Portis "gave notice" and came back to Arkansas in November of 1964, crossing a "cold" and "rough" Atlantic on "the *Mauretania*, a Cunard liner."

When *Norwood*, by report the work of six months, appeared in 1966—its publication in book form preceded by two installments printed in the *Saturday Evening Post*—its author had scores if not hundreds of bylined journalistic pieces to his credit, but the "Fiction" category on his CV carried a single short story called "Damn!" (Academics characteristically keep assiduous records of their publications, but journalists may be more cavalier, affecting disdain for such bean counting given their exponentially greater productivity.) "Damn!" was published in 1957 in *Nugget*, a *Playboy* wannabe with glossy lingerie pics, racy cartoons, and just enough fiction and lifestyle prose to supply a veneer of "class"—"How *Do* You Cook a Steak?" appears just before "Damn!," and pieces on cars and golf are scattered among the epidermal close-ups. Portis did luck into good company—Grace Paley's wonderful "Goodbye and Good Luck" ran in the same issue.

The story itself is a comic, first-person account of an episode in the life of the unnamed narrator and his carny pal Sanford T. McClerkin, following the untimely death of Sanford T.'s father and the group's breadwinner (he billed himself as Jesse James in a circus) in a drunken fall from a Ferris wheel. Abandoned by the circus in (fictional) Montezuma, Arkansas, the boys buy out a patent medicine maker's sixty-proof "Bethel Liver Emulsifier," rebrand it as "Damn!," and sell it in dry counties. They have a good run until greed trips them up—Sanford T. doubles the alcohol to boost sales, only to run afoul of "church folks" and end up busted for selling "untaxed liquor." At the close they're considering new ventures, Sanford T. betting on a "hillbilly singer with greasy sideburns he picked up in Memphis" while his less sanguine partner worries they'll end up wishing they'd opted for a "traveling exhibition show with a stuffed whale on a flat car and a mermaid and a 1,400-pound hog."

Norwood's central character is not in show business at any level, though he harbors dreams. Norwood Pratt is a Marine from Ralph, Texas, just awarded a hardship discharge to take care of his sister, Vernell. By page two he's on a bus from Camp Pendleton, headed home. Ralph, unlike Montezuma, is not wholly fictional—there is, or was, a community of this name, previously known as Ogg. If not purely coincidental, the name seems like a Portis joke. "No population was reported under either name," reports the Texas State Historical Association's online *Handbook of Texas*, "and there was no post office." In any case, the Ralph/Ogg of real-world geography was in Randall County, south of Amarillo, far from Norwood's home. The Pratts moved frequently, especially in Norwood's youth, but never far, oscillating "back and forth along U.S. Highway 82 in the oil fields and cotton patches between Stamps, Arkansas, and Hooks, Texas."

If the Pratt dwellings thus sit unsteadily on Texas/Arkansas ground (a yurt would have been a wise investment), *Norwood* the novel soon displays several odd qualities. There is, for example, something insistently off-center in the presentation of the Pratt family itself. Vernell's need for Norwood to be home originates in the death of Mr. Pratt, an "alcoholic auto mechanic" whose family, so long as he lived as its head, clung to the "banks" of Highway 82 like "river rats." They were no less itinerant, that is, than Sanford T. and his pal before them or the fabled John Selmer Dix to follow in *The Dog of the South*, who "did all his best work on a bus," riding back and forth between Dallas and Los Angeles "for an entire year." Rootlessness is thus established early on as one pole in Portis's fictional worlds, poised against such opposite extremes as the "sessile" Mr. Jimmerson of *Masters of Atlantis* or *Norwood*'s own Heineman, the "free-lance travel writer" who goes nowhere, never leaving his Manhattan apartment while working up pieces (for "the *Trib*") on Provence and Peru "from handouts."

But Mr. Pratt was the subject here, before the itinerant-versus-sessile business broke in. This lit-crit enterprise can clog up the prose. Mr. Pratt is Norwood's father, though not only is his paternity explicitly stated only by Vernell, but the just-orphaned son gives not the slightest thought to Dad at any point. Norwood is upset as he boards his bus, but his "distress" centers not on Dad's demise but instead on what he perceives as the "shameful" early discharge and his failure to "go by Tent Camp 1" to collect seventy dollars owed to him by Joe William Reese. Why such conspicuous lack of grief (or even acknowledgment)? Were father and son on bad terms or even estranged? Was the old mechanic perhaps angered by Norwood's dropping out of high school, his enlisting in the Marines, or his taking a job at the Nipper gas station instead of a Pratt and Son position as Pratt Sr.'s assistant?

Additional oddities surface upon Norwood's return to Ralph. Having invited the Remley family, encountered on the bus, to stop over for a visit, he installs them in "Mr. Pratt's old bedroom" and moves "a cot for himself" into the kitchen, though a "sleeping porch bedroom" is mentioned later. Was this Norwood's room, before his enlistment? After the Remleys' surreptitious departure, apparently on their first night, in which they somehow steal a television set and a shotgun in addition to toting their infant son, does Mr. Pratt's old bedroom then remain empty?

Then there's the bathroom, built by Norwood for his mother. It's described in detail, especially the bathtub, bought "new from

Sears," with a "built-in thing for the soap" and "a raised wave design on the bottom." Mom was appreciative "and said so," but she's been gone "these many years." Many years? What's happened to the incessant moves?

Number crunching adds additional fog. Norwood's initial conversation with Grady Fring the Kredit King takes place in Grady's "big new Buick Invicta," a model introduced in 1959. Norwood's just-truncated military service included a tour in Korea in some period between 1950 and 1953. Before this, dropping out of school upon arrival in Ralph, he'd gone to work and used his first paychecks to finance Mom's bathroom. Add it up and the Pratts emerge as settled folk if not community pillars, resident in Ralph for a decade or more. Close scrutiny of Norwood's later train ride from Indianapolis to Philadelphia uncovers analogous incongruities. It is dark for some time before Norwood even boards his boxcar, plus the train "stopped and started all night long"—yet he arrives in Philadelphia, replaces his stolen stovepipe boots with a hobo named Eugene's "house shoes" after a trackside scuffle, and boards a "commuter special" to New York. Indianapolis to Philly is a 650-mile trip. Let Norwood be rolling by 9:00 p.m. Let him average forty miles per hour even with the stops. Give him two hours to relieve Eugene of his shoes, acquire a ticket, and make it to the platform. Already it's at least 3:00 p.m. The "commuter special" is long gone. (The bus today takes sixteen hours, and the Amtrak Cardinal makes the run in just over twenty.)

Readers would be mistaken to take these incongruities as accidental, resulting from carelessness alone. Portis was an experienced journalist, well drilled in the importance of fact-checking. There's also the report from his mother that in choosing Mattie Ross as the name for the heroine of *True Grit* he checked nineteenth-century Yell County census records to ensure against offending early settler families. No, deliberate slippage should surely be the default assumption. This author is up to something—"That fog was there for a purpose," says *Masters of Atlantis*'s narrator, defending the felicities of "Gnomonic obfuscation." What's going on here? Might we have a fundamentally postmodern suggestion of ultimate elusiveness at the heart of narrative exactitude, of a universe where linkage of cause and effect fails to be absolute and exhaustive elucidation of temporal duration, spatial location, and human motivation proves impossible?

Might the first-time novelist, in short, have entered the quality lit game already sending it up, playing perversely if unobtrusively with its conventions? *True Grit*, novel number two, will be an outlier here as in other signature attributes—it generally pays scrupulous attention to consistency of voice and plausibility of narrative—but *The Dog of the South*, *Masters of Atlantis*, and *Gringos* are rich in additional expressions of authorial impishness.

Such puzzling elements, however, do not impede efficient deployment of a clear narrative arc. *Norwood* opens with a bus trip, and its protagonist is soon on the road again, this time to New York, the novel thus achieving full west-to-east, Pacific-to-Atlantic continental scope. He's the driver, this time, at least at first, hired by the Kredit King to transport a car (two cars, it turns out, plus a surprise passenger) to Brooklyn. His motive is double—he'll get paid for the driving, and he's learned, via a call to the Reese residence in the ominously named (and fictional) Old Carthage, Arkansas, of Joe William's recent departure for New York. He'll have a second chance to recover his seventy dollars. More on the Reese family later. The trip fills the novel—Norwood next pulls into his Ralph driveway in its final paragraph. But Norwood's odyssey cannot get properly underway without a closer look at Grady Fring, its sponsor and the novel's second most prominent and easily most odious character.

He's beyond odious, finally, a true bad actor. Con man just starts the list of appropriate labels. Sex trafficker ends it. But he is also a recurrent Portis type, cut from the same basic cloth as *The Dog of the South*'s Dr. Reo Symes ("not in active practice at this time") and *Masters of Atlantis*'s Austin Popper ("a gift for hopeful statement combined with short-term tenacity of purpose"). They're unregenerate reprobates—racists, misogynists, frauds. Popper is a stolen-valor draft dodger who brags of being "number eight on Herr Hitler's American execution list," while Symes takes pride in the profits accruing from his bogus asthma diagnoses: "I certified many a one at a hundred and fifty bucks a throw."

They're a bad lot, all three, to be numbered at last among "the most depraved" members of the species. But like Milton with Satan or Shakespeare with Iago, Portis often gives his worst characters his best lines. Accosting Norwood at Ralph's outdoor roller-skating rink, Fring opens by handing him an insurance policy brochure, also listing "a good many business interests"—insurance, mobile homes, debt collection, used cars. To these rackets are added at various points cut-rate wedding sets sold by mail, personal loans, and, most ominously, a "New Orleans talent agency" on the lookout for "lovely young girls" eager for "a career in show business." It's this enterprise, it turns out (insurance here just a moment's side hustle), that brings Fring to Ralph. "I've had my eye on her," he says of a young skater pointed out by the unsuspecting Norwood as "about the best one around here." "She's a dandy," Fring adds. "And sweet too." He's disappointed when his query about her age elicits a guess of "about seventeen" from Norwood. "I think she gets out of high school this year," he says. Too young, Fring replies—"I'd rather not fool with them if they're under nineteen or twenty. You will understand, Norwood, I am not necessarily looking for skating skills."

What has been up to this point a warmly comic scene—the boys at the rink are "skating fast, working hard at it, as though they were delivering important telegrams"—here unveils a loitering evil. "She's a dandy," from Fring's mouth, might challenge for the creepiest line Portis ever writes. This "Cresswell girl" with a pleated skirt and lights on her skates—she's a potential East Texas Lolita. Fring's even worse than Humbert, and her girlish voice, if not for the saving grace of her age, might soon be missing from the roller-rink concord. Fring is a blighting presence; in Portis's modest roster of fictional villains only the Manson-wannabe Dan of *Gringos* and the murderous Tom Chaney of *True Grit* edge out the Kredit King for ninth-circle bottom spots.

Defeated for the moment in his "talent agency" quest and failing in a first pitch to employ Norwood in his debt collection company (to "make those profligate bastards cough up"), Fring finally turns his expedition to Ralph to good account by lining Norwood up to drive one of his "surplus" cars to New York.

THE HATEFUL TOWN

As Fring's too-credulous hired man, then, Norwood departs Texarkana for Arnold's Garage in Brooklyn, piloting a "big 98 Oldsmobile" and towing a just-repainted Pontiac Catalina. "We always give them a coat of Duco," Grady tells him. There's also a surprise passenger, an unhappy Yvonne (*"Yuh-von"*) Phillips, perhaps not long ago as young and dandy as the Cresswell girl but now disappointed to learn she won't be "going up on a Delta jet." She, along with the cars, is to be delivered to Arnold—"You are not authorized to deal with anyone except Arnold," Norwood is told. "If he's not there then wait on him." Norwood has dressed carefully for the trip in a sharply pressed Nipper uniform, topped with a black cowboy hat and anchored by thirty-eight-dollar stovepipe boots, "coal-black 14-inchers with steel shanks and low walking heels." Fring tells him he looks like the Durango Kid; Yvonne calls him, with the emphasis of italics, a *"peckerwood."*

They don't make it halfway. Just outside Evansville, Indiana, after a long day and half a night filled with bickering and misadventure (they get rear-ended in Memphis and flee the scene), Norwood breaks the hitch connecting Oldsmobile and Pontiac with a jack handle and hands Yvonne the keys to the Olds. She departs "without a word or a wave" for Calumet City, Illinois, anticipating welcome from Sammy Ortega, a formidable bartender who "can press two hundred pounds over his head." Norwood then abandons the Catalina in "what looked like a blackberry patch" in an Indiana field and hikes back to Evansville, where he greets the dawn as a hitchhiker.

He continues to New York by bread truck (its driver sporting an "official bread hat" as easily visualized as a Colorado ranchette), boxcar, and passenger rail, arriving two days later much the worse for wear. His fancy boots, like Miss Phillips and both cars—no deliveries for Arnold—are gone, lifted from his sleeping feet on the boxcar leg of the journey but soon replaced by a pair of too-large "old timers' high-tops with elastic strips on the side" strong-armed from the hobo Eugene (Norwood gives him two dollars). It is not the entrance Norwood planned: "He *was* a mess, no doubt about it. The sole of one shoe was flopping and he had B.O. pretty bad." But at least one hard lesson has been learned. "Grady told me a lie," he tells Miss Phillips shortly after the flight from the rear-ending in Memphis. She mocks his gullibility—"You are the peckerwood of all peckerwoods"—despite her own prior victimization. She's a tougher customer now, who makes knowing reference to the Mann Act of 1910, which outlaws the transportation across state lines of "any woman or girl for the purpose of prostitution or debauchery, or for any other immoral purpose." "Now they can send you to the Federal pen," she crows when they cross the state line into Shelby County, Tennessee, on the Mississippi River bridge, causing Norwood to slam on the brakes and precipitating the rear-end collision that sends them fleeing.

Now Norwood's in New York, both peckerwood and dandy (Fring will call him one when they next meet), and it doesn't take him long to work through quite a list of yokel-in-the-city moves. His lame joke banter with a waitress at a Penn Station coffee stand nets him an "Oh fer Chrissakes" brush-off, and he does little better with a telephone company supervisor queried over Joe William's current whereabouts (his number has been disconnected). A man in his first day on the street in a Mr. Peanut suit has little to say despite Norwood's interesting comparisons to his more generous Dallas counterpart—no free cashews in the Big Apple. Norwood catches himself on screen at Ripley's Believe It or Not! Odditorium in Times Square (closed since 2021) and watches, but does not engage in conversation, a man across the street with a beanie on his head quacking like Donald Duck as he sews names on customers' beanies. An attempted conversation with a shoeshine man is cut off almost as summarily as Norwood's joke at Penn Station. "Go bother Mayor Wagner," says the shine man. "He needs advice." On the subway he acts the short-term Good Samaritan by propping a man seen "stretched out on the concrete" at the Union Square subway station up against a wall. Meanwhile he congratulates himself for the savvy displayed in avoiding a man he takes for a "dope fiend" who wants a dollar for "a four-color ball-point pen." "What did they think, that he was somebody who would buy something like that on the street?" he wonders.

Things improve markedly once Norwood makes it to Joe William's apartment, even though he's gone, evidently headed back to Arkansas. Norwood ends up staying four days with the apartment's new occupant, a generously hospitable travel writer named Heineman who, asked by Norwood if he knows "any beatnik girls," introduces him to Marie, "a beatnik by any definition." Norwood is no midnight cowboy, but Marie is a big-city woman, sophisticated and exotic, "always wearing the same loose orange silky blouse." She also turns out to be strikingly generous, feeding her guest, guiding him to Staten Island and the Cloisters, though resistant to amorous initiatives: "Once on the boat Norwood put his arm around her waist and she removed it and said he took a lot for granted and that she would let him know when she was ready to be 'pawed.'" Readiness never arrives, but Marie does read aloud from her favorite book, Kahlil Gibran's *The Prophet*, a sea of sonorous platitudes available in gilt-edged editions that made it the great collegiate breakup gift of the sixties. Attractive sorority sisters must have ordered copies in bulk, the better to send rejected suitors on their way gently, as many a frat boy graduated with three or four copies inscribed with florid valedictory wishes.

Marie is thus "agreeable in many ways," but "nothing ever got off the ground in the way of funny business," despite Norwood's repeated if easily parried efforts. With Heineman, too, there is good conversation and a couch to sleep on, but on day five, following a final dustup at an Automat (Norwood is evicted without having eaten), he flees the "hateful town" on a southbound Trailways bus, "thinking about purple hull peas sprinkled down with pepper sauce." The trip, despite the pleasant interludes with Heineman and Marie, is at midpoint mostly a disaster. He's 0-2 on the balance sheet—no car delivered and no seventy dollars collected. (Speaking of purple hull peas, Portis everywhere features a low-key but persistent note of praise for food, especially rural southern food. Ray Midge, on the road to Mexico, spends an afternoon hoping for chicken-fried steak "with white gravy and a lot of black pepper," and the Mr. Palfrey of *Delray's New Moon* answers expansively when a waitress asks for his order: "What I want is a fat yearling coon roasted with some sweet potatoes. What I want, young lady, is some salt-cured ham that's been hanging in the smokehouse for about two years, along with five or six big cathead biscuits.")

SOUTH TOWARD HOME

Things take a sharp turn for the better almost immediately. A pretty woman named Rita Lee Chipman boards between Washington, DC, and Richmond, and this time things in the way of funny business get off the ground promptly. (*Norwood* can be casual with the handling of time but is generally painstaking with the treatment of space—"He slept for 335 miles, leaning back at the maximum Trailways angle.") Rita Lee is bound for Jacksonville, North Carolina, to sort things out at Camp Lejeune with a boyfriend named Wayne, recently gone AWOL on the correspondence front. But Norwood is immediately smitten—"*What a honey!*" he thinks—and his courtship moves, so ineffective with Marie, here speedily reduce Rita Lee to confusion: "Norwood, I think I'm falling in love with you. If you were sick I would look after you and bathe you." Matrimony enters their conversation with astonishing speed, even before the early a.m. arrival in Jacksonville, and Rita Lee's cheeks are so reddened by the long night's nuzzling as to require application of "some powerful Noxema."

Norwood, left with half a day to kill while Rita Lee boards the Camp Lejeune shuttle for her showdown with Wayne, wanders through town, outgoing as ever, rattling the doors of locked stores, quizzing a window washer about the quality of T-shirts on sale. These overtures, too, mirroring his greater success with the Georgian Rita Lee than with the New Yorker Marie, meet with warmer responses than their Manhattan predecessors. "Beat it," said the shoeshine man, where the Jacksonville squeegee guy opens by allowing that the bargain shirts will "draw up some" when washed and closes the amiable exchange by agreeing with Norwood's admission of perpetual T-shirt shortage: "Man can't have too many of 'em." No explicit generalization is offered, but a regional contrast is put forward—not just outdoor temperatures are warmer in Dixie.

Norwood eventually gains entry to a shuttered beer joint—"We closed, hat man," says the proprietress, busy painting a wall, even as she lets him stay—where he falls into conversation with a "midget of inestimable age" named Edmund B. Ratner. Once a widely traveled performer (the Cirque d'Hiver and the Moscow State Circus are mentioned) billed as the world's smallest perfect man, Ratner admits to being "on the way down" due to immoderate weight gain: "Pizzas, thick pastramis, chili dogs—nothing was too gross." The "curious pair" end up lunching together at Ratner's hotel, where Ratner, himself headed west with hopes of "getting some television work," enlists Norwood as an unofficial and unsalaried bodyguard on the Memphis leg of the journey. "I'm just a bit apprehensive about traveling cross-country in the States alone," Ratner explains. "It's silly, I know. Civilized country and all that."

"Glad to have you," Norwood replies. But on their way to the bus station, they are "diverted" into an arcade where they encounter an "imprisoned" hen ("a Dominique," says the narrator; "Dominecker," says Rita Lee later) in a "circus-looking cage." A signboard, soliciting a nickel and billing her as "JOANN THE WONDER HEN THE COLLEGE

EDUCATED CHICKEN," offers her answer to "ANY YES OR NO QUESTION." Norwood inserts the coin and receives in return, when Joann pulls a lanyard, a slip of paper inscribed with more of a maxim or adage than a yes or no answer. *"Charity Endureth All Things,"* it says, offering in what will be Portis's standard low-key, easily missed register a thematic cue to one of the novel's and his fictional world's central topics.

Joann's proffered response is not only scripture, as the Portis who referenced Matthew in his "Fires of Hate in Jackson" report would know, but also a most apposite quality lit reference, which Portis the omnivorous reader would also know. The opening pages of *The Confidence-Man*, Herman Melville's embittered sign-off screed as a novelist, introduce a figure bearing this slogan on a placard aboard a Mississippi River steamboat named the *Fidèle* on April Fools' Day. The "novel" that follows is a fiendishly convoluted shaggy-dog story featuring a bewildering succession of scoundrels and con men (or a smaller number of tricksters variously disguised)—arguably as saturnine a work of fiction as anything in the American canon. The reference to it here shadows *Norwood*'s landscape as sharply as the appearance of Grady Fring at the Ralph roller rink. Such open allusions to canonical works, however, are rare and unintrusive, as here, especially in comparison to the much more frequent references to works of popular culture, which are often developed at greater length. There is, for example, Norwood's extended comparative discussion of *The Road Runner Show* and Noveltoons cartoons with the bread truck driver back in Indiana, as well as the briefer references to *Tarzan's New York Adventure* and the *Bowery Boys* series in New York. The former, a 1942 Johnny Weissmuller feature from Metro-Goldwyn-Mayer (MGM), exhibits similarities of both structure and detail to *Norwood*—Tarzan and Jane journey to New York and successfully rescue Boy from bad guy Buck Rand, who has put him in a circus. From Melville to MGM to the matchbook covers and potted meat labels read with such attention by Heineman and Norwood—the whole commercial and pop-culture gamut, ivory tower to Hollywood to TV shows to grocery-aisle fare, is grist for Portis's fictional mill. Bill Bird's "searching mind" nourishes itself on once-popular newspaper *Grit*.

(There's also a close-to-home real-world model for *Norwood*'s "JOANN THE WONDER HEN" in Hot Springs' IQ Zoo, a once-popular

Ad for IQ Zoo in Hot Springs, Arkansas. *Courtesy of Dr. J. Arthur Gillaspy.*

tourist attraction featuring rabbits, pigs, raccoons, and other animals, opened in 1955 by Keller and Marian Breland. Chickens were among their biggest stars, featured in "Bird Brain" exhibits marketed coast to coast and celebrated in the *New Yorker* by writer Calvin Trillin, who reported that he would bring out-of-town friends to New York City's Chinatown to play tic-tac-toe against a chicken in its Bird Brain box.)

Norwood, Edmund in tow, the larger man "throttling back on his normal pace" to accommodate the smaller man ("accommodation" is closer to the scriptural *agápē* than "charity"), arrives at the bus station to find a tearful Rita Lee already arrived. "I thought you'd gone without me," she sobs, reporting her mission's failure. Wayne's letter-writing lapses are made clear—he's "out in the Mediterranean Sea," far from Camp Lejeune. "But I didn't care any more," Rita Lee adds. "I wanted to go with you. I should of listened to what my heart was telling me last night." Norwood wants to kiss her but hesitates "with so many people around" and contents himself with bestowing "an Indian brave clap on the shoulder instead." It is an apex, life-altering instant, right out of Hollywood movies and romance magazines, and Rita Lee, its leading lady, is overcome: "She looked up at Norwood through tear-misted eyes and her hands were trembling in the magic and wonder of the moment." It's a warmly comic scene, but it would be a mistake to regard Rita Lee at this moment with condescension, despite the one-night courtship, the bus-station ambience, and Norwood's awkward gesture of affection. Such confluences of time, space, and hoped-for outcome are experienced as instances of just-for-me miracle, and her response is at bottom wholly appropriate, a pitch-perfect rising to occasion. We conduct our lives in corners where we are, build our loves among the company we meet. Joe William Reese, hearing the news the next day over the telephone, allows as how wives are "just wherever you find 'em. Buses, drugstores, VFW huts." Wiser than he looks, Joe William, and warm too, despite his own mother's "poolroom clown" assessment.

Norwood's final act before leaving Jacksonville, Rita Lee and Ratner safely stowed on the bus, is to borrow Rita Lee's shopping bag, return to the arcade, and rescue Joann, opening the trap door behind the cage and boarding the bus with her stored among Rita Lee's clothes. Rita Lee worries about mites, but Edmund is audibly impressed. "Norwood, how very plucky!" he says. Only then, two rescues completed (three if Rita Lee is included), is the wanderer at last directly on his homeward way, returning with a stolen chicken as he departed with two stolen cars, accompanied by a willing Rita and a grateful Ratner instead of the querulous Yvonne.

DESIRED COUNTRY

This is already excellent, and it only gets better. From this point *Norwood* hews closely to a standard epic return template, though Portis's Odysseus brings his Penelope with him, and the most fully developed homecoming scene is deflected from Ralph/Ithaca to the Reese farmstead in Old Carthage. Joe William, reached by telephone from the Memphis bus station, expands his invitation list to a "family fish fry" at comic length without the slightest hesitation. "Is there anybody else. Any Japanese exchange students?" he asks after learning first of Rita Lee and then of Ratner. When Joann is mentioned, he asks if he should perhaps charter a bus.

The fish fry is described at length, from setting to menu to specific conversations. The home itself is "a sprawling 1928 story-and-a-half nature's-bounty farmhouse" with a wraparound front porch furnished with two swings overlooking "twenty acres or so of Johnson grass with some polled Herefords grazing on it." It's a palace, a nearly prelapsarian Eden, after two weeks of boxcars and couches and bus stations. The catfish and frog legs are prepared by Mr. Reese, who "knew his business with the meal sack and the grease and the fish, never turning them until it was just the right time." The food is terrific, Norwood's "purple hull peas" bus dream come true. The conversation flows, hosts and guests mingling easily—Mr. Reese's offer of a tour of his "eighty paper-shell pecan trees" is eagerly accepted by Ratner; Joe William's girlfriend, Kay, listens patiently if uncomprehendingly to Norwood's detailed instructions for the repair/replacement of her Thunderbird's U-joint; and Rita Lee, the evening's champion listener, lends a willing ear to Mrs. Whichcoat's detailed account of the Butterfield family, previously unmentioned (and apparently unrelated to anyone present). Everyone is considerate ("consideration" is also closer to *agápē* than "charity") of everyone else.

Old Carthage, then, the hint of doom in its name a false lead for symbol hunters, is for the moment a fruited plain, crowned with brotherhood, one corner of nation and planet at their best. Nice weather, good food, comfortable shelter, warm company, no Grady Fring in view—it's hour upon hour of the blessed times for which people everywhere offer prayerful thanks. Portis, we'll see, will make such interludes a standard feature of fictional worlds and of his personal world as recollected in his 1999 essay "Combinations of Jacksons." Happy domestic settings that serve as appropriate backdrops highlighting the embedded ethic will also prove a standard Portis device in future works. More on this later. In *Norwood* its most explicit articulation is found in Joann the Wonder Hen's response to Norwood's nickel, the quality of enduring understood as a core element of charity's practice. Norwood himself is never not something of a goof, but like Leopold Bloom he at last wins the day by his invincibly upbeat outlook, his easygoing amiability, and most of all by his accommodation of others. When the bread man departs with ill wishes for his future—"I hope don't nobody pick you up"—Norwood is unruffled: "No use in you hoping that. Somebody will." Fring is out there, but so is Rita Lee. In what may be his worst moment, flustered at the loss of his boots and footsore from the "rocks and clinkers" under his stocking feet, when his appropriation of the hobo Eugene's "house shoes" could accurately be labeled a theft—even here Norwood stuffs two dollars into the other man's shirt pocket. (And "house shoes" itself a roofless man's sorry bit of *Hausbesitzer* pride—there's pathos!) The wonderful scene at the Reese farmstead, where this ethic appears to be house rules, only serves to emphasize its centrality.

    The next morning Ratner is up early and gone, after borrowing fifty of Norwood's just-recovered seventy dollars. Mr. Reese, excellent host to the last, gave him a lift to the bus. Norwood and Rita Lee stay through lunch, he enjoying a relaxed a.m. outing shooting snakes and cypress knees with Joe William, she accepting congratulatory prenuptial gifts from Kay and Mrs. Reese, who adds "a little talk." More consideration. Finally, a suitable carrier for Joann located (a mink trap so "humane" in its design that "no mink had ever entered it"), the new couple ride to the bus station in Kay's Thunderbird.

    The final homecoming, after this climax, is handled with breezy dispatch. The bus to Texarkana is nicely air-conditioned, and Vernell, two small presents having been purchased for her at Rita Lee's suggestion (yet another modest gesture of consideration), is summoned from Ralph. (The gifts bear more than passing resemblance to those the discharged serviceman buys his mother in Portis's *Arkansas Traveler* spoof of country-stringer reports. Where the earlier piece has Mom receiving "a beautiful satin-covered pillow from Fort Chaffee with a picture of a tank on it," Vernell's pillow features "a picture of the post office standing astride two states, and the words 'Greetings From Texarkana, U.S.A., Home of the Red River Arsenal.' ")

Into this scene slithers Grady Fring, alerted by his brother Tilmon. This time Norwood is ready. Their meeting is rancorous from the start, but only when Fring mentions the possibility of a nocturnal fire at the Pratt residence does Norwood's temper flare. He's on the Kredit King "like a bobcat," and Fring is left bloodied and gasping, slumped on his Invicta, wordless for once. "Just stay away from me," Norwood orders. "Don't come messing around me or my house or anybody over there." When Vernell arrives, her new husband, Bill Bird, is handled with similar dispatch. He says the trunk is the place for livestock, but he rides back to Ralph in the back seat "with his feet up on Joann's mink cage." Norwood is home, his arrival announced by the one-word sentence in the final paragraph, the place itself recognizable by the "pea gravel driveway with the white rock borders" he installed himself. It's a low-key return to close a low-key narrative—modest *bildung* in Portis's debut *roman*. (Scholarship has contrived an even bigger mouthful than *bildungsroman—Entwicklungsroman*—to cow the unwashed, but it was applied to *True Grit*, not *Norwood*, and need not detain us here.) The novel's final spoken words are Norwood's home-owner admonition: "Mine your own business, Bill Bird."

THE AUTHOR AS LACONIC CUTUP

Returning from such overarching generic observations to words-on-the-page issues again brings up matters analogous to the pronounced absence of filial attachment in Norwood's response to Mr. Pratt's death and the several apparent contradictions in the narrator's presentation of Pratt family living arrangements.

Two things stand out, both suggesting considerable insight behind Wolfe's off-the-cuff "laconic cutup" tag for Portis. What but a weakness for authorial mischief, a wiseacre disregard for literary convention, could account for the sudden register break in the description of the passing encounter between the just-arrived Norwood and a "woman in the Times Square Information Center" who provides a subway map and directions to Joe William's East Eleventh Street apartment? She's described as "about forty but with a smooth powdered neck he wouldn't have minded biting." What? Biting? There's no prep for this, or follow-up, unless the reader is tempted to view Rita Lee's early morning need for "powerful Noxema" after her night's nuzzling in a more sinister light. Nothing whatever of Norwood is revealed here. It's a throwaway line, a flippant, wiseacre move tied to the author and no other. Norwood's distinctly uninsistent courtship style is twice on extended view, in New York with Marie and on the southbound bus with Rita Lee—there's zero of the vampire evident.

An equally abrupt though less striking instance occurs later in the narrative, in the description of Mrs. Reese at the fish-and-frog-leg feast. She's presented comically, above all for her pretensions of gentility (to her fellow "Confederate Daughters" she brags of connection to "the usurper Cromwell"). "She often managed to leave the impression," the concluding paragraph of her sketch begins, "that she was in Arkansas through some mistake and it was her belief, perhaps true, that only common people had piles." What? Only "common people" afflicted with hemorrhoids? "Perhaps true"? Our narrator, scrupulously unintrusive in default mode, here interrupts his syntax to dart to the side of this pretentious biddy with her gross reference to perineal itch? Once again, the narrator's addendum offers another glimpse of the author as grinning scamp.

Portis also displays early on a fondness for and skill in the portrayal of characters who are masters of an antique, ornately elevated rhetoric easily caricatured but once also widely admired as a badge of the genuine article in oratory. Rich in classical allusion, historical reference, and recondite Latinate vocabulary, though often lacking in content, it rolls impressively off the tongue. Portis usually, but not invariably, attaches this lingo to bloviating reprobates, those who rob not with pistol but with pen. Dr. Reo Symes of *The Dog of the South*, full of high sentence but described by his own mother as "a sharper and a tramp," stands at the head of this group, with *True Grit*'s stockman Colonel Stonehill in a cameo role, warning Mattie Ross of the Indian Territory as a place of "sanguinary ambuscade" and telling her he would not pay $325 "for winged Pegasus" even as she has her way with him in their dealing. Thus Grady Fring, in the space of a two-page spread, first describes his ex-pal Nipper as "richer than the fabled Croesus," then confesses he "took him" in a business transaction "like Stonewall Jackson took Nathaniel P. Banks in the Valley of the Shenandoah." Norwood, listening, unfamiliar with both Croesus and Banks, is meant to be impressed, the better to mistakenly recognize Fring as a man of culture and substance. Ratner, *Norwood*'s other silver tongue, is a more benign presence, gallant in being introduced to Rita Lee but imperious when a Western Union clerk is slow to disburse his money order funds. "You're altogether too kind," he replies when Rita Lee praises his attire, but with the clerk he is sharply dismissive. "You *functionary*," he shouts. Cosmopolitan name-dropping substitutes for classical reference in his repertoire—he's enjoyed "jugged hare at Rule's" and appeared professionally with the Moscow State Circus and the Cirque d'Hiver Bouglione.

Fring's Nathaniel Banks reference is also a debut-novel instance of a yet more prominent Portis compositional trick. Reading his novels in sequence, one cannot miss an obsessive fondness for references to military history in general and to the American Civil War in particular. This, too, may be comprehended as yet another laconic-cutup move, joining the casual attention to emotional ties, patterns of residence, and consistent narrative voice as send-ups of quality lit practice. The Battle of First Winchester, after all, was not Gettysburg, just as Banks was not Grant. The arcane allusion seems more suited to a history buff like *The Dog of the South*'s Raymond Midge than a tawdry scam artist like Fring. Portis gives generous rein to Civil War history references in both *True Grit* and *The Dog of the South*, and the larger world of military history remains a regular presence throughout his work. "I Don't Talk Service No More" is the title of a short story published in 1996, five years after *Gringos* closed out his career as a novelist, but in fact Portis talks service insistently from start to finish. Even his passing metaphors are sometimes military—here's *Gringos*' Jimmy Burns on Louise Kurle's sudden suggestion of matrimony: "Here was another grenade, blinding white phosphorus this time." Norwood and Joe William Reese are just the first among many veterans among Portis's protagonists and secondary characters. Rooster Cogburn, the Texas Ranger LaBoeuf, and Mattie's murdered father Frank Ross will soon join them. Even Cogburn's cat is named for a Civil War general. More on the darker implications of the talking service focus later.

I LET IT GO

A Pauline "charity," understood as socially enacted accommodation of others, as forbearance, thus emerges as a core virtue embodied in Norwood Pratt and put forward, however implicitly, by the novel as a whole. This will be developed into a signature gestural marker of the stringently understated Portis hero. "I let the matter drop. That was my way," says Ray Midge. Jimmy Burns, narrator and protagonist of *Gringos*, opens with a Christmas wish "to be more considerate of other people in the coming year" and reports multiple instances of "I let it go" in the telling of his story. Burns is also an inveterate bringer of gifts, a walking Santa in all seasons. Even Mattie Ross, for all her characteristic insistence on her prerogatives, lets at least two issues go before she leaves Fort Smith on her errand of vengeance. "We will let it go," she replies when Yarnell Poindexter warns her that the undertaker is "trying to stick you" in the arrangements for shipping her father's body back to Dardanelle, and she also (though less willingly) sees "nothing to be gained from making a fuss" when Mrs. Floyd makes her share her rooming house bed with Grandma Turner.

A matching verbal accommodation is there from the beginning in Portis's nonfiction—"Somebody else said they were jack pines," he writes in a 1959 Our Town column for the *Arkansas Gazette*, "and we felt that was wrong but we didn't say anything." Similar passages occur at least three times in the 1967 "An Auto Odyssey through Darkest Baja." "I thought we'd *never* get here," says the "talkative sport from Las Vegas" of Portis's afternoon flight down the peninsula, addressing two guys who just spent nine rough days driving its nearly twelve hundred miles. "We let that one slide, with difficulty," Portis reports.

Letting things slide is thus across the board, in fiction and in fact, a central element of charity's enduring. It's a cardinal virtue, a manifest sign of goodness. The old coot at the wheel of his beat-up jalopy in "Combinations of Jacksons" offers a general assessment of the middle-level virtue achieved in their fallen fictional worlds by Norwood, Rita Lee, Midge, Louise, and Jimmy: "While not an ornament of our race, neither was he, I thought, the most depraved member of the gang."

The treatment of race, now that the word has surfaced, may be in the current cultural climate a major obstacle to a wider appreciation of Portis's fiction generally and of *Norwood* and *The Dog of the South* in particular. At least eleven "******" usages surface in *Norwood*. (There may be more—the text was not scanned and word-searched. Numbers are not at the heart of the issue.) Such usages are at long last strongly proscribed. The term is indelibly pejorative, but closer examination reveals a surprisingly broad tonal range. *Norwood*'s major offender, for example, is Rita Lee, who in the space of two pages registers five instances, almost half the novel's total (and she has at least one other). Her presentation of Wayne's friendship with his African American "best friend" Otis Webb is entirely positive, though her surprise at the immaculate condition of the Webb home (she and Wayne were dinner guests) reveals her familiarity with demeaning stereotypes. "I'll say this," she concludes, "the world would be a better place to live and work in if everybody was as nice to ******* as Wayne." The other appearances of "******" are shared between Grady Fring (two), the deceased Mr. Pratt (one), the narrator (one), and an unnamed "famous athlete" on the homebound bus (one), who complains that "******* have taken over every sport except swimming." "They don't know how to swim," he reports. "******" is not uttered by Norwood.

So: the athlete is an idiot, Mr. Pratt and Grady Fring flesh out their already-unsavory portrayals with their retrograde language, and even the narrator, by a single slipup (a geographical marker in Jacksonville, describing Norwood's pedestrian move from "white town" to "****** town"), signals an insensitivity to evolving standards. Rita Lee, despite being by a wide margin the worst offender in terms of usage, emerges by attitude as the best of the lot. Before leaving *Norwood* and race behind, it should be noted that the Miss Phillips who accompanies Norwood on the first leg of the New York journey is identified on her initial appearance as "a long tall redbone girl." Nothing is made of this, the word "redbone" is not repeated, and Norwood opens the trip with sustained if unsuccessful attempts to cultivate her good will: "He told her fifteen or twenty jokes and pointed out amusing signs and discussed the various construction projects along the way but she wasn't having any." But "redbone," sometimes capitalized, sometimes not, sometimes one word, sometimes two, is in all variants a term describing a mixed-race person, a varying combination of Anglo-American, African American, and Native American background. There are scores of such terms existing mostly as regional variants, used both within the groups themselves and by outsiders. Academics used "triracial isolates" as a scholarly catchall label in the sociological literature not so long ago. The word "peckerwood," showered repeatedly on Norwood by Miss Phillips, is also an ethnic tag, always one word, never capitalized except by placement, and always describing a white person, usually with implications of southern rural background and low social station. "Redbone" is most often not derogatory; "peckerwood" invariably is. *Norwood* is thus a production of a sociocultural milieu now dramatically changed, in which ethnic tags and slurs were tossed off much more freely. Encountering these usages now, a half century and more after their first appearance, one can only note them, avoid them, describe the contexts of their deployment, record the wish that they weren't there.

Norwood's close echo of the ancient return-song trope, linked to the novel's recurrent fulfillment of the Joann-proffered Christian precept, might lead readers to understand other recurrent elements of the novel in their light. Perhaps the most prominent of these is Norwood's persistent interest in a wide variety of jobs. Debt collector, bread truck driver, beanie salesman, travel writer, shoeshine-stand operator, Mr. Peanut, cotton acreage checker—every worker encountered is peppered with questions, especially about pay. The disquiet behind these inquiries is obvious enough—although he "picked up his old job at the Nipper station" upon his return to Ralph, Norwood is soon unhappy. "Every time you grease a truck stuff falls in your eyes and your hair and down your back," he complains. Things only get worse when Vernell begins waitressing at his insistence and ends up shaming him by bringing home "choice downtown gossip" and dropping "familiar references to undertakers and lawyers and Ford dealers." Norwood can't match this—"No one you could quote traded at the Nipper station." Vernell even earns more money than he does when her tips are good.

It's not good. The uncollected seventy dollars looms larger than ever, his half-formed dreams of country music stardom on KWKH seem impossibly remote, and Bill Bird arrives as a last straw in an already intolerable situation. The Kredit King thus appears to Norwood at the Ralph roller rink as an answered prayer, offering first an unlooked-for opportunity to recover his seventy dollars at no cost to himself and second (as he learns as he prepares to depart for New York) an introduction in Shreveport from a mover and shaker who knows "everybody on the *Louisiana Hayride*." It's too good to be true—even Norwood wonders if the car he'll be driving is stolen. But Fring knows his man's vulnerabilities, and the downbound, often humiliating ride to the "hateful town" is soon underway. *Norwood*'s protagonist, seen in the light of these quality lit and scriptural overtones, emerges as more of a Telemachus than an Odysseus, a young man getting something of a hard-knocks education.

But by the end of the novel, the rube is back, a marginally wiser man, and his job-related interrogations emerge, for all their hilariousness, as baby steps in his real-world instruction. Where both Fring and Bill Bird once bamboozled him, Norwood now handles them with ease. Ditto for his brief encounters with Yvonne and Marie, understood as prep for his meeting with Rita Lee. "Marginally wiser" seems a good descriptor for the protagonist at *Norwood*'s close. Portis carefully refrains from too grand a finale. The world is not Norwood and Rita Lee's oyster—he lacks even a high school diploma, and her professional aspirations top out with "beautician school"—but Bowie County is all before them. Stardom on the *Louisiana Hayride* may be a bridge too far, but Rita Lee's hopes for a trailer (perhaps used) where the newlywed couple could "play records all night" seem within reach, as do Norwood's plans to take his bride-to-be out for dinner at a sit-down restaurant. "I'm twenty-three years old," he says, "and I never taken a girl out to dinner in my life except drive-ins."

Don't be fooled. A used trailer may appear at first glance dangerously close to homelessness, the rootless life of railyard bums Eugene and the Cardinal in New York. Rita Lee, looking at a snapshot of Vernell from Norwood's wallet, first takes the Pratt home in the background for a "junkyard." But Jimmy Burns, articulating his primary criterion for long-term domestic accord in *Gringos*, knows compatible personalities trump external settings every time: "We didn't get on each other's nerves in close confinement." Like a cross-country bus trip with Ratner and a chicken? Norwood and Rita Lee? They've already passed the close confinement test. (The wallet photo is also there for a purpose. Vernell may drive Norwood bonkers, but she's his sister and he's a good brother.)

Dinner out and music all night? A place of their own with no Bill Bird hogging the hot water? Fring scared off and Joann safe in her tidy coop with fenced-in run? Sounds pretty nice. Once the idea of an overnight courtship on a cross-country bus is not dismissed out of hand as incapable of leading to durable relationship, additional details of the earlier stages of that relationship snap supportively into place. For one, there's the passage where Rita Lee describes a story from one of her "confession magazines" about a woman abandoned in "Lewisville, Kentucky" by a "good looking novelties salesman." Norwood pays close attention, asking questions, and when he later changes his ticket to lay over a day in Jacksonville, he brings back the story to illustrate by contrast his own dedication: "Right here," he says, "is where your novelties salesman would back out." He doesn't use the word, but Norwood is telling Rita Lee here, in a language natural to him, making use of literary allusion in an appropriate register, that he will not "crawfish" (as Mattie Ross says of herself), that he is a man of "true grit" (the quality she seeks in Rooster Cogburn). "Novelties" are lightweight items, frivolous toys, gone tomorrow. Norwood offers by contrast his own dependability. He will be there. His wait, his faith in her return, is thus another form of Pauline charity, an act of accommodation, however low-key the confession-mag milieu of its articulation. In the same vein, Norwood's bus-step farewell invitation to Joe William, if overheard by Rita Lee, would by its reiterated plurals convey long-term intent: "Yall will have to come see us when we get us a place." "Yall," "us," "we," "us." He's got plans for hosting visitors, Norwood must have at least a double-wide in view.

3 —

"HARD, ISOLATE, STOIC"

TRUE GRIT

PEARL OF GREAT PRICE AND ALMIGHTY TRIAL

True *Grit*, published two years after *Norwood*, in 1968, as Portis's second novel, is an outlier in the company of five. Its female protagonist is also its first-person narrator, its primary action occurs in the nineteenth century, and its success was immediate, spectacularly profitable, and enduring. Like *Norwood* it appeared first in the *Saturday Evening Post*, but unlike *Norwood* it spent twenty-two consecutive weeks on the *New York Times* Best Sellers list, the apparent beneficiary of a promotional stunt on behalf of the 1969 film adaptation. An audiobook version recorded by Donna Tartt with Portis's blessing appeared in 2006, and a second film version by the Coen brothers carried the book back to the bestseller lists in 2011. *True Grit* has outsold by a factor of at least five the author's other four efforts combined. Copies in print have passed two million. If Portis the cub reporter found it "hard to dress as a gentleman on $57 a week" in 1958, the novelist with $300,000 in his pocket for movie rights a decade later could afford bespoke haberdashery delivered to his door by the tailor himself, ready to alter as needed.

Mattie Ross is also an outlier for forcefulness of character, easily the alpha in the roster of Portis-novel protagonists. *Masters of Atlantis*'s Lamar Jimmerson has the klutz niche to himself, his slumping Poma a sartorial marker, with the Ray Midge of *The Dog of the South* just a rung or two above. Both are bookish nerds, monkish figures born to the scriptorium. Midge's "I had to get on with my reading!" could serve nicely as a motto for both, bannered in Latin over a seated

45

figure on the heraldic shield. A recliner for the coat of arms! Norwood and *Gringos*' Jimmy Burns hold the middle tier as affable interlocutors capable of holding their own with the Bill Birds and Eugene Skinners of the world (only shooting will do for Tom Chaney and the Dan of *Gringos*), but Mattie stands alone at the top, running the show, watching the money, keeping even Popper, Symes, and Fring on tight leashes with the threat of Lawyer Daggett.

True Grit is a tightly plotted narrative from the outset—no more playing loose with time and space. (Though there is at least one spectacular violation of narrative point of view when Lucky Ned Pepper, wounded but still mounted after the gun battle that leaves Cogburn pinned under his horse, prepares to shoot him with the revolver still held in his good hand. "Well, Rooster, I am shot to pieces!" he says, but Mattie could hardly report this, as she is by her own estimate more than six hundred yards away.)

Mattie Ross's characteristic mode of address is nothing if not direct—she orders the reader around with the same brusque address used for the other characters. She actually wields two distinct voices, that of the fourteen-year-old in the reported dialogue and that of the sixty-something woman narrating the story, though the single spirit behind both is easily recognized in each. "Here is what happened," the mature voice says twice in the first chapter alone (with additional instances to follow) after warning doubters not to refuse their "credence" on account of her youth or gender. The child's recollected voice surfaces most audibly in moments where Mattie proposes a strategy for capturing Chaney or offers to pass the time around a campfire by telling ghost stories. "When we locate Chaney," she tells the marshal and the bounty hunter, "a good plan will be for us to jump him from the brush and hit him on the head with sticks and knock him insensible." The offer of ghost story entertainment around the campfire is made with similar enthusiasm: "Would you two like to hear the story of 'The Midnight Caller'? One of you will have to be 'The Caller.' I will tell you what to say. I will do all the other parts myself."

These inanities elicit (and deserve) no response from the lawmen, but Mattie dispenses them with the same confidence her older self exhibits half a century later in commending the "Southern Presbyterian" doctrine of election. Four New Testament scriptural citations are followed by the "good for Paul and Silas" line from "Old

Time Religion" (a new song in the 1870s) and a closing sentence explicitly for the reader: "It is good enough for you too."

Mattie characteristically reports both what she sees and how she reacts to it—"My thought was" is a standard indicator of the shift from event to assessment. Chronology is frequently explicit—"We reached J. J. McAlester's store about 10 o'clock that morning"—and location is often spelled out in considerable detail: "Our course was northwesterly on the Fort Gibson Road, if you could call it a road. This was the Cherokee Nation." Paragraphs often open with "Now I will," and similar introductions, clarifications, edifications, and admonitions dot her "true account." Were her syntax scored, it would be in march time, in straightforwardly declarative sentences sparing of commas and clauses. Mattie speaks and writes precisely, avoiding the laxity of contractions, the luxury of semicolons, colons, and dashes. But within these boundaries, compositional equivalents of lines and columns in an accountant's ledger, hers is hardly a rhetoric of restraint. She is conspicuously fond of exclamation points and emphatic italics—both are signature markers of her voice. Her vocabulary is rich with wide-ranging scriptural and literary sources. Her father, remembered on horseback, is likened to "a gallant knight of old," and even the scruffy Cogburn's trusty horse, Bo, is elevated to a "plunging steed" in the climactic gun battle. Knights are traded in for equally archaic pastoral shepherds when she recalls her now-lost father in idyllic Arkansas settings: "nor would he ever again harken to the meadowlarks of Yell County trilling a joyous anthem to spring."

Not a word of this is self-conscious. Mattie can at fourteen worry about her appearance, although she's reluctant to admit it—"I must own," she reports when the dashing Texas Ranger LaBoeuf first appears at the Monarch boardinghouse supper table, "that he made me worry a little about my straggly hair and red nose." But she at no time exhibits an analogous fretfulness or insecurity about her writing. Mattie the author knows how to tell a "true and interesting tale" in "a 'graphic' writing style combined with educational aims." She provides early on the fifty-nine-word title of her "good historical article," never for a second doubting its excellence despite an editor's dismissal of the piece as too "discursive."

When Norwood Pratt, eager to impress Rita Lee, casually allows as how he might drop by a studio in Shreveport and "cut some platters," he's immediately embarrassed, sensing his tongue has cut a check his shoes can't fill. The closest he's come to a recording studio are imaginary backstage dialogues with Lefty Frizzell and "howdy folks" star poses in his bathroom mirror. *"Cut some platters?"* he thinks. Mattie is prey to no such doubts. Ray Midge, despite his professional experience in the newspaper business, is also less sure of himself. Rebuffed in his attempts to relate the story of his adventures to the (temporarily) retrieved Norma and bail bondsman Jack Wilkie on the return journey, he realizes he'll need "to write it down, present it all in an orderly fashion." But where Mattie signs off with a clear declaration of achieved success—"This ends my true account of how I avenged Frank Ross's blood"—Midge exits with a confession of shortfall: "I can see that I have given far too much preliminary matter and that I have considerably overshot the mark."

True Grit is thus at its heart the story of brave and headstrong Mattie Ross, as told by herself. Everyone except the occasional academic bent on arraignment at all costs eventually bows before her. "She has got the best of us," Cogburn says, and the LaBoeuf adamant against her presence in the beginning supports her when Cogburn attempts to leave her with Mrs. McAlester. "She has won her spurs," he says. The Colonel Stonehill she worsts in their horse trades, the Grandma Turner entertained by her reading of *Bess Calloway's Disappointment*, the Lawyer Daggett whose letter calls her a "pearl of great price to me" even as he describes her as "an almighty trial to those who love you"—all are won over. Even the outlaw Lucky Ned Pepper ends up sympathizing with her, warning Tom Chaney against harming her. Generations of readers have joined in.

WHEN SNOW WAS ON THE GROUND

The tale told by Mattie Ross's two voices is a straightforward revenge narrative. Blood vengeance is her topic from first to last, a single focus governing her actions as a fourteen-year-old and her memories as an old woman fifty years later. The central story arc spans something close to a single week, with nearly half of it given to preparation and the climactic action confined to a single day. The setting is as bleak as "Journey of the Magi," horses and mules substituted for camels, and the action as bloody as *Hamlet*—"the weather sharp, / The very dead of winter" linked to "bloody, and unnatural acts, / Of accidental judgments, casual slaughters, / Of deaths put on by cunning and forced cause." No births here either, only deaths, lots of deaths, of men and animals, including the sought-after man, the "Louisiana cur" Tom Chaney.

The action of *True Grit*, echoing *Norwood* earlier and *The Dog of the South* to follow, occurs along the track of an out-and-back journey. Its effective starting point is Fort Smith—Mattie actually departs from the Ross family farm in Yell County intending the retrieval of her father's body—but the novel's larger quest, requiring a great deal more of the "grit" featured in the title, begins when she swims the Arkansas River into the Cherokee Nation of the then Indian Territory astride Little Blackie. She travels as an unwelcome companion of her hired deputy marshal and the bounty-hunter Texas Ranger. Their journey is traced with some care—an initial northwesterly track along the Fort Gibson Road is followed by a southern turn back to the Arkansas River and the (apparently fictional) store run by a Mr. and Mrs. Bagby. Their first night out is spent some fifteen miles past the river crossing, in the Choctaw Nation now but still by Cogburn's estimate some forty-five miles from J. J. McAlester's (certainly factual) store on the Missouri, Kansas and Texas rail line ("the Katy"). The next day's travel, slowed by a snowstorm in what Mattie takes to be the San Bois Mountains, ends violently with the trio seeking shelter in a sod-roofed squatter's dugout, rousting two outlaw occupants, and waiting through the night in ambush for the arrival of their comrades (six in number, led by Lucky Ned Pepper). By sunup the third day, four are dead, two shot by Cogburn, one by LaBoeuf, and one outlaw fatally stabbed by another. Chaney has not yet been seen, though a gold coin stolen from Frank Ross's body turns up on the body of a dead outlaw, and a cartridge case from a Henry rifle he was known to carry has also been found. "Thus we had another clue," says Mattie.

The four bodies left at McAlester's with the Choctaw Light Horse tribal police, the threesome moves on, "traveling east and slightly south" into the Winding Stair Mountains for fifty miles before stopping "well after midnight." Things quickly come to a head the next day: Chaney, at last run to earth, meets a gruesome end; LaBoeuf saves Cogburn's life by ending Lucky Ned Pepper's with a spectacular shot from his Sharps rifle; and Cogburn in turn saves the snakebit Mattie by racing her back to Fort Smith (Little Blackie dies on the way) for treatment. So: Mission accomplished, right? Dad avenged, bad guy dead, his bullet-riddled and snakebit body headed for Texas with the ranger who will produce it to collect his long-sought bounty? The "true grit" of the title is rewarded, understood long before the end as applying more widely than to Cogburn and most especially to Mattie herself. But a terrible price has been paid. Mattie loses her arm, and seven men in addition to the sought-after Chaney have died, along with Little Blackie, Cogburn's Bo, and several other horses. Collateral damage is today's euphemism, but there seems a great deal of it.

As labeled on today's maps, the entire round trip takes place in a trapezoidal tract of east-central Oklahoma, narrow at the top, much wider at the bottom, running from a northeast corner at the Arkansas line at Fort Smith to a southwest corner at McAlester in Pittsburg County to a southeast corner south of Poteau in Le Flore County. A chunkier New Hampshire would have something of the basic contour. *True Grit*'s days and distances come off as more plausible than *Norwood*'s, and the historical setting also seems vetted with some care, though a determined nitpicker could find holes in it. Mattie's references to Rutherford B. Hayes's presidency (1877–1881) and Jay Gould's control of the Missouri, Kansas and Texas Railway Company (1880–1888) lock the pursuit of Chaney into a two-year (1880–1881) window, yet a look at the register of hangings overseen by Judge Isaac C. Parker shows none for 1880 and no winter or late-fall executions for 1881. The author himself, responding in 2000 to questions from the superintendent of the Fort Smith National Historic Site, described his background research as "alternately intense and slapdash."

One element of its "intense" phase seems to have been Glenn Shirley's *Law West of Fort Smith: A History of Frontier Justice in the Indiana Territory, 1834–1896*. Judge Parker is the central figure of this volume, which includes an appendix listing in chronological order the seventy-nine hangings conducted under his authority between 1875 and 1896, but Shirley's narrative includes an impressive list of persons, events, attitudes, and even scriptural passages that find their way into *True Grit*.

George Maledon, a flamboyant figure in his own right and for most of Parker's tenure the regular hangman of his court, shows up in just this role in Portis's novel. Mattie describes him as a Yankee, for

George Maledon, jailer and hangman of Judge Parker's court. *Courtesy of Center for Arkansas History and Culture, University of Arkansas at Little Rock.*

the no-doubt valid reason that he served in Union forces (but in an Arkansas regiment) during the Civil War, but he was born in Germany, immigrated to Michigan as a child, and was in Arkansas working in the Fort Smith police force in the 1850s. Mattie is also right to describe him as wearing "two long pistols"—he apparently used them to shoot, sometimes fatally, would-be escapees (though Shirley's account lists Maledon's "rifle fire" as responsible). Maledon, like Frank James in real life and Rooster Cogburn in Portis's fiction, ends his days in the lower echelons of the limelight as a circus attraction, going on the road with his own tent show, spicing his execution narratives by displaying bits of noose rope and gallows wood along with photographs of recently dispatched miscreants. A pathetic decline, as Mattie presents it: "Now this was all they were fit for, to show themselves to the public like strange wild beasts of the jungle."

Portis might also have encountered Mattie's ascription of Odus Wharton's penchant for "black murder" to his "half-breed" background in Shirley's study, where "a mixture of Creek and Negro" is reported as "considered the most dangerous of all the types of 'mixed-blood' desperadoes to infest the Indian country." Mattie Ross, wrapping the canard in a "they say" generalization, voices a nearly identical view: "Creeks are good Indians, they say, but a Creek-white like him or a Creek-Negro is something else again." (The presence of tabooed terms in *True Grit* is sharply reduced from their presence in *Norwood* two years before. ****** usages may be as low as two, one from a brutish train conductor, addressed to Mattie's neighbor Yarnell Poindexter, the other from LaBoeuf in reference to an allegedly increased vulnerability to cholera among African Americans. Mattie rebukes the conductor, adding later that she and Poindexter later exchanged "letters every Christmas" until his death in the 1918 flu epidemic. LaBoeuf of course knows nothing of cholera's epidemiology: it's a waterborne disease. Folks without access to clean water contract it; folks with such access don't. It's tied to class, to money and what money buys, not to ethnicity. One outlaw carries a "Greaser Bob" nickname disparagingly indicating Hispanic background. As before, one can only note the appearances of such slurs, describe the varied contexts surrounding their use, and repeat the wish for their absence.)

Certainly the most high-profile echo of Shirley's study in *True Grit* is the vivid episode centered on Mattie's (and later Chaney's and finally LaBoeuf's) plunge into the *"pit"* (Mattie's italics) already occupied by "the corpse of a man!" (Mattie's exclamation point) and a *"ball of snakes!"* (Mattie's italics and exclamation point). Shirley's fourth chapter, focused on the dangers faced by Parker's marshals and deputies, recounts at some length the story of Deputy Marshal John Spencer, lowered by ropes into "a deep crevice at the back of a cave on top of the Arbuckle Mountains" to recover the bones of a murdered couple needed as evidence in Judge Parker's court to corroborate the killer's confession. "What Spencer didn't know," Shirley continues, "was that a den of rattlesnakes had set up housekeeping in the bones of the two victims." Greeted on his first descent by the sight of "the skeletons crawling with the mass of scaly reptiles," Spencer screams to be hauled up: "For God's sake, pull me up quick!" he cries. But "his nerves soon steadied," Shirley reports, and Spencer descends again, this time with "a lantern in one hand and his revolver in the other," shooting one snake and successfully gathering the victims' bones and clothing before being pulled up again. Presented in court, they secure conviction. The murderer hangs.

 The crevice in the mountains, the bones, the snakes, the underground shooting, the man lowered by ropes—Portis makes his own novelist's use of these elements, turns them into something more mythically resonant than Shirley's straightforward narrative of a lawman's courage contributing to a successful prosecution. The crevice of bones and snakes, opening beneath Lucky Ned Pepper's outlaw hideout, is the novel's triple-headed nadir locale. At once a literal grave and den of thieves, the *pit* is an Indian Territory Avernus, both entrance to the underworld and eventually that underworld's ninth circle. It's a metaphorical bottom of bottoms, where the heroine endures a close encounter not only with death (she's been sojourning with death ever since her father's murder, beginning with her identification of his body) but also with evil. Chaney as her father's killer is for her evil's ultimate embodiment, and in one of *True Grit*'s most Dantesque moments Mattie watches as "two rattlers struck and sunk their sharp teeth into Tom Chaney's face and neck." "Those serpents were my friends," says Dante the pilgrim when the spirit of the still-defiant thief Vanni Fucci is similarly assailed at the beginning of *Inferno*'s twenty-fifth canto. Mattie's Cogburn-assisted ascent from the crevice thus becomes something more than a physical rescue.

The bodily lift is also a spiritual resurrection, a rebirth into something like adult understanding, with Cogburn, LaBoeuf, and Little Blackie as attendant midwives. "Sunlight and blue sky!" Mattie exults, "so weak that I lay upon the ground and could not speak." *Inferno*'s Dante, in the poem's final lines, emerges from hell's larger crevice with similar responses to a similar view, seeing the nighttime stars as "things of beauty heaven bears" (*le cose belle / che porta 'l ciel*).

Finally, to conclude with much briefer possible uses of Shirley's study, there is the shared scriptural citation from Proverbs 28, the first verse, "The wicked flee when none pursueth," and the reference to the celebrated Cherokee bandit Henry Starr. The two references are linked. Both authors give the proverb prominence—Shirley makes it the title of his penultimate eleventh chapter ("The Wicked Flee"), while Portis, placing it in a somewhat different context, puts it in Mattie's voice at the close of his initial chapter. Shirley's chapter head introduces a discussion of Judge Parker's thirty-seven Supreme Court reversals, with the fuller King James verse appearing within as part of his instructions to a jury in a trial (the second of two) featuring Starr as the defendant. The verse's import is the suggestion that flight in the absence of pursuit is itself a useful indicator of wickedness (and therefore guilt). The Supreme Court disagreed, twice overturning guilty verdicts, holding that Starr's flight (he was apprehended in Colorado) "did not raise a 'legal presumption' of guilt."

In Mattie Ross's narrative this emphasis shifts—Tom Chaney flees in haste because he "had mistaken the drummers for men" and anticipated pursuit when "he might have taken the time to saddle the horse or hitched up three spans of mules to a Concord stagecoach and smoked a pipe." Judge Parker's emphasis falls on the defendant's flight; Mattie's stress is on the absence of pursuit. Shirley labels Starr a "notorious desperado," though his account covers only the two trials presided over by Parker. (Starr was finally convicted of manslaughter in a third trial in 1898, though Parker, who died in 1896, didn't live to see it. Starr's flamboyant career—he'd starred in *A Debtor to the Law* and other "crime does not pay" silent films—covered nearly thirty years, not ending until he was fatally shot in 1921 while robbing a bank in Harrison, Arkansas. "I've robbed more banks than any man in America," he reportedly bragged to the doctors who could not save him.)

"THEY CALLED IT THE BULLET DEPARTMENT"

From one admittedly eccentric angle of view, Portis's first two novels could be classified as soldier tales, with Norwood and Joe William Reese matching Rooster Cogburn and LaBoeuf, the former pair's warm though low-key exchange of goodbyes and invitations matching the even briefer farewell of Cogburn as he races off with the stricken Mattie Ross. "Come back when you can stay longer," says Joe William. "I'll see you sometime, tush hog," replies Norwood. "You take it easy."

Cogburn's valediction, for all its rushed brevity, ends with fully explicit affirmation of ties forged by shared experience of peril: "I am in your debt for that shot, pard." Once noted, the nearly ubiquitous military presence in Portis's work becomes ever more evident: Norwood and Joe William are Korean War veterans, and even Bill Bird apparently served in Panama; Rita Lee is first encountered on her way to visit her uncommunicative beau Wayne at Camp Lejeune, and her initial conversations with Norwood include accounts of his own and Gunny Crankshaw's roles in the "tail end" of the fighting in Korea. Both LaBoeuf and Cogburn served in the Civil War, and *True Grit* makes repeated shorter and longer references to military matters—for a longer one turn to their protracted bickering over their stints in "supply" and "bullet" departments; for shorter ones note Cogburn's cat Sterling Price (governor of Missouri, Confederate general) and his nickname Admiral Semmes (Confederate naval officer) for the boy who pilots the ferry in the Indian Territory.

Military references in *The Dog of the South* are more oblique—though neither Ray Midge nor Reo Symes is a veteran, Symes the quack physician brags of using asthma as "the slacker's friend," Midge is inordinately proud of a personal library anchored in "more than four hundred volumes of military history," and both men carry on extended conversations about specific battles and the generals responsible (or not) for victories and defeats. One of these is a biography of the same Admiral Raphael Semmes named by Cogburn.

Readers must also be mindful of Wolfe's Portis, the laconic cutup, in approaching his bibliographic references. Caught by a "desert rainstorm" on his first day in Mexico, Midge waits it out "reading *The Life and Glorious Times of Zach Taylor* by Binder." Both title and author are Portis's fiction—Google the pair and you get nothing—but some twenty-five pages later, Symes now on board, the two men argue about another author named Pollard, familiar to both. Searches this time pay off. The reference is to Edward Alfred Pollard's *The Lost Cause: A New Southern History of the War of the Confederates*, published in 1867 and kept in print today by die-hard adherents of its racist views. The cutup appears here in a darker vein. When Symes identifies Pollard as a particular favorite of his father ("Pollard was his man"), knowing readers will understand more fully the sources of his son's retrograde views.

Masters of Atlantis has, if anything, an even richer cast of soldier characters, led by its central protagonist, who served in the Great War's Allied Expeditionary Force and was supported one world war later by most of the Gnomon Society's leadership (though there's also a very high-profile slacker in Austin Popper). Finally, military veterans are so well represented in *Gringos* that comic reference is made to the "Private Slovik Post of the American Legion" in Mérida. This, again, is the laconic cutup in a somber register—Eddie Slovik was the only American soldier executed for desertion in World War II. One of Portis's last published fictions, the 1996 short story "I Don't Talk Service No More," puts the title's claim in the mouth of Neap, a Korean War veteran. But Neap goes on to "talk service" at length, and he's far from alone. LaBoeuf and Cogburn, more than a decade after their war's end, talk service incessantly. LaBoeuf, who enlisted on his fifteenth birthday, was "almost sick when I heard of the surrender" that prevented him from experiencing more of the "real fighting." "I have always regretted," he adds, "that I did not get to ride with Stuart or Forrest or some of the others. Shelby and Early." Here's *Gringos* narrator Jimmy Burns reacting to an encounter with a Guatemalan army patrol along the Usumacinta River: "It's just as well to step lightly around teenage boys in uniform carrying automatic weapons. I had been one myself and I had known, too, with my heart knocking against my ribs and my finger on the trigger of that BAR, that there was nothing sweeter than cutting down the enemies of your country."

From start to finish, then, Portis found ways to "talk service" at every turn, in both fiction and nonfiction. As late as the 2003 magazine piece "Motel Life, Lower Reaches," he drops in "the Ominato Inn" as his chosen alias for a motel in southern New Mexico where he "came to know celebrity" during an "onerous" two-week stay for his possession of "great jumper cables." The reader whose eyes perk up at the odd look of this is rewarded for investigating with the news that Ominato was both the major base for the Imperial Japanese Navy during World War II and the anchorage used by the USS *Panamint*, a US Navy amphibious force command ship that served for the formal occupation ceremonies after the Japanese surrender. From the Civil War forward at least to the Korean conflict—Vietnam is conspicuous by its absence—Portis's characters have borne arms against the nation's foes, and his references to their experiences, however brief in themselves and indirect in their context, make up in their aggregate a central theme. Soldiers, and more specifically the burdens soldiers carry long after their wars, are a persistent presence. Recollect Norwood as he boards the train in Indianapolis for his maiden hobo ride. "Better put the boots back on," he thinks. "Like getting caught by the gooks in one of those sleeping bags that zipped only halfway down. A suicide bag." Or recall Harold Bolus, like Norwood a Korean War vet, from *Gringos*:

> Bolus had lost his legs, the lower parts below the knees, in the Chosin retreat. "My heart's in Oklahoma," he would sing, "but my feet are in Korea." That was his song. He sat on park benches and showed his willow-wood shins to children. This is what came of too much dancing, he told them. As a foolish boy he had danced his feet off. Let this be a warning to them. Go easy on the dancing and particularly the spinning about, or when the music was over they would end up like him with nothing to stand on but two bloody stumps.

OF GRIT, SAND, PLUCK, AND GAME

The notion of "grit" is by title alone a central concern of *True Grit*. It is introduced into the narrative by Mattie Ross, whose original conversation with Cogburn offers his reputation for it as her motive for approaching him. "They tell me you are a man with true grit," she begins. Though she attributes the quality to him, readers will have already noted her modeling it herself from the beginning. She's barely boarded the train for Fort Smith on the trip to retrieve her father's body when she bristles at a conductor's racist insult to her helpful neighbor Yarnell Poindexter. The stock trader Colonel Stonehill, who meets Mattie before she encounters Cogburn, is already on his back foot within minutes of her arrival, though he has yet to fully appreciate it. He's soon expressing a genuine if exasperated admiration for her "sand." Before this, she has already witnessed a triple hanging, brushing Poindexter's hand aside when he tries to shield her from the sight, and gone straight from this scene to the undertaker's parlor to identify her father's body. "I would see it all," she reports.

Cogburn's favored synonym for grit and sand is "game," and he's confident in his lifelong possession of it. "Game? I was born game, sis, and hope to die in that condition." By the narrative's end the "grit" and "game" of both Mattie and Cogburn will be amply confirmed, but other characters, including some very minor ones, will be added. LaBoeuf is an obvious instance, as is Lucky Ned Pepper. Another example, the outlaw Haze, "killed where he stood" by Cogburn at the dugout ambush, is briefly eulogized (by Lucky Ned) when Mattie informs him of Haze's death: "He was tough as boot leather. I am sorry for him." Ned accords a similar respect to Billy, the young man who died riding back to save him in the dugout ambush: "I don't say he wan't game, I say he was green." Moon, another outlaw, fatally stabbed by his senior partner Quincy for revealing their association with Lucky Ned to Cogburn and LaBoeuf, accepts the justice of his fate: "Quincy was always square with me," he says. "He never played me false until he killed me." Mattie herself, so quick to dismiss others as "trash" (Tom Chaney, Frank James) and "criminal trash" (the whole Permalee family), can deploy grit as a criterion to judge other outlaws (she names Henry Starr among them) as "not altogether rotten."

As an aspect of character, grit is thus unshakably positive, invariably admired, but the very words describing it suggest a shading complexity. Portis's prose avoids for the most part the abstract descriptors typically associated with it (courage, tenacity, endurance, determination), sticking with concrete images to nudge readers toward a view of grit as a visceral, deeply somatic quality, essentially noncognitive. Grit and sand are both abrasives, and its most conspicuous possessors, in *True Grit* and elsewhere, are often difficult, even reprehensible characters. Haze and Lucky Ned are straight-up outlaws, and Cogburn's frontier equivalent of carpet bombing eventually produces a body count that costs him his badge. When he adds to his one-man wipeout of the Wharton family by killing Odus, he is "criticized" for killing a second man and wounding a third at the same time, both of them "not wanted by the law at that time."

Mattie herself combines her celebrated grit with a wide range of dubious attitudes and unattractive character traits. The relatively modest scholarly attention thus far paid to Portis's work has often focused on *True Grit* and most frequently on its protagonist's character. She does not come off well at all. Despite enthusiastic and almost universal approval from the general reading and movie-going public, Mattie Ross appears in academic eyes in a variety of very different but reliably unappealing guises. One critic describes her as "lovelorn" in his title and stresses "her incredible mean-spiritedness"; another, making her a good bit younger at the close (thirty-nine) than Portis did (at least fifty-seven), finds her "scarred for life" and prone to various "forms of self-deception": "The outlook that served her as a child can now be recognized as . . . a serious limitation."

Mattie's "descriptions of Chaney and other evildoers are often couched in terms suggesting the association of perverseness and crime with poverty, physical unattractiveness, laziness, and race." Odus Wharton, seen in manacles in Judge Parker's courtroom, offers a striking example: "He was a half-breed with eyes that were mean and close-set and that stayed open all the time like snake eyes. It was a face hardened in sin."

Mattie Ross, then, after a fifty-year run as a darling of reviewers, readers, and moviegoers, stands revealed by scholarly analysis as a complacent bigot. Even in captivity she retains a purblind confidence in her privileges. She tells everyone she meets about her lawyer, as if she has Daggett on retainer. "I am Mattie Ross of near Dardanelle, Arkansas," Lucky Ned is informed, as if this is relevant information to an outlaw in Oklahoma. "My family has property and I don't know why I am being treated like this." When Ned is also told of her lawyer, he replies, "I need a good judge."

These critiques are not wrong—they are both right in principle and in agreement with prevailing attitudes—but they have gained little traction outside the faculty lounge. The indomitable Mattie's hair-raising story, benefiting from archetypes readers respond to even against the grain of progressive ideals, continues to overwhelm ideological objections. Donna Tartt, voice of Mattie Ross in *True Grit*'s audiobook version and self-described lover of the novel "since I was a child," nevertheless senses Mattie's "implacable stoniness" and notes "the thunderous blackness of her wrath" before concluding she "is less Huck Finn's little sister than Captain Ahab's." Huck Finn, Buster Keaton—no wonder she voices Mattie so effectively. And still finds her irresistible.

Her creator surely intended this allure, but the "stoniness" Tartt noticed is conveyed in Portis's signature muted key, as easily passed by as "official bread hat" in *Norwood*, "ranchettes in Colorado" in *The Dog of the South*, and the "Private Slovik Post" in *Gringos*. Here's Mattie at the close bringing readers up to date on her now-grown siblings, Little Frank and Victoria: "I have never held it against either one of them for leaving me at home to look after Mama, and they know it, for I have told them." Pause over this and you'll wish you hadn't. Imagine yourself in Frank's or Victoria's shoes, your elder sister in front of you, her face a marbled, self-congratulating mask, awaiting your response. D. H. Lawrence, describing the "essential American soul" as "hard, isolate, stoic, and a killer," would have instantly recognized *True Grit*'s heroine as Mattie Bumppo, Leatherstocking born female, made younger, and brought forward in time. William Carlos Williams's *In the American Grain* portrait of the nation's founding Puritans also hews close to her ethos. She embodies their "tough littleness" along with their creed, the "jargon of God" with which they "kept themselves surrounded as with a palisade." Such spirits survive on rough frontiers where others perish. Men and horses fall in great numbers in the wake of Mattie's vengeance, but she lives on, sustained by her rectitude and her bank. She opens as an accountant and closes as an author, confident in her abilities as both. She lies, cheats, and sanitizes her epitaph of Cogburn even as she insists on Chaney's "roasting and screaming in hell." We cheer and cheer.

Portis has thus, in his most commercially successful novel, managed an unusual coup, combining a swashbuckling western adventure tale featuring a heroine as solitary as Shane with a sweeping critique of the personal and social costs of this same heroine's legal, ethical, and spiritual scaffolding. Against the grain of widespread admiration for Mattie Ross's grit and for Portis's vivid storytelling and mastery of southwestern frontier idiom, *True Grit* animates a substantially darker universe than its predecessor. *Norwood* certainly has its dark moments—none more creepily chilling than Grady Fring on the lookout for "lovely young girls . . . seeking a career in show business." But only "a suicidal owl" and possibly one "maybe dead" Elk from Little Rock die in *Norwood*, where *True Grit* opens upon a murder and three hangings, centers on two gun battles where seven men die, and closes upon the ignominious demise of its reprobate hero in a "Wild West" show exhibit. Where *Norwood* ends with its youthful protagonist safely home from his madcap adventures with his intended bride in tow and the huckster who duped him at the outset soundly thrashed, *True Grit* concludes with its now-elderly heroine savoring her austere virtues in solitude while tending the grave of Cogburn, her partner in her life's great adventure. At its coldest, austerity descends to sterility—the vestal tale of a hearth guardian who brings home, buries, and tends the graves of two men, her murdered father and the unlikely rescuer who saves her life and calls her "sis."

At a thematic level the two books also differ greatly. *Norwood* explores in detail various behavioral manifestations of the "charity" at the heart of Christian ethics, finding its core enactment in accommodation of others, in patience and forbearance. The catfish dinner at the Reese residence exhibits these behaviors in full flower. *True Grit* devotes comparable attention to the more visceral quality of grit, locating its very different center in an unyielding confrontation with others, in tenacity and uncomplaining endurance, perhaps finding this a more requisite character trait in a rough-hewn frontier society. The climactic scene at Lucky Ned Pepper's bandit hideout exhibits this trait at its height. "No grit?" thinks Mattie as she watches Cogburn gallop unwaveringly toward four opponents, pistols blazing. "Rooster Cogburn? *Not much!*" LaBoeuf at the same time displays his own courage by returning to the bandit camp alone to rescue Mattie.

Assuming both qualities to be inherently desirable in themselves, one might examine specific moments in both novels in search of moments where the two circles of the thematic Venn diagram overlap, revealing character at its most exemplary, displaying both virtues at once. Norwood's behavior during the Jacksonville layover shows him both "throttling back on his normal pace" to accommodate Ratner's stride and then returning to the arcade to rescue the caged Joann. "I got to give her a shot," he says when challenged. "Norwood, how very plucky!" says the impressed Ratner. Pluck—here's an unequivocally benign face of grit. And here's Mattie Ross near the beginning of her adventure, just arrived in Fort Smith to arrange for the return of her father's body to Yell County. In a matter of hours, she runs a gauntlet of grit-testing trials. First comes the public hanging, where one prisoner's repentant last words bring her to tears and another's drawn out suffering is an even worse "bad part." "Perhaps you can imagine," she confesses, "how painful it was for us to go directly from that appalling scene to the undertaker's where my father lay dead."

How painful, indeed—but Mattie does not waver. "Nevertheless it had to be done," she says. "I have never been one to flinch or crawfish when faced with an unpleasant task." Less prominent in the same two episodes, however, are her acts of accommodation. Her attendance at the hanging is motivated by her desire to oblige Poindexter, whose very presence in Fort Smith is in turn a gesture undertaken on her behalf. "Yarnell wanted to see the hanging," Mattie reports, adding that she "did not much care to see it." The visit to the undertaker ends with Poindexter taking Mattie aside to warn her of his exorbitant charges: "Miss Mattie, that man trying to stick you." But again she steps back from confrontation: "We will not haggle with him," she says. "We will let it go."

A "bandit chieftain," as Mattie repeatedly calls him, might seem an unlikely bearer of Christian qualities of forbearance, but Lucky Ned Pepper, much later in the story, displays a similar mix of grit and consideration. Having just captured Mattie near his hideout, he uses her as a bargaining chip to force (he thinks) Cogburn's and LaBoeuf's departure. "If I see you riding over that bald ridge to the northwest I will spare the girl!" he says. "You have five minutes!" But once returned to his camp Lucky Ned turns solicitous host. "Help yourself. Have some coffee," he responds when she asks for some bacon. He also extends the five-minute time limit, despite reminders of its expiration. "Five minutes is well up," Chaney says, but Ned insists, "I will give them a little more time." He remains in charge and remains dangerous—"I will do what I have to do" is his credo—but even as he struggles to arrange for Mattie's care, he also accommodates fellow outlaw Greaser Bob's wish for immediate distribution of the train robbery haul. "Very well then," Ned says. "It suits me. I want you to feel easy." He eventually leaves Mattie with Chaney, promising to send a fresh mount and ordering him to deliver her safely to a "meetinghouse" where a "dummy called Flanagan" will take her to McAlester's.

Ned's final words to Chaney are repeated warnings. "Make yourself agreeable to this child," he says, having earlier taken a more threatening tone: "If any harm comes to this child you do not get paid."

"MY TRUE ACCOUNT"

True Grit no doubt owes much of its popular success to its purely narrative appeal. It's a recognizable Western, an action-filled story with engaging characters set in a convincingly realized frontier setting. But under this surface, sustained thematic questions are at issue. Mattie Ross not only repeatedly stresses her ability to tell her story well but also insists again and again on the truth of her account. "People do not give it credence," she begins, the clear inference being that they should. "Here is what happened" is the confident lead sentence of her second paragraph, repeated several times, and her curtain line is a straight-up claim of achieved purpose: "This ends my true account." The novel itself, however, continually develops an undermining counterpoint calling truth's ultimate accessibility into question.

Even Mattie, for all her self-assurance, admits her knowledge is incomplete: "I cannot say how he knew about them," she says of Chaney's theft of the gold pieces from her father's trouser band. "There is no knowing what is in a man's heart," she says of Judge Parker, in a more sweeping admission of limited access to complete understanding. Other departures from "true account" are knowing, deliberate fabrications, ranging from Mattie's childish bluff to Lucky Ned—"Marshal Cogburn and fifty more officers"—to the rosy epitaph she creates for Cogburn: "A RESOLUTE OFFICER OF PARKER'S COURT." "Resolute" (yet another good descriptor for grit) is clearly deserved, but whole chapters of less savory "truth" have been swept under a large carpet.

The larger novel's presentation of jurisprudence (at least as practiced on the Arkansas-Oklahoma border in the final decades of the nineteenth century) is filled with comparable instances of shortfall. Attorney Goudy's cross-examination of Cogburn in Judge Parker's courtroom catches the resolute marshal in obvious contradictions, his handling of expense vouchers is presented as comically improvised, and the "newspaper record" Mattie relies on for her narrative is by her own account "not an official transcript" despite her assurance that it is "faithful enough." The legal system in general and attorneys in particular are a recurrent presence in Portis novels—*Norwood*'s Grady Fring is a lawyer, and *Masters of Atlantis*'s Pharris White is a law student—but *True Grit*'s deeper critique seems more generally epistemological in nature, resulting in a wide-ranging though remarkably affable skepticism. Where *Norwood* at its core persistently if unobtrusively puts forward an upbeat ethic based on consideration of others, *True Grit* makes one of its centers a dark-minded insistence on the limits of knowing itself.

Both themes will receive sustained attention in later works, most especially in *Gringos*, but Portis's next effort, eleven years in the making, will stand out very differently for freeing his comic gifts from *True Grit*'s short leash. They'd been let out before for short romps—Edmund B. Ratner's hilarious autobiographical sketch in *Norwood*, Stonehill's brief "sanguinary ambuscade" riff in *True Grit*—but *The Dog of the South*'s repellent silver-tongued grifter Dr. Reo Symes ("not in active practice at this time") will lift this high-octane rhetoric to another level. A scathingly critical subplot will serve as Portis's most sustained political statement, even as another at least semiyouthful protagonist embarks on a road trip adventure, but laugh-out-loud comedy, however dark, will be the new book's dominant mode.

4 —

"HORDE CONTROL" AND "THE ANCIENT FEAR"

THE DOG OF THE SOUTH

"I HAD TO GET ON WITH MY READING!"

Portis's third novel gets underway straightforwardly enough—it's another trip novel. Home base this time is Little Rock. Ray Midge's wife, Norma, has run off with Guy Dupree (her ex-husband and Ray's ex-friend), taking Ray's Ford Torino and financing their trip with his Texaco and American Express credit cards. Dupree, like the Mr. Remley of *Norwood*, also swipes a shotgun. The runaways do leave Dupree's "shamefully neglected" 1963 Buick Special in Midge's apartment parking space. It's a junker, with slack in the steering and a hole in the floor between the driver's feet. Dupree's wife-napping is also a bail jump—he's facing threatening-the-president charges, and Midge himself has put up the front money with a bondsman pal named Jack Wilkie. Big bills are coming in, and Amex is calling about payment arrangements. It gets worse—Midge has just quit his newspaper job, and his father and source of support is "floating somewhere on a lake near Eufaula, Alabama, in his green plastic boat, taking part in a bass tournament."

What's funny beyond the bare facts is that Midge is in terrific humor. "I love nothing better than a job like that," he says of plotting the Torino's path by matching credit card charge dates and locations on a map. "The last position was the Hotel Mogador in San Miguel de Allende," he continues, "where I drew a terminal cross on the map with my draftsman's pencil and shaded it to give an effect of depth." From the start, then, we know we're in the hands of a goofball narrator/

protagonist, an anti-Mattie who for starters must be the least discomfited cuckold this side of Samuel Beckett's Otto Olaf bboggs, whose horns "sat easily upon him." Otto Olaf's stance toward Walter Draffin, his wife's longtime paramour, is rooted in gratitude: "Any man who saved him trouble, as Walter had for so many years, could rely on his esteem." Midge stops short of this extreme but admits culpable inattention: "I should have paid more attention to Norma," he says. "I should have talked to her and listened to her but I didn't do it."

And why not? "I had to get on with my reading!" Three pages in, and the fundamental incompatibility of husband and wife is directly articulated. Norma is eager to "play a more active part in life." She joins a cycling club and dreams of being a stewardess. Make that flight attendant. Her mother is "crazy about dancing" ("I mean smoking soles!"), a captain of an all-female "city obstruction" squad devoted to snarling traffic and supermarket checkout lines, and Norma grew up close to the maternal tree. She needs a world, with people in it. Ray wants none of this—his Eden is a cloistered alcove. He owns "more than four hundred volumes of military history" and "sixty-six lineal feet of books" but experiences zero urge to join any army. He owns "a drawer full of pistols" and takes a Colt Cobra with him on his trip, but it stays in its ice-chest storage until confiscated at the Mexico–British Honduras border. So much for Chekhovian craft! Just reading about "the great captains of history" is for Midge entirely sufficient, so exhilarating that "I would have to get up and walk around the room to catch my breath." A snug reading nook—four properly plastered thick walls capable of warding off the sonic intrusions of the motorcycle owning "rock-and-roll twerp" next door ("Noise was his joy")—this is Midge's dream. Norma's mother has him pegged—he's a "pill."

No wonder he's such an upbeat jiltee! He's alone in the apartment with no job responsibilities to interrupt his mapping. "I was biding my time," he says, in the voice of a biding adept. He's twenty-six, a holder of no college diploma despite credit hours sufficient for "at least two bachelor's degrees" spread out across multiple majors at several universities—"some pre-law at Southwestern and some engineering at Arkansas." There was also a stint of history at Ole Miss, "where I studied the Western campaigns of the Civil War under Dr. Buddy Casey." Over the course of the novel Midge reports having "looked into" a roster of occupations matching or perhaps exceeding Norwood's inquiries, though Midge's reveries substitute lifestyle considerations for Norwood's focus on pay scale. "I thought about the happy and decent life of a forest ranger," Midge says at one point. "A fresh tan uniform every morning and a hearty breakfast and a goodbye peck from Norma at the door of our brown cottage in the woods. It was a field well worth looking into." Midge also has a conspicuously low bar for "looking into"—at another point he mentions medicine as a possibility: "I once looked into medicine myself. I sent off for some university catalogues."

The basic structural comedy of the novel's opening—Midge as a mild-mannered Menelaus remembering to bring along his Helen's lower-back medicine ("She would thank me for that")—is complemented by a wide range of shorter riffs and gags. Crowds of children in the capitol for a "sort of youth congress" described as "Junior Bankers or Young Teamsters" returns readers to the world of "ranchettes in Colorado." Young Teamsters? Just try to picture them. Kiddie-size trucker wallets? Keynote address from Red Sovine? And the Junior Bankers? Still worse—perhaps a motto from Brecht on the plenary session podium: "What is the burgling of a bank to the founding of a bank?" (There's another of these mini gags in *Gringos*, where Jimmy Burns remembers a three-day salesmanship course in Shreveport where students earned "League of Leaders certificates" and "speckled yellow neckties." League of Leaders? How could such a group accomplish step one, in any direction? A cohort well worth looking into.)

Then there are Midge's worries about his reputation: "The paper didn't run cuckold stories as such but I thought it best to keep my name out of any public record." What a phrasal gem, "cuckold stories as such"! And where would they fit? The society section, with weddings and engagements? "Ms. Beauchamp to Wed" and "Midge Bed Sacked" on the same page? Midge has many such worries—the slack in the Buick's steering requires him to turn the wheel "wildly back and forth in a childlike burlesque of motoring" that "made me look like a lunatic." His elaborate barroom protocols are rooted in similar fears of public humiliation: "When the beer came, I dipped a finger in it and wet down each corner of the paper napkin to anchor it, so it would not come up with the mug each time and make me appear ridiculous." Norma is prey to similar anxieties—she disapproves of her husband's practice of checking into cheap motels adjacent to classier establishments with in-house restaurants and bars where they can then drink and dine: "She was afraid we would be caught out in the better place and humiliated before some socialites we might have just met. The socialites would spot our room key, with a chunk of wood dangling from it like a carrot, or catch us in some gaffe, and stop talking to us."

This riff is typical Portis in that the basic ludicrousness of the scene is amplified by a more specific comedy centered on "socialites." Jokes within jokes, like laughing matryoshka dolls—a signature move. Ever meet a socialite in a motel dining room? Meet a socialite at all? Does any person on the planet self-identify as a socialite? What might be a serviceable definition? An expensively groomed nonentity?

The most extended comedic sketch of *The Dog of the South*'s opening section may be Midge's admiring description of his Ole Miss history prof's "famous lecture" on the siege of Vicksburg. Midge plays a tape recording of this "bravura" performance often—while shaving, during drives with Norma. Another impetus for Norma's flight? "I had heard the tape hundreds of times," Midge reports, "and yet each time I would be surprised and delighted anew by some bit of Casey genius." Listening to a master like "Dr. Bud" is evidently every bit the equal to reading about the "great captains of history." Here's a sample: "With nothing more than his knuckles and the resonating sideboards of his desk he could give you caissons crossing a plank bridge, and with his dentures and inflated cheeks and moist thick lips he could give you a mortar barrage in the distance and rattling anchor chains and lapping water and hissing fuses and neighing horses."

There's a difference, too, beyond the greater length, in this sketch. It's warm, genuinely admiring, along with the exaggerated comedy of the pedagogue carried away by his performance. It's a fortunate Professor Casey who gets Ray Midge on his roster. There's a Dr. Bud in Portis the author's DNA too, though kept very much under wraps in the fiction. He gives something of a panel presentation in the "Combinations of Jacksons" essay, but only "The Forgotten River," his 1991 account of a leisurely tracing of the Ouachita River's six-hundred-plus-mile journey from its headwaters near the Scott County–Polk County line in far western Arkansas to Jonesville, Louisiana, shows Professor Portis really ascending the lectern. He's more than good, sustaining a relaxed travelogue pace while packing the prose with informational nutrients. A single two-page spread offers references to two (Elvas and Ranjel) of the four accounts of De Soto's expedition, a discussion of the differing lengths of Spanish and Portuguese leagues, and an inconspicuous sampling from *Hamlet* ("aslant the brook" from Gertrude's report of Ophelia's death) in a lament for the lack of a Hakluyt-derived reference to De Soto's travels in Shakespeare's plays. This arcana is combined with observations of the passing contemporary scene—two hundred million "sturdy bricks" are the pride of Malvern manufacture, while the Ag-Cat crop duster is an "excellent workhorse" despite a "bulging cockpit canopy" lacking the "pleasing lines of the old Stearman." The casual Shakespeare allusion is matched by an equally unintrusive Tony Orlando reference (the yellow ribbons that "girdled the shade trees" at the Rockport United Methodist Church). All this in two pages.

"ODD THINGS HAPPEN WHEN YOU GET OUT OF TOWN"

His money problems solved by a trove of twenty-five-dollar savings bonds left to him by his mother, Midge at last gets on the road. Right off, events or thought patterns that seemed odd or off kilter in Little Rock—Mrs. Edge's geriatric "city obstruction" patrol, Midge's ruminations on Dupree's chances in bar fights with American presidents (next to zero except against "tiny James Madison")—appear wholesomely normal in comparison to the madcap escapades awaiting in Laredo, San Miguel de Allende, and points farther south. "Tiny things take on significance when I'm away from home," Midge observes. "I'm on the alert for omens. Odd things happen when you get out of town."

More than odd. On his first full day's drive he notes "three interesting things" (a small child driving a car, an old man with a placard pulling a wheeled cross down the highway's median strip, and a line of trucks "piled high with loose watermelons and cantaloupes"). The last is especially astounding: "Topology!" he exclaims, marveling that "the bottom ones weren't being crushed under all that weight, exploding and spraying hazardous melon juice onto the highway." The melons, pilgrim, and junior motorist are mere appetizers. That night, in Laredo, he is surprised at the bar of the "better motel" first by "an old man wearing clown shoes" and second by the unanticipated and unwelcome arrival of Wilkie, also on the hunt for Dupree. "I'm a party to the action," Wilkie says. He will be a persistent presence, though temporarily ditched the next day when his car breaks down. The old-timer in the clown shoes, however, with only a cameo role, introduces a darker tone. His first two appearances are brief streaks through the bar, making noise on a toy trombone and shouting, "Phone call for the Sheriff of Cochise!" but the final encounter, following his knock at Midge's motel-room door, is more extended. This time he's added a white smock that "looks like a pharmacist's coat" and has a "bad eye" that reminds Midge of Mr. Proctor, a loner watching television and eating peanuts in a shed back in Little Rock. "I'm just fooling around," the man says, proffering a card. He's Mr. Meigs, he explains, husband of the "shopping-cart lady" Mrs. Meigs. "She picks up bottles all day and I do this all night," he says. Mrs. Meigs made the smock "so the cars and trucks could see me at night and not run over me."

Meigs then departs, after a two-chord harmonica solo, but Midge, alert for omens, examines the card carefully. The front, with the Meigses' names at the bottom, features American flags with "the ever-popular 'Kwitcherbellyachin' " as its headliner imperative. This seems clear enough, but the penciled-in salutation on the back is more gnomic: "adios AMIGO and watch out for the FLORR."

"I couldn't make anything out of this," Midge confesses, but his heightened anticipation of out-of-town omens imprints the bizarre phrase deeply. At least twice, both times in Belize, at the trip's point of greatest distance from Little Rock, the phrase comes back to him. "Watch out for the florr!" he thinks, waking up after a lunch of Jell-O and peanut butter cookies. He's not thinking well of himself. "I was heavy and sodden with jello," he says. "What a piddler!" he concludes. Days later, besieging Dupree at his father's farm outside of town, Midge throws a "big rock the size of a cantaloupe onto the porch" and exults, "Watch out for the florr! Dupree would soon be whimpering for his pills."

So, "FLORR" is read as "floor," at least by Midge, and the card's warning takes shape as comic shorthand for nadir, bottom-of-the-well, end-of-the-rope exhaustion and despair. FLORRs, once recognized, are recurrent presences in Portis's work, functioning as hell did for Dante, Satan's own head for Milton, other people for Sartre. Mr. Proctor might be forgiven for taking his shed for a FLORR, too confident of his lease and forgetful of the potential loss of his television set and can of peanuts. Norwood hits something of a FLORR in the New York Automat, losing his seat, chili, and *Argosy* magazine before being ejected. Mattie hits a more serious FLORR in Lucky Ned Pepper's Winding Stair Mountains hideout, snakebit and trapped in a crevice with bats, a broken arm, and a dead man. Portis's ultimate FLORR will appear in *Delray's New Moon* as Avalon, cruelly disguised as a "home" but more accurately pictured as a crematorium's vestibule, especially on the "Special Value Package." More on FLORRs later, but it's time now for a character at once so dissipated and so extravagant as to make Mr. Meigs and Mr. Proctor appear as mainstream citizens by comparison.

Midge is "a resentful drunk" in a bar in San Miguel de Allende when Dr. Reo Symes appears in search of a ride. His vehicle, an old, now-inoperable school bus with "The Dog of the South" crudely painted on its side, was acquired in haste in Corpus Christi during Symes's flight from a vanity-publishing scam gone bad. Midge has seen it earlier, bogged down in a trailer park he visited in his search for Dupree and Norma, thinking it a "suitable place for their meretricious relationship." A "hippie wagon," he calls it (not a compliment). Both men are headed to British Honduras (Belize since 1973)—Midge because he's realized a farm there owned by Dupree's father is the runaways' destination, Symes because his mother lives there. "*¡Misión cumplida!*" Midge thinks at the time, as he enters a bar called the Cucaracha to celebrate.

Big mistake. Mission is far from complete. The outbound journey of *The Dog of the South* takes shape as an underworld descent comparable to Norwood's trip to "the hateful town" and Mattie Ross's fall into the snake pit at Lucky Ned Pepper's hideout. Long falls to multiple FLORRs. The worst is yet to come, and there in the bar's expatriate company ("a curious mix of retired veterans and hippies and alimony dodgers and artists") Midge ties up with a truly nefarious conductor for the lower tiers of his downbound ride. Symes enters in the novel's third chapter and dominates its action until his departure in the thirteenth—he's center stage for two-thirds of the book. In his company Midge is lured into acting as: a driver of a getaway car (abetting Symes's flight from the allegedly dangerous Ted "Ski" Brunowski), a human trafficker (of Symes himself, from Mexico into British Honduras), a spy/informer (on Symes's mother, abetting his plans for her Mississippi River island), and a drug dealer (obtaining

Demerol, among other drugs, for Symes, using his bogus prescriptions). The doctor is a thoroughly reprehensible character, with two arrests in California (for impersonating a naval officer and for disrupting divine service) and his medical license suspended in Louisiana for administering a "Class B irritant poison" to a patient in his arthritis clinic. (The "disturbing divine service" bit may be an instance of Portis's slyly attaching an item from his own bio to his Falstaffian creation. There's a spot in the *Looking Back at the "Arkansas Gazette"* volume where Portis's former Little Rock housemate Jack Meriwether recalls summertime suppers at a restaurant called Lido's: "There was generally a tent meeting going on at Twelfth and Main in a vacant lot not far from Granoff's. And [Charles] Portis was the one who always had to stop, and he would make signs from the back of the crowd that indicated that he thought the preaching was heretical and often draw attention to himself and then quietly slip away.")

Symes even makes a habit of robbing his mother. "This makes thirty some-odd I've found so far," he exults after discovering a year-old insurance check made out to her. "Your mother will have to endorse them," says the still-naïve Midge, but Symes doesn't miss a beat: "They'll be well endorsed, don't worry about it." Mom, however, is onto her worse-than-wayward son: "I remember you standing up there in the choir in Ferriday in your robe, just baying out, 'I'd rather have Jesus than silver or gold!' and all the time you were taking advantage of the deaf people of Concordia Parish. You were taking their money and putting those enormous Filipino hearing aids in their ears that squealed and buzzed when they worked at all, and in some cases, I believe, caused painful electric shock."

When the Buick finally makes it into Belize, with Symes in a sodden coma in the back, Mrs. Symes and her pal Melba at first take Midge for a lawman. "Are you with the postal authorities?" Mom asks, remembering an earlier visit in connection with a "Gifts for Grads" scam. "Has he got some old floozie with him?" is her second query, a suspicion also rooted in prior experience. Suspicion three, not phrased as a question, is that he's drunk. Symes is also, and not coincidentally, Portis's most frequent utterer of "******" slurs, less murderously deranged than the Dan of *Gringos* but fairly described as a wholly parasitic presence. Slime, or more precisely snot, is the signal indicator of his presence, like the "fruity breath" of the diabetic

Ski. Every page of his copy of *With Wings as Eagles*, a salesman's manual produced by the John Selmer Dix revered by Symes as "the greatest writer who ever lived," is spotted with "bits of gray snot" that have "dried and crystallized." Even his prescription slips have "amber nose deposits" on them, Midge reports as he goes to fill them. "The old man left a mucous track behind him like a snail," he says.

But this same Symes is also his author's second most memorable character, eclipsed only by Mattie Ross, and easily his funniest. And this is saying something, given Portis's Dickens-level gift for creating the dozens upon dozens of sharply delineated major and minor characters who throng his books. *The Dog of the South* deploys a cast of more than fifty. *Masters of Atlantis* musters close to sixty-five. *Gringos* may top one hundred. Pulled from the page into the world, given a mic and stage with a stool to sit on, Symes would make a fortune in stand-up. He's a cracker-barrel Belial, a silver-tongued devil fallen on hard times but still a spellbinder. Chaucer's Pardoner, Twain's duke and king, *The Confidence-Man*'s herb-doctor—these are Symes's quality lit peers. Their lowbrow colleagues are on television twenty-four seven—the litmus-paper tag line is "the . . . family of products." Every word is sheer patter, every anecdote a hustle and shuck. "Just pay separate shipping." "But wait!" Appalled and held, we laugh and laugh.

It's a challenge not to be trapped into endless citation, unable to select, such are the riches of Symes's blather. We'll stick with two samples for now. Here's just one of Reo's plans for Mom's island:

> How about a theme park? Jefferson Davis Land. It's not far from the old Davis plantation. Listen to this. I would dress up like Davis in a frock coat and greet the tourists as they stepped off the ferry. . . . I'd have Lee too, and Jackson and Albert Sidney Johnston, walking around the midway. Hire some people with beards, you know, to do that. I wouldn't have Braxton Bragg or Joseph E. Johnston. Every afternoon at three Lee would take off his gray coat and wrestle an alligator in a mud hole. Prize drawings. A lot of T-shirts and maybe a few black and white portables.

And here's a California cross-border denture venture, Symes helping his pal Rod Garza ("just like David and Jonathan") make legal contacts:

Rod had an interest in a denture factory in Tijuana and he was trying to get a U.S. patent on their El Tigre model. They were wonderful teeth. They had two extra canines and two extra incisors of tungsten steel. Slap a set of those Tiger plates in your mouth and you can throw your oatmeal out the window. You could shred an elk steak with those boogers.

There are dozens more (at least) where these came from—the City of Life nursing home (also on Mom's island), strawberry farms in California, the arthritis clinic in Ferriday, Louisiana. Hilarious stuff, all of it, sidesplitting, but dark currents connected to horrors at the center of the nation's history run underneath. Jefferson Davis Land is a "Lost Cause" throwback celebrating a band of slavers dedicated to the republic's overthrow, the oldsters in the nursing home are drugged ("Put a halfgrain of phenobarbital in their soup every night and they won't give you much trouble") and the strawberry farm relies on leased-convict labor ("Those pimps were dropping in their tracks"). The arthritis clinic, for its part, pushes "The Brewster Method" ("gold salts and nuxated zinc followed by thirty push-ups and a twelve-minute nap"), a regimen echoing the once enormously popular though therapeutically worthless "Double Chloride of Gold" alcoholism cure that from the 1880s through the 1930s brought thousands of inebriates each year to Leslie E. Keeley's treatment centers. The obvious literary tie is again to Melville, to *The Confidence-Man*'s herb-doctor, with his "Samaritan Pain Dissuader" and "Omni-Balsamic Reinvigorator." Scams, every last one—and in the end crime fails to pay. Rod Garza meets a terrible fate—"You can't talk your way out of an exploding car"—and Melba's prophetic gifts foresee an equally grim end for Symes himself.

Even Symes's self-proclaimed FLORR moment is a scam (and a well-worn scam at that, another paltry chief-of-sinners routine), the huckster evangelist presenting himself as the alpha reprobate prior to his road-to-Damascus moment. ("I was a bigger hog for women than Leon ever was. Talk about your prisoners of love. Talk about your boar minks.") But even here, in the weeper mode mined so profitably by Tammy Faye Bakker and Jimmy "I Have Sinned" Swaggart, Symes is a top-octane performer. "It's time for plain speaking," he says, meaning anything but. He then opens with a list of negatives, delivered in

THE KEELEY INSTITUTE
WHITE PLAINS, N. Y.
FOR THE SPECIAL MEDICAL TREATMENT OF
Alcohol and Opium Inebriates.

This institution is founded on the well recognized fact that inebriety is a disease and curable. Experience has shown that 95 per cent. of the cases treated here are permanently cured.

CHARLES E. PERSONS, W. H. VAN DEN BURG, M. D.,
Superintendent. Medical Director.

Cash or Credit—Furniture, Carpets, Shades, etc. **FRIEL & HAND**
110 South Fourth Ave., MT. VERNON, N. Y.
54th St. and Third Ave., New York City.

Advertisement for Leslie E. Keeley's Keeley Institute. *Reprinted from E. F. Turner,* 1891–1892 Turner's New York and Harlem Railroad Directory *(Yonkers, NY: E. F. Turner, 1892).*

short, declarative sentences. "Let's face it, I'm a beggar. I'm old and sick. I have no friends, not one. Rod Garza was the last friend I had on this earth. I have no home. I own no real property." The "Dog of the South" bus, he says, grounded in San Miguel, is his "entire estate." So far, so good—hard truth straightforwardly told. But now the penitent con man is off his knees and running, a Pardoner resurrected, ready to close the deal: "If I did have a home and in that home one room was set aside as a trophy room—listen to this—the walls of that room would be completely barren of citations and awards and scrolls and citizenship plaques. Can you imagine that? Can you imagine the terrible reproach of those blank walls to a professional man like me? You could hardly blame me if I kept that shameful room closed off and locked."

An extraordinary leap up from the FLORR, this, from no home at all beyond a derelict bus to a showcase residence opulent enough for a "trophy room" in less than a page. There follows a good bit of back-and-forth about the doleful influence of "low companions" (Melba's term) on the once-promising medical student. "I had a massive executive head and a million-dollar personality," Symes claims. "I was wide awake. I was just as keen as a brier. Mama can tell you how frisky I was." Mama's reply doesn't exactly focus on friskiness: "I was always afraid you would be burned up in a night-club fire, baby." The doctor meanwhile downshifts into a register drawn largely from old hymns. "Just as I am, without one plea," he cries, lecturing "Speed" (Symes never learns Midge's name, calling him Speed throughout) on the song's redemptive themes. " 'Just as I am, though tossed about, with many a conflict, many a doubt.' Can you understand the appeal it has for me?" he asks. "Can you see why I always request it, no matter where I am in my travels?" It's all sidesplitting, but the somber undercurrents keep running. How does Symes know he's a has-been? He hasn't been sued in four years. When his shift to hymnal language includes a mention of "land"—"My face is now turned toward that better land, but much too late"—we know his deeper reference is to Mama's island.

The language is mad, from the phrasal level up. "Massive executive head"—who but Portis? His Symes is a monster creation, every venal impulse endowed with manic verbal panache. And earnest Midge is his perfect foil, a sucker even for the inferior version he overhears in his hotel's adjoining room: "I paid particular attention to a California evangelist who came on each morning at nine. I looked forward to this program. Was the man a fraud? He was very persuasive and yet there was a Satanic note in his cleverness. I couldn't work it out." Vulnerable even to this minor leaguer, no wonder Midge falls into a whole rap sheet of crimes under Symes's spell.

DIX

I can see Uranus? My mother was a Tubb? A character named Dix? Where are we here, the fifth-grade playground? Under the grandstand with Seymour Butts? A horse named Harass announced as scratched from the field as it heads to the post? The comic genius sources its humor where it will, often in the *inter faeces et urinam nascimur* sweet spot, but John Selmer Dix, despite his name and his absence, both occupies a central niche in *The Dog of the South* and points forward to the central preoccupations of *Masters of Atlantis*. Both Symes and Midge spend time with Dix's *With Wings as Eagles*, a motivational tract and how-to guide for salesmen—Symes praising his well-worn, coverless, and deeply smarmed copy and earnest Midge, hesitant to "judge it too quickly," struggling to make sense of its often-contradictory maxims. In this effort he prefigures Lamar Jimmerson's initial attempts to decode an ancient work of Atlantean wisdom illustrated with geometric figures and written in a language he does not understand.

Dix as he's presented in Symes's rambling accounts emerges as an itinerant figure, a bus-riding sadhu or wandering philosopher in a tradition older than Democritus and as recently hip as Neal Cassady. The scant published accounts of Dix's life and work fit this profile, appearing in *Motel Life* and *Trailer Review* (fictional periodicals both), and he apparently produced *Wings* during repeated coast-to-coast journeys: "Do you know that express bus that leaves Dallas every day at noon for Los Angeles? That's the one he liked. He rode back and forth on it for an entire year when he was working on *Wings*."

Such extravagant praise ("Dix puts William Shakespeare in the shithouse") and detailed accounting for the origins of what, despite the biblical sonorities of its title, is a pep-talk sales manual is inherently comic. But Dix himself, according to Symes's offhand account, eventually rejected *Wings* as "nothing but trash" and either fell silent or spent his last years "filling up thousands of sheets of paper with his thoughts" before disappearing without publishing again. A bizarre lost-wisdom thread is thereby added to the novel's already crowded thematic mix, joining the Midge-centered stolen-bride narrative, the Symes-centered land-grab plot to steal the Mississippi River island from his mother, the Jack Wilkie–centered bounty-hunter tale, and the Mr. Meigs–based "watch out for the FLORR" warning. "Find the missing trunk and you've found the key to his so-called silent years," says Symes. "You've found a gold mine is what you've found." What you've found is a Route 66 *Codex Pappus*, but Portis put that in his next book.

Here no actual search for wisdom is underway, by Symes or anyone else. In *The Dog of the South*, the action is mostly motivated by short-term goals achievable by real-world action. Midge wants to recover his Torino and his wife. Jack Wilkie wants to capture Dupree. Dr. Symes wants a "warranty deed" to Jean's Island. Even Mr. Meigs's concern about the FLORR, his more abstractly intellectual inquiry into what conditions might constitute the absolute worst the world could inflict on the living, seems a more present quest than that for the ultimate ruminations of a hermit-sage whose juvenilia reduced all prior writing to "foul grunting."

But then, as the trip moves to its final leg and the novel to its inconclusive close, additional issues of just this sort move to the fore. Jack Wilkie, long admired by Midge "for being a man of action," suddenly "became solemn" and "began to pose rhetorical questions. 'What is everybody looking for?' he said." Love gets Norma's immediate vote, with Midge, after "some thought," weighing in with "a good job of work to do" before Wilkie opts for a basic-survival position: "a place where he could get food cheap—on a regular basis." We're a page from the end at this point, but sweeping questions of this sort will be on tap from the opening paragraphs of *Masters of Atlantis*.

HORDE CONTROL

Politics is rarely a central concern in a Portis novel. Rutherford B. Hayes and Al Smith are mentioned in *True Grit*, and Hitler, Tōjō, and New York City's Mayor Wagner are referenced in *Norwood*, but the spotlight in both is focused elsewhere, on the private sphere instead of the public, on family matters. In *The Dog of the South*, bribes to border and customs officials may be offered and accepted at several points, but the corruptions of Mexican officialdom are far from the novel's core interest. Unlike the first two novels, however, Portis's third, appearing at the end of the 1970s after an eleven-year interval (the longest of his career), exhibits a persistent if rarely explicit interest in larger social issues.

The most obvious of these deforms the novel's structure in its closing sections by departing from Midge's first-person narrative for his summary of the just-located Norma's hospital-bed report of Dupree's misadventures among a crew of "radical photographers" during their stay in San Miguel. Dupree's credentials had been vouched for with this group by "a third party in Massachusetts" who told them he "had threatened to kill the President and was okay." Also mentioned, either by the third party or by Dupree himself, was his ownership of "a shopping center in Memphis which produced a vast income that was now available to the radical movement." Portis's contempt is clear enough, but the critique is too crudely drawn, and the entire episode is by a substantial margin the novel's weakest stretch. Here's the account, Midge reporting Norma's report, of "Come Dream Along with Me," a "famous speech" delivered by Jay Bomarr, one of the photographers: "It was a dream of blood and smashed faces, with a lot of talk about 'the people,' whose historic duty it was to become a nameless herd and submit their lives to the absolute control of a small pack of wily and vicious intellectuals."

They're subpar Portis, these scenes, the sarcasm overloaded with signposts ("nameless herd," "wily and vicious intellectuals") directing reader response. Portis at his best gets in his digs in passing, offhandedly, as when Christine Walls, an "artist from Arizona" Midge encounters in Belize, moves through a hospital ward "in the confident manner of a draftdodger athlete signing autographs for mutilated soldiers." (This is the laconic cutup in very dark top form, with perhaps a belated dig at John Wayne, who died the year *The Dog of the South* was published. Wayne was in fact booed off the stage by wounded Marines at Aiea Heights Naval Hospital in Hawaii. Would Portis have known this? Very probably.)

Norma's appendectomy occurs "a week or ten days" before Midge finds her, and much has happened in the interval. Midge has confronted Dupree at his father's farm, Jack Wilkie has arrived and been jailed for threatening a local ranch manager, both Mrs. Symes and Melba are in the hospital, and Dr. Symes, taking his mother's imminent death for granted ("church is out this time"), has departed, challenges to Mom's will in the offing. "Let me tell you how it is, Speed," he explains. "I need to be on the ground in Louisiana. All right? Nuff said." All this social upheaval is then eclipsed by natural disaster—a hurricane sweeps through town, killing people and flooding the streets. Midge is twice ordered into emergency service, first as a member of a sandbagging crew composed in part of prisoners (reuniting him with Wilkie) and second as a hospital orderly (reuniting him with Norma).

Midge is surprised to learn in his initial encounter with Dupree that his ex-friend and newsroom colleague is at work on a book. (*The Dog of the South* is chock full of authors: Midge was a newsman. John Selmer Dix was an author. Symes and Leon Vurro are working on a vanity book when Leon absconds with the money. Belize itself is crawling with aspirants—an equatorial Yaddo or Bread Loaf! Melba has penned several short stories, including one about a "father-and-son rape team who prowled the Laundromats of New Orleans," and an Episcopal missionary named Father Jackie is busy composing "new Christmas carols" and "a new catechism for the modern world." Even Mrs. Symes has produced a longish poem about a hurricane.) The surface, with Dupree as elsewhere, is comic—there is no book; only an "outline" is "almost complete"—but the subterranean line could hardly be more ominous.

    His work in progress, Dupree tells Midge, is devoted to "horde control." The point is restated several times. He's interested in "Shaping up the Skraelings. Getting them organized." (More on "Skraelings" later, but for now we'll take the term as synonymous with "subhumans.") Dupree's book will be a how-to manual involving "low-voltage strobe lights and certain audio-visual techniques," but the driving economic motive for the planned "shaping up" is stated with chilling clarity: "What you have to know is how to make ******* work. That's the hard part." The "hard part," fortunately, still has lots of bugs in its programming, as Norma's report describes a serious Skraeling uprising during her four-day stay at the Dupree farm: "Terrible things went on outside. The workers shot the cows and beat up Dupree and destroyed the water pump." And with this whole episode the recurrent if largely unstated dystopian element in *The Dog of the South* is for once made starkly visible. Dupree's "horde control" dream; Rod Garza and Symes on their failed strawberry farm, their convict labor force felled by the heat; the radicals with their dream of a "people" ruled by "wily and vicious intellectuals"—all are linked by their vision of a many ruled by a few, the divide organized along class, ideological, and ethnic lines. For Aldous Huxley's pharmaceutical "soma," Dupree would substitute a technological hypnotic.

    Mrs. Symes's Unity Tabernacle, this perspective opened, emerges as yet another institutional relic of a senescent neocolonialist regime. When Mrs. Symes shows off her favorite pupil by having her explain "effectual calling" to Midge, the poor girl parrots by rote, in language as old as Cotton Mather, an equally antique doctrine straight out of the seventeenth-century Westminster Confession of Faith. The effectual caller is none other than God, and by his call's bestowal the called soul is not only saved but also made both cognizant and welcoming of its salvation. God, being God, does not make ineffectual calls, and those he calls thus constitute the whole company of the saved, also known among Westminster confessors as the elect.

Mattie Ross, called upon by Mrs. Symes, would acquit herself well. Here's Elizabeth, in the first of her two prompted recitations: "Effectual calling. Effectual calling is the work of God's spirit, whereby, convincing us of our sin and misery, enlightening our minds in the knowledge of Christ, and renewing our wills, He doth persuade and enable us to embrace Jesus Christ freely offered to us in the gospel."

Not a word here against the Westminster Confession, a thorough and impressively sonorous articulation of its creed. For Mrs. Symes and for Mattie it's a facet of inherited cultural tradition, cherished as a bulwark tenet of their conception of the world. But even in the comic context of *The Dog of the South* it comes awkwardly off the tongue of a young Afro-Caribbean woman assumed by her tutor to be previously sitting in darkness. "He doth persuade"? An air of coercion, not by God, who persuades, but by Mrs. Symes, who instructs, pervades the whole scene. What sort of social structure, after all, licenses an old white lady, however sincere in the profession of her beliefs, to insert her scary notions ("convincing us of our sin and misery") into the heads of other people's children? And isn't it also true that the doctrine of effectual calling itself, rigorously applied, renders superfluous to the process of salvation the entire company of clerics and their lay assistants, including Mrs. Symes? She, by her own lights, need not worry over young Elizabeth's soul—the unassisted "work of God's spirit" will make her blessed. Or not.

Then there's Tarzan, already familiar from *Norwood*. The phenomenally popular creation of pulp-fiction writer and would-be English nobleman Edgar Rice Burroughs (an enthusiastic eugenicist who never set foot in Africa), Tarzan is the grown-up son of the English Viscount Greystoke, marooned and orphaned in Angola and raised there by apes. He's an undisguised white-supremacist fantasy, and even Midge is perplexed by his enduring appeal: "I didn't see why this white lord of the jungle should be such a favorite with Negroes," he thinks, noting that "the chapel was packed with excited boys" for a film that eventually disappoints. (The film is *Swamp Fire*, from 1946. Johnny Weissmuller stars, but not as Tarzan, and it's set in Louisiana, not Africa, and thus lacks the hoped-for "Tarzan action with vines and big cats and crocodiles.")

Put all this together—Dupree at work on new methods of "horde control" designed to "make ******* work," the shameless use of Tarzan films to lure children within range of Mrs. Symes's notions of "effectual calling," Dr. Symes's alarm at the insufficiently controlled behaviors of minority (for the moment) citizens in California—and what repeatedly emerges, under the comic surface, is white folks both assuming preeminence and fearing its loss. One of Dr. Symes's racist rants, upon closer examination, reveals this unease with particular clarity. "They're running wild out there, Speed," he says of California's African American residents. "They're water-skiing out there now." The phrasing here is brilliant, isn't it, identifying "water-skiing" as a form of "running wild" when nonwhite folks are involved? Waterskiing is normally understood first as a leisure activity requiring of its practitioners at least modest material means—you need a boat and a motor with a trailer to pull it, along with skis and ropes and life jackets. Water-skiers do not typically move in havoc-wreaking packs, like soccer fans or biker gangs. They hang on to ropes in a spectacularly unthreatening form of suburban vacationing. The speaker, meanwhile, is a twice-booked seller of "hi-lo shag carpet remnants" and "vibrating jowl straps." He's a bottom-feeder, looking up with envy at the affluent at their play. They could be playing polo or buying yearlings at thoroughbred auctions, so remote are they from his station.

Even Midge is not immune. Caught in a crowd of drunks celebrating "life spared for another day" by the passage of the hurricane, he senses in himself "the ancient fear of being overwhelmed and devoured by a tide of dark people. Their ancient dream!" What? Whose ancient dream? Do light people endure white supremacist nightmares of a "great replacement" where they are eventually overcome and absorbed by nonwhites? Or does Midge, by a sharp shift of perspective, ascribe to "dark people" an equally ancient revenge fantasy, a violent if long-delayed retribution for colonialist subjugations? This whole passage is either very adroitly or very clumsily phrased. Midge can report with confidence his own fear, though he cannot be certain either of its antiquity or its universal distribution among "light" people. But of the "dream" (dreams) of "dark people" he knows nothing, and not even the emphasis of the closing exclamation point can hide his absolute ignorance. Here, in a sadly revelatory moment, he seems at greatest remove from the "*gringo of goodwill*" who enters Mexico promising to "*try to observe your customs!*"

There are other such moments—at his most deranged Midge doles out US savings bonds with lavish hand to bewildered locals like a down-at-the-heels conquistador distributing beads. He's also the source of the novel's only homophobic slurs, referring to a Canadian paper-rabbit artist as a "queer" and including "fruits" in his list of invasive *norteamericanos* ruining Mexico ("Creeps! Nuts! Crooks! Fruits! Liars! California dopers!"). One surprise here is the omission of hippies, often pilloried elsewhere. Portis, one gathers, was not fond of the flower children (or their rock-and-roll brethren). At first glance Midge's plan to set up Webster Spooner, the Fair Play Hotel's "bell captain," in the "snow-cone business" might appear as a generosity. Midge certainly sees himself as a benefactor, even calculating setup costs—"A small cart and an ice scraper and some flavored syrups and conical paper cups and he would be ready to roll"—and noting the advantages of mobility in competition with the shopkeeper Mr. Wu: "He could take his refreshing ices directly to the chicken fights and harvest festivals." But just a moment's thought reveals the whole daydream as a patronizing fantasy—not a second is devoted to inquiry as to young Spooner's aspirations for himself. Midge might as well be togged out in a pith helmet! A "small cart"? Really? Young Spooner is assumed capable of no larger dream?

Belize, it turns out, is overrun with outsiders—the Unity Tabernacle is a colonial-era holdover with two old white ladies haranguing children; Leet's Motor Ranch is "three columns of derelict cars their hoods and trunk lids raised as though for a military inspection," its "headquarters shed" a pitiful manor. The "House of Leet was winding up here in this tropical junkyard." Then there's Dupree and Father Jackie, plus Christine with her "Arizona art," Jack Wilkie in the prison, Spann (or Spang), and the "guys and chicks from the Peace Corps."

The closest thing to *Norwood*'s Reese-residence haven in *The Dog of the South* might be the Mayan ruin located between Belize itself and the Dupree farm, where three brothers described as "Indian men" live in what seems to be total contentment, living on the site and spending their days in an endless cycle of ruin maintenance. One of the three is "always hiding in the woods and was seldom seen by outsiders." Smart man, this fellow with Sentinelese leanings, given what these loco outsiders bring in their wake. The other two are by quite a margin the happiest locals in the book, always eager to conduct tours and never not delighted to have company. One occasion stands out for its exuberant hospitality. When Midge and his two child companions arrive early one morning, exhausted and famished after a miserable night besieging the empty Dupree farm, they are warmly welcomed. The two brothers (the third has already fled) are "as merry as ever": "They greeted us with shouts of laughter and they gave us some coffee and tortillas and canned white lard from their meager stores. We spread the lard on the tortillas. After breakfast we toured the ruin."

What to make of all this? How to fit these scattered but thematically persistent elements into a comic novel that devotes most of its narrative bandwidth to its mostly earnest but often hapless narrator/protagonist? For starters, let's suggest a double focus, one a sustained psychological portrait of Midge as he copes with his wife's departure and his inability to find a stable occupational niche in the world and the other an intermittent social and cultural description of Mexico and Central America as they cope with the presence within their borders of so many "strange birds down here from the States." There's a Portis twist to everything, of course—the bildungsroman is comically undermined throughout by the not-so-young youth's off-the-charts cluelessness, even as the *One Flew Over the Cuckoo's Nest* echoes in Symes's City of Life scheme and the *Heart of Darkness* vibe of Dupree's plans for his father's farm are blurred by the crazed ineptitude of their would-be directors. Dupree with his program to "make ******* work" comes off as the closest thing *The Dog of the South* has to a bush-league Kurtz, but Symes, too, is envisioned as meeting a horrific end, run over on a sleet-slicked highway by semitrucks "tossing him about like a bullfighter" in one of Melba's prophetic visions (Doctor Symes, he dead). Too bad Mrs. Meigs didn't make him a coat. But Portis at last confines the crackpot intrigues of Dupree and Symes, however sinister, to subplot status, reserving the spotlight for his hapless protagonist.

MIDGE

Ray Midge, despite sharing his surname with miniscule bugs, is *The Dog of the South*'s first-person narrator for a reason, and he's finally the novel's core interest. If he begins in loss and confusion, deprived in a single stroke of spouse, car, and credit cards, he nevertheless presents himself as the earnest enactor of a coherent self, projecting as best he can an air of rational proceeding. He's "biding my time" at the

"HORDE CONTROL" AND "THE ANCIENT FEAR"

narrative's outset, preparing to "make my move." He negotiates the world armored with a truly enormous list of "rules" designed above all to protect "my reading" and guard him from appearing ridiculous in the eyes of others, though he looks spectacularly inept to the reader from start to finish. He makes lists, checks them twice, then forgets all about them.

Consider for example the Heath bar wrappers left behind in Dupree's Buick, "at least forty of them, all over the floor and seats." It's a bit of a surprise, given Midge's general fastidiousness, that his elaborate trip preparations do not include their removal—"It wasn't my car and I despised it"—but on his way to Laredo he realizes his speed must stay under sixty "because at that point the wind came up through the floor hole in such a way that the Heath wrappers were suspended behind my head in a noisy brown vortex." This must be it, you'd think—that at the next stop the bothersome rubbish, once again at rest, would be removed. But you would be mistaken. The next day, in Mexico now, he pushes the Buick to "around ninety" in a futile attempt to outrun Wilkie's powerful Chrysler. "Candy wrappers were flying everywhere."

There's also the matter of the Edge family silver service, bequeathed to Norma by her mother. Midge is on the verge of departure when he remembers it with dismay: "If some burglar nabbed the Edge forks I knew I would never hear the end of it. My note would invite a break-in!" A major delay results. He returns to his apartment, retrieves the silver, rips down the invitation to passing burglars he'd tacked to the door—"*I will be out of town for a few days. Raymond E. Midge*"—and then spends the rest of the day in a futile search for Mrs. Edge. (The note alone reveals him as an awkwardly formal figure—who signs a full name, let alone a middle initial, to such a brevity?) Mrs. Edge has a "good job with a lot of seniority at the Cotton Compliance Board," but she's not in the office, and night has fallen by the time he gives up his search in frustration: "I was furious with myself at having wasted so much time over it. I didn't feel like going all the way back to the apartment, so I just left the chest in the car trunk."

And there it stays, for the most part forgotten, until Midge attempts without success to pledge it as collateral for a loan from Dr. Symes in Belize. It's somewhat worse for wear from being "knocked around in the trunk. It was greasy and scuffed and the leatheroid skin was peeling and bubbling up in places from glue breakdown." (Does Portis crack a smile as he types out "leatheroid" and "glue breakdown"?) Symes, not impressed, turns him down: "Why would I want to tie up my money in spoons? You'd do better to take this to a pawnbroker or a chili joint." Following his hurricane duties on the sandbagging gang and at the hospital, Midge returns to the tabernacle for the silver, intending to surprise Norma by feeding her with one of the set's spoons, thus triggering "happy domestic memories, by way of the well-known principle of association." Nice idea, but he doesn't follow through here either, instead impulsively bestowing the whole set on Webster Spooner, perhaps as a substitute for the already-forgotten plan for a snow-cone cart.

Midge is thus in every way a dizzyingly volatile if invariably well-intentioned conductor for the novel's bizarre trip, with occasional moments of acute self-appraisal mixed in with exaggerated extremes of self-condemnation and smug superiority. The condemnations easily outnumber the brags—at one low point he refers to himself as the "world's number one piddler." On the plus side, he stresses throughout his nearly superhuman vision: "I can read road signs a halfmile away," he announces at the outset, "and I can see individual stars and planets down to the seventh magnitude with no optical aids whatever." We later get a more detailed description of these "prodigies of light-gathering and resolving power" in action: "I was always good at catching roach movement or mouse movement from the corner of my eye. Small or large, any object in my presence had only to change its position, slightly, by no more than a centimeter, and my head would snap about and the thing would be instantly trapped by my gaze."

The comedy here, aside from the purely verbal dramatics of a phrasing suggesting a "gaze" capable of not only perceiving the rodent or insect but also freezing it in its tracks, lies in the multiple levels of seeing, in perceiving as compared to understanding. Where mice and roaches fear to tread, Norma walks out (and drives off) unnoticed. During the hurricane, the immaculite prospector Spann (or Spang) asks Midge to "keep an eye" on his bag when he's impressed into a "ladder gang." But Midge soon leaves it unattended, and it's gone by the time he thinks to check. (Immaculite, like the Binder who wrote about Zachary Taylor, doesn't exist.)

Even worse is his performance when tasked by Christine to "look after" her son, Victor. Christine herself has a lot to answer for here, dumping the kid to run off for hanky-panky with Father Jackie, but Midge's level of ineptitude is astonishing, a clear instance of child endangerment. He takes both Webster and Victor with him to the Dupree farm, drives at night with reckless speed, wrecks the Buick, and ends up ordering the boys to "lie down, against the possibility of a shotgun blast." What? The babysitter from hell has driven his charges to a makeshift siege! All three eventually spend the night outside Dupree's house after unsuccessfully trying to flush him by throwing rocks onto the porch and through the windows. The house, thankfully, is empty, with Dupree maybe gone for days. Midge wakes to abject failure: "I was lying in the middle of the road and I had slept for hours." Even "prodigies of light-gathering and resolving power" don't work so well when closed, and it's by now frighteningly clear that if Raymond's a woefully inept husband, he'd be even worse, dangerously incompetent, as a parent. The single occasion when he daydreams himself intent on fatherhood reveals his bedrock cluelessness with shocking clarity. He and Christine would marry and live in Vermont. But then he remembers Victor. What about him? No problem: "Send him to Dean. Tag him for Phoenix and put him on an express bus. Then Christine and I could have our own son, little Terry, a polite child, very nimble and fast on his feet."

An aside here. If graduate students in a Portis seminar constitute a reliable sample, female readers are measurably harsher on Midge than males. He was perceived as an utterly hopeless husband by all on several counts, social inertia among them, but even this ran a distant second to his "rules" and what was understood as the condescending attitude behind them. Here's why: "Two of my rules did cause a certain amount of continuing friction—my rule against smoking at the table, and my rule against record playing after 9 p.m., by which time I had settled in for a night of reading." It was these, coupled with the shocking maltreatment of Webster and Victor and Midge's willingness to put the latter on a bus to Phoenix in favor of an imaginary Terry, that did it for the women—the commandments themselves were mostly immaterial, though the "night of reading" was connected scornfully to his later reference to "weekly embraces." "This guy is twenty-six," one scoffed, "not seventy-six." Norma had a roomful of allies.

Speaking of "weekly embraces," here's what might be the novel's most revealing and perhaps saddest moment: "Then I saw the answer," Midge reports of his reunion with Norma. "I'm slow but sure. I had read things and heard many songs about people being poleaxed by love and brought quivering to their knees and I thought it was just something people said. And now here it was, true love." True love, yes, but it is Norma who experiences it, and the heart of the insight here is not that Dupree instead of him was its focus but that the experience itself is known to Midge only at second hand. Midge is not immune to the attractions of women: He's interested in the Australian "cuties" in the Cucaracha. He thinks of "squeezing" Christine and imagines a life with her in Vermont. He is clearly devoted to Norma. But he is not and has never been "poleaxed" by love. He's poleaxed by reading and by Dr. Buddy Casey's lectures. When things are at their best for the reunited pair, when they're going "to football games and parties" and Midge goes so far as to admit having "danced a little"—even here there's a shadowing caveat: "which isn't to say I became overheated."

The "weekly embraces" preceding Norma's flight match perfectly the tepid "We reaffirmed our affection for one another" on their magical night on the beach south of Tampico (fresh broiled shrimp, the sound of surf, and stars overhead) on the return trip, and both harmonize smoothly with the "which isn't to say I became overheated" back in Little Rock. He didn't—he was underheated every time. Midge, all this says, is Midge, was Midge, can only be Midge. What's true of his love life is also true on the occupational front. Every field is "very exciting." All are "well worth looking into." But he's never "overheated," never "poleaxed." There always comes a point "when I withdrew from the field."

But how exactly to read this? It sounds grim, but might there also be found in defeat's rubble a more fundamental acceptance of himself, a recognition that nothing in the larger world excites him so reliably as the sagas that unfold in his head as he reads about the "great captains of history" or marvels at "nature's tricks with curved surfaces" as a stake-bed truck loaded with melons passes by? "Topology!" "Strength of materials!" The world is a huge place—might it have ample room both for those best suited for statics (Midge) and those more inclined to dynamics (Norma, Jack Wilkie, Mrs. Edge)? Midge is at his core a loner, a perpetual student forever withdrawing from this or that field but also perpetually attracted to another "very exciting and challenging field of . . ." It's "plate tectonics" this time, the slow shifting of continents, as the novel ends. Supersize helpings of statics, a nearly imperceptible hint of dynamics. Could this be the perfect occupational fit, taking Dad off the hook at last? Not likely, but . . .

And Norma too—perhaps even Midge sees she's better off without him, as he is without her, running (or perhaps cycling) around with Marge in Memphis, her own future in "city obstruction" looming. Mrs. Edge, however, may be in for tough times, as dancing, especially among the senior set, disappears from the scene. Where are they now, the "big red-faced men" with the requisite dance-floor stamina, the "smoking soles" of today? Are they still to be found anywhere, the twenty-first-century analogues of the once-weekly Veterans of Foreign Wars and Legion Hut gatherings where golden-age couples moved smoothly, if slowly, to Western swing or big band oldies? Are the strollers and twisters and fruggers of the 1950s and 1960s even now milling away in some nursing home rec room? What ghastly future looms for the twerkers of the new millennium?

It may therefore be a somewhat wised-up Midge we see at the novel's end. "Marginally wiser" was the tag I chose for Norwood returned to Ralph, and it might work as well for Midge back in Little Rock. At least he has a BA, though the teaching career has been put on hold, and Dad is apparently willing to sponsor yet more schooling. Midge's "I didn't go after her again" at the close may even connect him to the then-odd note of elation of the beginning, his "biding my time" excitement before the great misadventure. There's little of the "great Cortez" in him, rather more of the Díaz or Prescott who chronicled the conquistador's deeds, and most (a perfect fit) of the reader so "poleaxed" by their accounts that he must "get up and walk around the room to catch my breath."

So here he is at last, as he was at the start—a nearly overheated Midge, perhaps even a half-poleaxed Midge, certainly an out-of-breath Midge, in love not with "the great captains of history" themselves but with the vivid accounts of their deeds. At the start he was also Midge alone, reading in a room recently made wholly his own. What he's learned, perhaps, is that this can be satisfactory, that he (like his maker?) is not in his solitude necessarily "the most depraved member of the gang." He's been himself, the whole time, even before the trip, but it took the trip for him to know it. He had to find his own FLORR, perhaps in his "Then I saw the answer" moment. Now, returned, he may know—in what is at once the end of exploring and a newly validated affirmation of his armchair mode of vicarious travel—the shape of his restored Eden. They also serve who mostly sit and read.

THE DOG OF THE SOUTH

So what about the title—anything deep going on here? Absolutely, very deep and very dark, though the reference is strikingly arcane, even for a learned laconic cutup. Nobody seems to have asked, but the "dog of the south," we're guessing, is better known in English as the extinct Falkland Islands wolf (*Dusicyon australis*). The operative word is "extinct." A "double focus" for the novel was suggested earlier, with Midge at the center of a main-plot "psychological portrait" and the struggle of Mexico the overarching interest of a subplot "social and cultural description." Midge we've just discussed, suggesting a maximally upbeat reading, but this vanished canid, comprehended as emblem for the fallen world Midge inhabits, anchors a substantially darker tale. The Falkland Islands wolf was first reported by European explorers in the late seventeenth century and had been hunted to extinction before the nineteenth century ended. Big as a coyote, nice fur—the stuffed specimens in museums resemble foxes more than

Dusicyon australis (the foolish dog of the South). *Courtesy of Otago Museum, Dunedin, New Zealand.*

wolves. The scientific name translates as "foolish dog of the South" (and one specimen from the Otago Museum in New Zealand does look appealingly doglike), though behavioral attributes were likely responsible for the initial association.

From the first encounters, the animals struck visitors as remarkably tame—they had no prior experience with creatures they needed to fear. Charles Darwin, who visited the Falkland Islands in 1833 and 1834, reported that "the Gauchos also have frequently in the evening killed them, by holding out a piece of meat in one hand, and in the other a knife ready to stick them." There's also a research principle emergent here: when a Portis reference is opaque, Occam's razor is exactly the wrong way to go. You search not for the simplest but for the most arcane source. Learned on top of laconic, heckling the Modern Language Association panel instead of the Little Rock tent revival.

The foolish, too-trusting dog of the South!—a thematically apposite if strikingly obscure choice of totem, possessing a breathtakingly deadpan savagery. This poor beast, made vulnerable by millennia as an isolated archipelago's only land mammal, wagging its tail in greeting on initial contact only to be clubbed and shot and poisoned into extinction in the next two centuries—it makes an unsurpassable emblem for a Mexico similarly ravaged by hordes of *norteamericano* lowlifes and a whole continent pillaged and despoiled by centuries of European colonialist incursion. But how, deliberate authorial reference provisionally conceded, did Portis encounter it? *Dusicyon australis* is a much-tunneled rabbit hole, but if two Icelandic sagas are almost inevitable sources for the "Skraeling" references, Darwin's *The Voyage of the Beagle* is at least a good one for the Falkland Islands wolf, labeled there as *Canis antarcticus*, and Barry Lopez's popular *Of Wolves and Men*, published a year before *The Dog of the South*, had it as *Dusicyon australis*, straight-up "foolish dog of the South." Portis read stuff like Darwin and Lopez—Dupree's "Skraelings" drop is matched by Midge's praise of the "great Humboldt." Few specimens of *Dusicyon australis* survive (if this is the word), but at least two are in London's Natural History Museum (might the *Herald Tribune*'s bureau chief have seen them?). These are flat skins (while other institutions have mounted specimens). The sneering *Dusicyon australis* label originated in London too, bestowed in 1914 by Oldfield Thomas, the museum's curator of mammalogy.

Not a bit of this nails anything down, and the general interest in and concern for animal welfare by Portis's characters (Norwood for Joann, Mattie for Little Blackie, even Cogburn for the mule and Popper for Squanto) is even more tangential. But the buried pieces—Skraelings, Cortés, *Dusicyon australis*, Squanto—make a very snug thematic fit, and their connection, once noted, seemed (still seems) irresistible.

The "strange birds down here from the States" are under the novel's "foolish dog" sign cast onto a larger stage illuminated by sinister lights, appearing as pale echoes of the conquistadors and *filibusteros* who turned a tropical near paradise—"What a life!" exclaims the newly arrived Midge at his relaxed alfresco luncheon with the Hotel Mogador's owner—into an apocalyptic wasteland. Dupree has been in residence less than a month, his "horde control" plans still a mere outline, but already the "Skraelings" have rebelled and departed, having "shot the cows and beat up Dupree and destroyed the water pump." Leet is a less malignant gringo, but his "Motor Ranch" is a "field of weeds," littered with "three columns of derelict cars." Symes's snot may be the least toxic of the strange birds' secretions—they poison all they touch, these yahoos, and they've been doing it for a very long time.

There's not a syllable of portentous theorizing in any of this, but Manifest Destiny and the last best hope of earth get both barrels of Portis's LC Smith twelve-gauge in the breeches. The reviewer Ed Park's comparison to Cormac McCarthy here finds its deep application, with the murderous bounty hunters of *Blood Meridian* in the 1850s, wielding rifles and bowie knives to trade in severed heads and scalps of murdered Indians in Sonora and Chihuahua, succeeded by huckster descendants a century later, wielding Tarzan movies, cheap watches, and the Special Value Package in Texas, Louisiana, Arkansas, and Belize, to trade in effectual calling, stolen cars, parent disposal, and knock-off hearing aids that "squealed and buzzed when they worked at all."

Midge's trip south is among other things a historical review of Mexico's tumultuous history—near Saltillo he looks for but does not find the site of the 1847 Battle of Buena Vista from the Mexican-American War (which ended with Mexico ceding a third of its territory), and he searches in Celaya for "some shell-pocked buildings or at least a statue or a plaque" commemorating the bloody Mexican

Revolution battles in 1915 between Pancho Villa's cavalry and the entrenched troops of Álvaro Obregón. The last Falkland Islands wolf died between the first battle and the second, another victim of the big world's arrival in yet another little world. The future Belize became British Honduras during the same interval (in 1862).

Dusicyon australis's fatally trusting welcome of the first European sailors is also eerily similar to the initial encounter between Montezuma and "the great Cortez" as presented by William Carlos Williams's "The Destruction of Tenochtitlan," the third chapter of *In the American Grain*. The sophisticate in this account is Montezuma, embodying what Williams calls "the orchidean beauty of the new world" on which the Old World, incarnated in the conqueror Cortés, "rushed inevitably to revenge itself." Cortés is presented as a blunt instrument "superbly suited to his task," while the Aztec ruler is characterized as "full of gentleness and amused irony," a "suave personality," a model of "tact" in his dealings with the bellicose intruder who demands that his host "declare himself a subject of the Spanish King forthwith." Where the native "foolish dog," unsuspecting, is soon extirpated, the Aztec cacique's gracious-host attempts to placate his bellicose guest only get him killed (perhaps by his own people, as a collaborator) and his city destroyed. Four hundred years later his descendants are still being catechized on effectual calling by Mrs. Symes, who thus stands revealed as demanding an analogous declaration of subjection by Elizabeth.

The Dog of the South, despite relegating its mostly indirect addressing of these themes to subplot level and disguising it still further by the astonishingly recondite reference of its title, launches Portis's most persistent social and political critique, sustained over his final three novels. The world of *Norwood* is for the most part inhabited by characters who appear to know little and care less about politics, and while Mattie Ross is as tartly partisan on political matters as she is on religious ones, the central attention of *True Grit* is focused tightly on her resolute pursuit of her father's killer. Portis will be back in Mexico for *Gringos*, his final novel, where "strange birds down here from the States" will appear in even greater numbers. But before this he'll turn to his most geographically wide-ranging work of fiction, *Masters of Atlantis*, where the subplot critique initiated in *The Dog of the South* will be continued and deepened, despite Mexican locales playing only cameo roles.

5 —

"AMERICAN PYTHAGORAS"

MASTERS OF ATLANTIS

JIMMERSON'S CALL

With the 1985 *Masters of Atlantis,* Portis departs for the first time from the out-and-back road novel format he'd used from *Norwood* on. There's plenty of travel, over a much larger world, but the return motif is gone. The timeline also expands, from the weeks of the earlier novels to years and decades—the narrative opens in France in 1917 and closes on the Rio Grande in the 1960s.

The central character for this one, present at beginning and end, is Lamar Jimmerson, another mostly sweet guy but at once so credulous and abstracted as to make even his day-to-day survival a surprise. The title alone suggests a focus on the biggest ideas, on intellectual history's great quests after systems of ultimate knowing, and Portis wastes little time in pulling poor Jimmerson into their depths. By the novel's second page, a soldier serving with the American Expeditionary Forces in Chaumont is gazing at a copy of the *Codex Pappus,* "a little gray book" exhibited by a down-and-out Albanian refugee named Nick whom Jimmerson is treating to dinner. Grateful, the indigent reveals his true identity as Mike, a Greek from Alexandria. The *Codex,* moreover, is also not what it seems—the work of Pappus, a fourth-century Greek geometer who wrote commentaries on Euclid and Ptolemy—but a copy of "the secret wisdom of Atlantis," rescued after nine hundred years afloat in an ivory casket by none other than Hermes Trismegistus, "the first modern Master of the Gnomon Society." Mike is thus no ordinary bum but a man on a mission, an Adept in the

Gnomon Society assigned by its current Master, one Pletho Pappus, now resident in Malta, to locate a suitable apostle to the New World. In Jimmerson he has found his man.

Everything, of course, is wrong with this preposterous tale, but Jimmerson, already introduced to "secret wisdom" lures back home in Indiana as an "Entered Apprentice in the Blue Lodge of the Freemasons," swallows it whole, eschewing even the standard "reluctant prophet" motif of Moses's protest to God, Aeneas's to Mercury, and Dante's to Virgil. Before he finally makes it back to Indiana, numerous Gnomon-inspired adventures occur. Nick/Mike goes through two more names (Jack and Robert), ethnicities (Armenian and Roma), and places of residence (Damascus and France), and under the next-to-last identity guides Jimmerson through a complex initiation regimen (there's a "Night of Figs" and "Night of Utter Silence" sequence before the utterance of the "ancient words from Atlantis—*Tell me, my friend, how is bread made?*"). Under the last, Robert, he collects a $200 ceremonial-robe fee before departing for Malta to report his success. He'll return soon, he promises, with the robe, additional "secret books," and "sealed instructions from Pletho himself."

When he fails to show, does Lamar at last realize he's been had, cut his losses, and return to Gary? Not a chance. His only worry is for Robert's safety—his ship perhaps "torpedoed or lost in a storm." His skipping town with the $200 is impossible, Jimmerson thinks, "because he, Lamar, still had the *Codex*, along with Robert's 'Poma,' a goatskin cap he had left behind in his room." Eventually discharged following the armistice, Jimmerson takes a mail boat to Valletta, where he fails in persistent efforts to locate any sign of Gnomons but does become acquainted with a like-mindless Englishman, Sydney Hen, who "read strange books as well, and speculated on what he had read, hoping to piece together the hidden knowledge of the ancients." Jimmerson tutors him, finding him an "apt pupil," and soon moves at his invitation into "Villa Hen," where the new pals "talked far into the night about the enigmas of the universe." ("Enigmas" may be a carefully chosen term here, as Portis's name for his novel's secret society is itself a slippery label. As a noun, "gnomon" is known most widely as the projecting element of a sundial, derived from a Greek root meaning "one who knows." As adjective, however, "gnomic" focuses on uncertainty and obscurity. A gnomic expression is "ambiguous or enigmatic," and the root itself thus oscillates between two opposed poles. A Gnomon is at once a sage, one who knows, and one who can't ever be sure, a perpetually befuddled goof.)

Masters of Atlantis, focusing its interest in the twilight zone where the two terms overlap, is its author's most sustained examination of the epistemological issues visited briefly in *True Grit*'s concern with the "faithful enough" character of its trial report (and Mattie's confidence in her "true account"). Jimmerson and Hen, each encouraging the other's attraction to "marvelous stuff" resistant to comprehension—"I can't make head or tail of it!" is an exclamation of highest praise—are soon wholly absorbed in the *Codex Pappus*, oblivious to the present world. Hen neglects his duties as "Keeper of the Botanical Gardens in Valletta," so all-consuming are his Gnomonic studies. The two men, perhaps meeting "behind the giant ferns," often "had to speak up over the shouting and scuffling that was taking place in the street. It was some political disturbance that did not concern them."

Fortunately for both men, Hen's sister, Fanny, is also in residence. When Jimmerson, who will eventually marry her, apologizes early on for his inability to share with her the secrets of Gnomonism ("he was under certain vows," he explains), she replies that "she understood and that, after all, women had their little secrets too." Her own greatest secrets, never fully appreciated by the brother and husband who benefit from them, are her wide-ranging competence, energy, and resourcefulness applied to their well-being. Deprived of her watchful care, both would soon perish. There's no real predecessor to Fanny in Portis's fiction—she possesses Mattie Ross's intelligence and grit without the wrath and zealotry—though the Louise Kurle of *Gringos* will be a worthy successor.

Their concentrated studies soon pay off in the sense of convincing both men of their arrival as Masters of Gnomons. Hen is first to proclaim it (though Jimmerson soon "knew in his heart that it was true"): "Can't you see it, man? You're already a Master! We're both Masters! You still don't see it? Robert was Pletho himself! Your Poma is the Cone of Fate! You and I are beginning the New Cycle of Gnomonism!"

These self-inflating truths apprehended, the new Masters (Hen also having awarded himself a "Hierophant of Atlantis" title, first of many) move quickly to evangelize the world, with Hen relocating to London to direct the effort in Europe and Asia and Jimmerson returning to Indiana to proselytize the Americas.

THOSE WHO KNOW

It's tough sledding at first for Gnomonism's American apostle. Nearly two years in, he's recruited only two new members, a traveling salesman named Bates (in Chicago) and a football coach named Mapes (in Valparaiso, Indiana). These pioneers establish the three initial pillars of the Society in the American heartland. Hen does much better in England—he is now "Sir Sydney," made a baronet by the death of his father—raking in new members at "his Gnomon Temple on Vay Street," including "very famous members of the Golden Order of the Hermetic Dawn and the Theosophical Society." (Real outfits, both, though the former group folded in 1903. The Theosophical Society is still going strong.)

Things in America are much better on the domestic front, with Jimmerson, "working out of Chicago under Bates with a line of quality haberdashery," doing well enough to make "a down payment on a small house in Skokie and a transatlantic proposal of marriage" to Fanny. The now dog-eared manuscript of the *Codex*, he decides, its pages bound by a shoelace, fails to "make a good impression," so he orders fifty copies from the printers of a Latvian newspaper in Chicago. Bates meanwhile acquires a mailing list with names and addresses of some seven hundred "Odd Birds of Illinois and Indiana" (Jimmerson is surprised to find his name on it), who are then winnowed via questionnaires to the "worthy few" who receive personal visits and copies of the newly printed *Codex* from Jimmerson or Bates (Mapes presumably being tied up with his football squad). The limited success of these efforts—they "even bagged a new member now and then"— come at a high cost. Both Jimmerson and Bates are fired (though "they hardly noticed," so immersed are they in their Gnomon labors), and the house in Skokie is lost to foreclosure. It's Fanny who saves the day, taking a job as a nurse's aide and speedily rising to supervisory and better-paid positions. She also takes "courses in accounting and hectograph operation" and prepares the typescripts for her husband's first promotional Gnomon books, *101 Gnomon Facts*, *Why I Am a Gnomon*, and *Tracking the Telluric Currents*.

These titles are no doubt a draw, but it takes the Great Depression to really give Gnomonism a boost. Vast numbers of unemployed Americans "now had time on their hands," and some of these, "so desperate as to seek answers in books," find refuge in the fledgling Society. "By the summer of 1931 there were more than forty Pillars in six states," and the Latvian printers, "reorganized as the Gnomon Press," are busy with an order for five thousand additional copies of the *Codex Pappus*. In 1936, Gary's most tony suburb sees the dedication of the Gnomon Temple, "a mansion of Bedford limestone"—a residence so fine that the Master "had to be persuaded by the Council of Three, Bates, Mapes and Epps, that it was necessary for the Master to live in the Temple."

The laconic cutup again—Epps enters the novel in this line, already raised to high office in some off-the-page dealing. Portis loves to send up narrative norms in various ways—we're in chapter 2 at this point, and a reference to Morehead Moaler has been dropped in even earlier, though he won't make it onstage until chapter 19, some two hundred pages on. Poor Kuggins surfaces only once, listed with Epps later as not returning from World War II, his enlistment, departure, and Gnomon affiliation unreported. Portis also delights in introducing plot elements that go nowhere. The Malta episode includes an unexplained ransacking of Jimmerson's room and at least one assault on his person, and Hen, on his ignominious postwar return to London, narrowly misses a meeting with an old man claiming to be Pletho Pappus when he's turned away by Noel Kinlow, Hen's "private secretary." Given his later animosity, Hen might seem an obvious suspect in both the break-in and the assault, but neither is ever solved or even mentioned again. The caller in London also never reappears and is never identified, though Hen castigates Kinlow, convinced the old guy was either Pletho himself "in his sly mode" or perhaps the Lame One. For all these mysteries (and several others) there are plausible if uncertain readings, though Portis's careful dispersal of whatever clues he lays down is itself the most prominent feature.

In a novel with its thematic center rooted in issues of knowledge, especially arcane systems of knowledge making noumenal claims, these fogs are present for a comic purpose. Loose ends stay loose. Heresies find unusually fertile ground in fields where all competing positions are subject to neither verification nor falsification. More than half a century ago Randall Jarrell described a novel as "a prose narrative of some length that has something wrong with it," and Portis clearly signed up to make hay with the rich comic potentials of these somethings. In yet another send-up of realistic novel conventions, he suddenly introduces Reo Symes from *The Dog of the South* into *Masters of Atlantis*, tying him to superhack author "Dub" Polton's *Slimming Secrets of the Stars* instead of the *Stouthearted Men* scam he'd worked on with Leon Vurro.

The schoolboy humor that gave us "I can see Uranus" and John Selmer Dix in *The Dog of the South* resurfaces in *Masters of Atlantis* with Constantine Anos, "unfortunate name, though apt enough," and Portis apparently liked Midge's riff about "gateway claims" being "thin stuff" because "they can only mean you're not there yet" so much that he repeats it. Texas state senator Rey complains that the titles of Mr. Jimmerson's books are overly reliant on question marks and "approaches to this, that and the other thing." It would be much better, he adds, if he could "tell us of his arrival somewhere." Portis also continues from beginning to end to find baseline chuckles inhering in names, especially but not only in cascades of one-syllable surnames—Pratt and Fring, Midge and Leet, Hen and Mapes, Mott and Sloat.

Speaking of Hen, Sir Sydney cables "fraternal congratulations" from London on the Gnomon Temple's opening, signing off with a flurry of additional self-conferred titles, some spelled out ("Theos Soter"), some abbreviated ("C.H.," for "Companion of Hermes"), and dating his missive "Anno, XVII, New Gnomon Cycle." Seventeen years after anointing himself a Master in 1919, the guy is getting the jump on Pol Pot's "Year Zero" notions. This mania for multiple titles never really catches on with Mr. Jimmerson, but the Council of Three's adoption of the initials "T.W.K." offers a wonderful instance of Portis's characteristically oblique external reference strategies, especially when the allusion is to a high-culture source. He'll come right out with extended discussions of country singers, Tarzan movies, and *The Road Runner Show*, but his quality lit or otherwise learned allusions, as we've already seen with the Skraeling (and perhaps the *Dusicyon australis*) references of *The Dog of the South* and Joann the chicken's Melville citation in *Norwood*, are both brief and indirect. Here "T.W.K." is at least spelled out as "Those Who Know," but the reference is both unmistakable to those familiar with the source text and easily passed over without pause by others. Portis's default strategy, here and elsewhere, is most fully elaborated in *Gringos*, where it's presented as an Olmec aesthetic: "The Olmecs didn't like to show their art around either. They buried it twenty-five feet deep in the earth and came back with spades to check up on it every ten years or so, to make sure it was still there, unviolated. Then they covered it up again."

Here the quality lit ancestor is Dante, who in the fourth canto of his *Inferno* identifies Aristotle as " *'l maestro di color che sanno*," the master of those who know. Another Grand Master! The claim is comically ludicrous—Bates the salesman, Mapes the football coach, and Epps, whose occupation is unlisted here, linked to the likes of Democritus, Empedocles, and Heraclitus, all named by Dante. But with Portis especially the comparison also works both ways, with the lofty Aristotle and his pre-Socratic predecessors suddenly demoted, cast as Odd Birds of Greece and Asia Minor. And Dante, too, with his own *Codex Alighieri*—what is his downward tapering *Inferno* but a Renaissance iteration of the Cone of Fate? The *Commedia* itself also shares at least its peripatetic compositional milieu with Dix's *With Wings as Eagles*. Dix rode his bus; Dante the exile lived as a guest in others' houses, climbing their stairs and eating their bread. Odd birds scribbling away everywhere, in hexameter verse (Empedocles), terza rima (Dante), and demotic prose (Portis).

Applied in this direction, the comedy might come across as sourly anti-intellectual, though *Gringos* especially will make clear its enveloping warmth. Scribbling away, by savants and crazies alike, is in Portis's work characteristically portrayed as a benign, finally reverential activity. Study, all study, the act itself, is understood as devotional, and the student, if inevitably a comic figure, is also revealed as lit by a broken-haloed grace. Doc Flandin, in *Gringos*, may get carried away in making the self-justifying claim "I've always had a love for truth and that in itself is a sign of grace," but Portis's obvious affection for his cast of earnest goofballs, from *The Dog of the South*'s Ray Midge through *Gringos*' Rudy Kurle, provides considerable support.

SKRAELINGS, BROWNE, BLAKE

A fuller consideration of Dupree's use of "Skraelings" was promised in the previous chapter, and here's the place to make it good, link the ultimate sense of this obscure usage to a baseline subplot theme of Portis's final three novels. The term is Old Norse, used by Scandinavian explorers and settlers in Greenland and North America in the eleventh and twelfth centuries to describe Indigenous peoples. The import, as usual with Group A tags for Group B, is derogatory—the modern Icelandic term translates as "barbarian" as an ethnic slur and "churl" or "coarse fellow" as a class badge. Most English-speaking readers today likely encounter the word in the two Vinland Sagas, *The Saga of the Greenlanders* and *Erik the Red's Saga*.

By merely inserting this word in Dupree's mouth Portis greatly enlarges the spatial and temporal range of his indictment. Not only is Mexico in the nineteenth and twentieth centuries overrun by Anglo armies and 1960s hippies, but this modern scourge is also by this move tied to the millennium-long apocalyptic assault by Europeans and Euro-Americans on the whole hemisphere. Here's the deep import of Symes's "mucous track"—the sliming of a continent. Arrive in an Eden, the "fresh, green breast of the new world," and devote half a millennium to befouling it, lacing its lands with poisons and its seas with plastics. Rivers on fire in Ohio, dead zones in Lake Erie, dioxin in Missouri, chat piles in Oklahoma, mine tailings in Colorado, underground fires in Pennsylvania, undrinkable water in Michigan and Mississippi—look no further for truly dystopian FLORRs.

In Portis's pages derelict vehicles and home furnishings on fire signal the disaster at local scale. The burning sofa in the Gnomon Temple's broken fountain in Burnette and the "smoldering mattress" in Brooklyn used to roast marshmallows in *Norwood* join Symes's wrecked "hippie wagon" and Midge's destroyed Torino as signals of continuing "Westward ho!" presence. There's also the "utterly lifeless ... mineral waste" of Hogandale's abandoned gold mines and the "bog" swallowing Neap's house in "I Don't Talk Service No More." Low-profile markers, as per usual, but notably recurrent.

Dupree, Symes, the hippies and throwback missionizers, even the malevolent Dan of *Gringos* and the Dr. Mole of *Delray's New Moon*—they appear in this expanded geographical and historical context as belated, decadent Vikings and conquistadors. First the soldiers, later the Bible beaters and the dopers. The scientific name of an extinct South American wolf, linked to an Old Norse label for threatened North American native peoples—rarely has so much been so succinctly suggested by such brief, obscure, easily overlooked references.

EPA radiation warning sign, Arizona. *EPA image.*

More on Buster Keaton was also promised some time back, in support of Donna Tartt's sagacity in noting a comparison with Mattie Ross's "deadpan manner." A yet deeper resonance might be found right here, in the fundamentally corrupt nature of the social world where Keaton's and Portis's protagonists pursue their earnest ends. Dana Stevens's *Camera Man* describes the "cosmos" of Keaton's 1922 *Cops* as "a place of random injustice and meaningless violence, where valor, industry, and even true love go unrewarded." Her description of the "essential solitude" of the Keaton character would also do nicely for Mattie, Midge, and the Jimmy Burns portrayed by Flandin as "solitary as a snake."

Before we leave the topic of Portis's highbrow references, a brief sketch suggesting their astonishing range might be helpful. Dante is an apex canonical figure, widely known among folks laying claim to assessing quality lit credentials, and the *Commedia* is by a large margin his best-known work, leaving even *La Vita Nuova* far behind. But he's an outlier figure in Portis's citational practice, where the default option is either less well-known works by canonical figures or authors themselves less celebrated. Let's settle for now with two of the former. Sir Thomas Browne, a seventeenth-century physician and polymath, and William Blake, an eighteenth-to-nineteenth-century poet and painter, are both highly regarded and much-studied figures, though Blake, largely ignored in his lifetime, is today much better known. They're both in the curriculum and have been for a long time—the most recent (tenth) edition of the widely used *Norton Anthology of English Literature*, a six-volume monster chronologically ordered, devotes nine pages of volume B (*The Sixteenth Century/ The Early Seventeenth Century*) to Browne's *Religio Medici* and fifty-two pages of volume D (*The Romantic Period*) to a selection of Blake's work. Portis's citation of Browne is unique for both its prominence and its length, serving as the fronting epigraph for *The Dog of the South*. No other Portis novel sports this ornament, though *Norwood* and *True Grit* feature dedications to family members. *Masters of Atlantis* and *Gringos* have neither. Here's the passage from Browne in its entirety (italics are from the text): "... *Even Animals near the Classis of plants seem to have the most restlesse motions. The Summer-worm of Ponds and plashes makes a long waving motion; the hair-worm seldome lies still. He that would behold a very anomalous motion, may observe it in the Tortile and tiring stroaks of Gnatworms.*"

    The first thing to note is that this comes not from *Religio Medici*, published in 1643, Browne's best-known work then (it made him widely known not only in England) and now, but from *The Garden of Cyrus*, published fifteen years later. Portis's epigraph makes up the concluding paragraph of its third chapter. At first glance it would seem a more appropriate epigraph for *Masters of Atlantis*, as Browne is as captivated by the quincunx (the "quincunciall" of the full title) as Jimmerson and Hen are focused on triangles and cones. The prominence of hermetic, alchemical, and kabbalistic elements (the "mystically considered" of the title) pushes *The Garden of Cyrus* way down the reading list even for graduate students of literature not focusing their research on occult topics. Rosenbaum is thus right on the money to center his "Of Gnats and Men: A New Reading of Portis" on an exploration of the passage's resonance in *The Dog of the South*. His emphasis, entirely in keeping with Browne's baroque leaps in *The Garden of Cyrus* from ancient tree-planting practices to the "Quincuncial order" of the "Rhomboidall protuberances in Pineapples," is on Portis's analogy between physical and mental movement: "The way the study of tiny motions, those restless tortile twists and turns, tells so much about the workings of a supposedly higher intelligence."

HYDRIOTAPHIA
URNE-BURIALL,
OR,
A Discourse of the Sepulchrall Urnes lately found in

NORFOLK

Together with the

GARDEN of *CYRUS,*

OR THE

Quincunciall Lozenge, or Net-work Plantations of the Ancients, Artificially, Naturally, Mystically Considered;

With Sundry Observations.

By *Thomas Browne* D. of Physick.

LONDON,

Printed for *Hen. Brome* at the Signe of the Gun in *Ivy-lane.* 1658.

Title page of Sir Thomas Browne's *Hydriotaphia, Urne-Buriall and The Garden of Cyrus*, published together in a single volume in London in 1658.

All this makes great sense—the physical movements of tiny organisms matching "the way the mind winds and twists, . . . the tortile twists and turns of the stream of consciousness." A less subtle comedy of scale seems also to be operating, *The Dog of the South* being in large part a chronicle of *"most restlesse motions"* by its human actors, from Midge in the Buick and Jack Wilkie in his Chrysler to Dix and Mrs. Edge on their marathon bus rides and dance floors. Popo on his "three-wheel motorcycle rig," the pilgrim with his rolling cross determined to make Jacksonville or bust, De Soto's "aimless trek"—the list goes on. Mr. Meigs dashing nightly through bars and knocking on motel-room doors with his cards of warning, Dupree hiking and flying to Tegucigalpa, Symes in his haste to "be on the ground in Louisiana," even the "tiny girl, maybe ten years old, driving a 1965 Cadillac"—to a panoptic cosmic eye this whole unhinged company would surely appear as *"Animals near the classis of plants."* The Keaton of *Cops* might come to mind again—he spends most of the eighteen-minute film sprinting.

And Dante, now that he's introduced, is he also a source for this perspective, the pilgrim now arrived in the *Paradiso*, looking down from the edge of the empyrean? From this lofty perch, far beyond the moon or any other vantage point ever occupied by humans, Earth's "narrow plot where we behave so savagely" (*L'aiuola che ci fa tanto feroci*) appears smaller even than the "plashes" ("streams" or even "puddles") that are home to Browne's "*hair-worm*" and "*Gnatworms.*" This seems a stretch, but Portis's sly insertions, for all their inconspicuous brevity, have the effect, once noticed, of amplifying audience vigilance. The three "T.W.K." letters appended to Hen's missive are easily skipped over, even with the help of the narrator's "Those Who Know" elaboration, miniscule in comparison to "Skraelings" and microscopic next to the forty-nine words of the Browne epigraph. But once noticed they move the *Commedia* into the picture, and it stays there, encouraging additional noticing, and the laconic cutup has already surreptitiously smuggled into two oddball novels three or four (Browne, Dante, Vinland Sagas, maybe Darwin) full-bore quality lit associations.

There's little surprise, either, the obscurity of the source text digested, in Portis's selection of Browne for his epigraph. Want another source for Symes, a truly Rabelaisian creation, mix of impressive if unfocused learning, overweening vanity, utter lack of scruples, and most of all a mad facility with language? Look no further for the linguistic component—it's a twentieth-century Browne who slouches into the Cucaracha in need of a ride. Portis clearly realized, browsing Sir Thomas, that he was both brilliant (everybody saw this—that's why he's been on reading lists for centuries) and bonkers. And thus hilarious. Here's the nominally orthodox Anglican doctor on human reproduction: "I could be content that we might procreate like trees, without conjunction, or that there were any way to perpetuate the world without this triviall and vulgar way of coition." Then check the bio: man fathered ten children. We'll be coming back this way when we get to *Gringos*, where Browne's dismissal of the "vulgar way of coition" meets the virtual absence of erotic drive in Portis's novels.

The Blake reference is, if anything, more puzzling. If *The Garden of Cyrus* was not Browne's best-known work, it was at least a completed and published work. Near the end of *Masters of Atlantis* Sir Sydney, newly arrived at the Moaler compound in South Texas and meeting the just-returned Austin Popper for the first time, insults him with a line from an untitled, unfinished work Blake almost certainly never intended for publication: "Lo the bat with leathern wing." This is the opening line of a song leading off the ninth chapter of *An Island in the Moon*, a mixed bag of short songs and prose dialogues most often described by commentators as satire or burlesque. Its appeal to Portis generally and its specific connection to *Masters of Atlantis* clarifies somewhat on closer examination—its overall tone is comic, there are scatological references ("Kiss my Roman Anus" from the same song as the "Lo the bat" citation), and many speakers are identified by their philosophical stances (one is a Pythagorean named Sipsop). But the main point, here as with the lengthier Browne citation, is to emphasize the shared obscurity of the sources, understood as yet another feature, along with hanging plot leads and oddball references to vampire impulses and class associations of hemorrhoids, of laconic-cutup comedy.

We'll soon get back to the Gnomon Society, last seen flourishing in the midst of the Great Depression's ravages, but just to enlarge the sample of Portis's quality lit references a bit, sticking with the same pair of novels, here's a bare-bones listing, far from comprehensive, of additional instances. From *The Dog of the South*: "Hawking and spitting, we lay waste our powers" (Wordsworth, "The World Is Too Much with Us"), "The sun came up out of the sea" (Coleridge, *The Rime of the Ancient Mariner*), "an ordinary turd indulging himself as the chief of sinners" (Bunyan, *Grace Abounding to the Chief of Sinners*). From *Masters of Atlantis*: "Hen furioso" (Ariosto, *Orlando Furioso*), "It's the House of Usher" (Poe, "The Fall of the House of Usher"), "the only begetter" (dedication page to the 1609 first printing of *Shakespeare's Sonnets*, where it is spelled "onlie begetter"). So: a temporal span from the thirteenth to the nineteenth century linked to a geographic range from the subarctic to the near-Antarctic, centered on English references but including Italy, Greenland, and the US. There will be more of the same in *Gringos*. Portis might have encountered a good bit of this in English department courses at the University of Arkansas, where Professors Duncan Eaves and Ben Kimpel were holding forth on both Browne and Blake, among others, during his student years, though he seems very quickly to have accelerated into intensely self-directed reading. Back now to *Masters of Atlantis*.

TROUBLE IN GNOMON COUNTRY

Chronicles of esoteric thought systems, like those of political parties and religious denominations, are littered with internal power struggles, doctrinal and ideological conflicts, heretical offshoots and schisms. Two such rifts trouble the Gnomon Society in its first growth, one rooted in the English Master's ill-health and growing megalomania, the other in his American colleague's inability to control an underling. Austin Popper is the difficult aide's name—he starts as a "mail boy" but is "quick in every sense of the word" and soon persuades Mr. Jimmerson to approve a "new probationary degree" (Neophyte) and a "simplified version of the *Codex*." Preached by Popper as Mr. Jimmerson's showman spokesman (he leads the crowds in cheers and engages "in comic dialogues" with a talking blue jay named Squanto), the diluted Gnomon pitch brings in "thousands of new members."

A different underling is responsible for Hen's ill-health—Evans is his name, he is listed as a "paid companion," and he has "been lightly dusting Sir Sydney's muffins with arsenic on and off over the years." When the Second World War breaks out in 1939, ahead of the

Luftwaffe's assaults on London, Hen decamps for Toronto, where sister Fanny visits and nurses him back to health. A healthier Hen, however, is a more dangerous Hen, and his reaction to the new developments in Indiana "rocked the Gnomon Society." In a letter published in a Toronto newspaper he threatens as "Grand Prior of World Gnomonry" to revoke the "charter" of the American Temple if it does not promptly "purge itself of Popper and Popperism." Mr. Jimmerson's response ("strong stuff too"), published in Chicago and scoffing at the very notions of a "charter" and an office of "Grand Prior," leads to open rupture—a "Jimmerson school" and a "Hen school," with insults and vandalism on both sides.

Once again, however, as with the Great Depression, the fortunes of the Gnomon Society get a boost from disaster. The shock of the Pearl Harbor attack galvanizes Popper: "First came the Gnomon blood drive, with the brothers laid out in rows, rubber tubes coming out of their left arms and their right arms raised in military salutes for the news photographers." Second came the idea for the Temple staff's enlistment—"They rallied to the colors *en bloc*," though Popper excuses himself, explaining his "strategic standby" assignment from the secretary of the navy.

This ludicrous claim is followed by an even more preposterous idea for a visit to the nation's capital by the Master, bearing plans for "winning the war through the use of compressed air and the military application of Gnomonic science." Popper is nothing if not a big-scale thinker—the itinerary includes a "courtesy call at the White House" and a "working session with General Marshall." This will be, he assures his hesitant Master, a publicity coup guaranteed to "cut the ground from under Sydney Hen." The trip is a catastrophe, a humiliation for Mr. Jimmerson, who meets neither Roosevelt nor Marshall and has his Gnomon "Rod of Correction" stolen by an aggressive Neophyte and future FBI agent named Pharris White. The trip's most significant event is Popper's meeting with Cezar Golescu, practicing alchemist and fellow seeker after occult knowledge. Odd birds find their fellows—as with Jimmerson and Hen in Malta, so with Popper and Golescu in Washington. Popper's subsequent adventures with Golescu will fill a three-chapter run, the longest segment in the book with neither Hen nor Jimmerson onstage. Popper and Golescu hole up in the abandoned mining town of (fictional) Hogandale, Colorado, and spend months living as Commander DeWitt Farnsworth and Dr. Omar Baroody cultivating creeping bagweed (*Blovius reptans*, also fictional) for its supposed ability to concentrate gold from the soil it grows in within its leaves. This venture ends as badly as the earlier trip to Washington, though now Popper is the humbled party, barely escaping arrest as a draft dodger and losing out to Golescu in the courtship of a waitress.

The restored Sir Sydney, meanwhile, now taken in tow by a wealthy Canadian widow named Babette, is turning to new projects. He's just published *Approach to Knowing*, an account of his own further enlightenment allegedly composed in a "three-day Gnomonic trance." He has now, he reports, " 'completed the triangle' and 'scaled the cone' and been granted 'the gift of ecstatic utterance,' " with the result that he has now passed "beyond Mastery and was no longer bound by law or custom." What's more, his example might be emulated by others at his newly opened "New Croton Institute for Advanced Gnomonic Study" in Cuernavaca, Mexico, where Babette owns a splendid house with a swimming pool and "blazing gardens." The tuition is steep ($1,200, paid up front and not refundable), and the rigors of the month-long course sound like Symes's arthritis clinic ("thirty push-ups and a twelve-minute nap")—weekly bleedings ("an imperial quart at each draining") and a diet of "alfalfa sprouts and morning glory seeds."

This venture doesn't last either, "the joys of quiescence" proving insufficient for "the Sphinx of Cuernavaca," and when peace is restored in 1945, Hen announces a return to England, his echo of Jimmerson's wartime visit to Washington, citing a responsibility to "help rebuild his country." Unlike the irresolute Jimmerson, Sir Sydney needs no Austin Popper to buck up his sense of self-importance: "He had prepared a White Paper for the government, having to do with the restructuring of English society along Gnomonic lines." But just as Popper before him was unable to arrange meetings with Roosevelt and Marshall, Hen is "ignored, written off as a bishop in some church or other." The whole trip is a disaster—"You're a back number, Hen," a British reporter tells him on his arrival. The London Temple, repossessed for unpaid taxes, has been repurposed as a home for unwed mothers, and his "current male companion," Noel Kinlow, serves him poorly on two occasions. First, instead of conveying it to the British Museum as instructed, Kinlow dumps in the Thames a "heroic bust" by a Mexican artist commissioned to produce "a sort of Aztec Hen, with jade eyeballs and coral teeth." Second, returning from this same failed errand, Kinlow turns away the unkempt caller claiming to be Pletho Pappus. The chastened English Master is soon back in Mexico, his failed plan for triumphant return marking his final attempt on the world-historical stage. Mr. Jimmerson, however, Popper once again busy at his ear, has additional Gnomonic humiliations in store.

INDIANA IS NOT ATLANTIS

Popper has of course learned nothing from the nightmare visit to Washington or his winter of discontent in Colorado. Returned to Gary after a mysterious four-year interval, he has plans as grandiose as ever: "Public service was the answer." Master Jimmerson is to present himself as a candidate for governor of Indiana. This whole episode is at least as zany as the visit to Washington touting compressed-air warfare and the addition of "*boktos*, or Pythagorean butting" to American basic training or the "Banco Plan" for bagweed-covered mountain ranges in Colorado. But once again, as with the split-level humor of the varied items sold by Symes from the back of a truck, the overall hilarity of Jimmerson's gubernatorial run is greatly amplified by several self-contained episodes. Two of these stand out—the production of candidate Jimmerson's campaign biography by the noted hack writer "Dub" Polton and Jimmerson's scheduled presentation before the annual retreat of the Busy Bees, a "very exclusive lawyers' club," at the (fictional) Rainbow Falls State Park.

Polton first. Writers have already been noted as frequent Portis targets—with *The Dog of the South* alone featuring more than half a dozen published and unpublished scribblers. But Dub is a hands-down winner on the quantity front—nine listed titles in many genres under at least four pen names. Jack Fargo's *'Neath Pecos Skies*? Dr. Klaus Ehrhart's *Slimming Secrets of the Stars*? Ethel Decatur Cathcart's *Billy and His Magic Socks*? Dub's—every one. For Jimmerson, Dub turns out with customary dispatch *His Word Is Law!* (though Popper ends up going with the less punchy *Hoosier Wizard*). Like his creator (and his fellow creation Mattie Ross), Polton is fond of exclamation— his "family memoir" is titled *Here Comes Gramps!* His compositional methods are spelled out in detail—he "rejected all suggestions from the subject," read not a word of any Gnomonic text, made "not a single note" in his hours of interviews, and thus completed the project with his "idea that Gnomonism had come out of the Andes" intact. Mr. Jimmerson is puzzled by the finished volume's references to "sacred macaws of Tamputocco" and "Peruvian metals unknown to science" until Popper explains that Polton, following "widely accepted" practice, "worked in some odds and ends he had left over from a book he did on South America." It's all hilarious stuff, but we're far enough along now, the "Skraelings" and *Dusicyon australis* of *The Dog of the South* under our belts, to sense in Polton's unhinged "campaign biography" a mordant critique of the biographer's art aligning nicely with Joyce's and Janet Malcolm's.

    The lawyers' retreat riff is written in a similar broad-strokes register, trained on a different target. Portis doesn't write about lawyers as frequently as he writes about writers, and both Daggett from *True Grit* and Nardo from *Gringos* come off relatively well, but the Hoosier barristers in conclave are portrayed as overfed chowderheads with one if not both eyes resolutely trained on the billable hour and dedicated as a group to consternation over the "far too many human activities that can be carried on without the intercession of lawyers." The Gnomon contingent arrives late, missing lunch, to find the stuffed attorneys "drowsy" if not already "dozing, the older ones blowing like seals" and Mr. Jimmerson's slot on the program hijacked by an "unexpected guest"—none other than ex-FBI agent Pharris White, last seen hot on the heels of Popper/Farnsworth in Colorado. Mr. Jimmerson is instantly forgotten. The cheering lawyers greet "Bulldog" White, now a "U.S. Attorney," in rousing Busy Bees style, their "glee club" hastily assembled for a welcoming serenade of a "good many stanzas." Before it's finished, White has recognized the fleeing Popper and marshaled a posse of lawyers into a "long line of beaters sweeping across the park," only to be foiled again by the elusive Popper, whose "burrow" behind the park's celebrated falls goes undetected. Portis leaves the driver Maceo and Mr. Jimmerson to find their way back to Gary on their own, and in this chaotic fashion the American Master's venture into state-level public life meets an end as ignominious as his World War II attempt to offer his services to the nation, as laughably delusional as Sir Sydney's planned triumphal return to London.

THE ORIGINS OF MASTERY

Masters of Atlantis, at this point nearly two-thirds complete, might be succinctly described as a chronicle of misadventures, the repeated pratfalls of two singularly credulous airheads, one American and one British, on their farcical mission, accompanied by a bush-league con artist who would be a power behind the Gnomon throne. The pretensions of the two would-be magi are lampooned throughout, not least by their association with the surprisingly detailed list of notable odd birds sprinkled throughout the text—Cornelius Agrippa, Madame Blavatsky, Cagliostro, Aleister Crowley, Robert Fludd, Nostradamus, Pythagoras, Hermes Trismegistus. The Portis who had Browne's *The Garden of Cyrus* under his belt in *The Dog of the South* has clearly stuck with his arcana reading. Figures of more mainstream reputation are occasionally mixed in, especially by Popper, whose newspaper-sourced fragments of learning are often comically mangled. Here's his account to the Texas state senators of Hen's attempt to attach his name to Mr. Jimmerson's breakthrough spiral: "Hen, an envious little man, jumped in to claim equal credit, citing the historical parallel with Newton and, who was the other one, Darwin, I believe, yes, the pair of them working in their own tiny cottages, and then one day, miles apart, clapping their foreheads in unison as they both hit on the idea of phlogiston at the same time."

This gumbo is silly enough—the life spans of Newton and Darwin do not overlap; calculus, not phlogiston, was at the center of Newtonian and Leibnizian priority claims; and Leibniz did not work in a tiny cottage (he spent his life in posh court circles in Mainz and Hannover)—but the deeper comedy is in the hearing room. No senator bats an eye. (Portis may be sending up several once-widely celebrated congressional bozo moments here—Bertolt Brecht's 1947 appearance before the House Un-American Activities Committee or the earlier Dies Committee hearing in 1938 when Alabama representative Joe Starnes asked Vassar theater prof Hallie Flanagan if Christopher Marlowe and "Mr. Euripides" were Communists.) Zeno and Archimedes also make it into Popper's patter, the latter invoked as a Gnomon Master in support of the Society's contributions to the war effort against the Axis powers ("Don't you recall how he jumped into the battle with all his scientific tricks to help defend Syracuse against, who was it, Tamerlane, I believe . . . ?"). Mr. Jimmerson, like the Texas legislators, offers no objections.

Masters of Atlantis makes its vastly greater temporal reach explicit at the outset—Hermes Trismegistus and Pythagoras appear on the second page, with the former described as "the first modern Master of the Gnomon Society." This "modern" may hold the record for antiquity, given that Hermes is mythical and death dates assigned for Pythagoras center on 490 BCE, but what's clear is that young Mr. Jimmerson's "keen interest" in the *Codex Pappus* involves him in a vast network of occultist figures and movements from many nations. The linchpin figure would be Minnesota utopian politico Ignatius Donnelly, whose *Atlantis: The Antediluvian World*, published in 1882, remains the most widely known work in modern Atlantean studies unless Plato's *Critias* and *Timaeus* (not mentioned by Portis) are judged modern by the Pythagorean standard. Donnelly gets

Ota Benga. *Photograph by Jessie Tarbox Beals. Courtesy of St. Louis Public Library.*

competition, however, from James Churchward's *The Lost Continent of Mu: Motherland of Man*, published in 1926 and vigorously championed in Europe and Colorado by Golescu: "Go to Bucharest or Budapest and say 'Mu' to any educated man and he will reply to you, 'Mu? Ah yes, Golescu.' In Vienna the same. In Zagreb the same." In Colorado the Christian Ute Indian Thomas is much less impressed.

And even at this point we're not finished with the lost-continent sweepstakes. The comedy of "Dub" Polton's confused sense of a South American origin for Gnomonism may be Portis's typically covert reference to an astonishingly convoluted tale of an Atlantis on the Bolivian Altiplano called Tiwanaku or Tihuanacu. In the 1920s and 1930s, now-obscure figures (Belisario Díaz Romero, Arthur Posnansky, Edmund Kiss) grafted Atlantean myth and Aryan-supremacist racial ideology to a Bolivian archeological site to create an origin myth for Euro-American cultures explaining and justifying colonial conquest. The very title of Posnansky's four-volume *Tihuanacu, the Cradle of American Man*, published in English translation between 1945 (volumes 1 and 2) and 1957 (volumes 3 and 4), makes the claim explicit. The Falkland Islands wolf of this narrative, as doomed to inevitable disappearance as poor *Dusicyon australis*, is the whole Indigenous population, the "Skraelings" in the north to the Aymara of the altiplano. Senator Gammage's one-line query to Popper, asking if Mr. Jimmerson is "the one who claims that the Chinese discovered America," may be an equally oblique reference to the once-widespread Fu-Sang theory that apparently caused something of an uproar at an 1875 conference of academic Americanists in France. Doc Flandin in *Gringos* is all in on this one, asking the party on its way down the Usumacinta to Likín to sign off on handwritten sheets affirming their acceptance of "Dr. Richard Flandin's theory of direct trans-Pacific Chinese settlement of Meso-America."

Such themes rarely break the surface of *Masters of Atlantis*, but they are a persistent, unnerving presence—one instance would be Thomas the Ute Indian's angry denunciation of Golescu. "Where are you from anyway, you Nazi devil?" he says. "You dog eater. You call me a fossil and you say I'm degraded, but I'll tell you something, mister, you're the one who's cut off from God." Thomas is quite right to be offended, and his "Nazi devil" charge is not far off the mark. Golescu is turning him into a lab rat, a relic of a bygone race, a fictional analogue of the infamous (and factual) display of the Yahi Indian Ishi in Alfred Kroeber's California museum exhibit or the Congolese teenager Ota Benga in the Bronx Zoo.

Thomas is human, like both Ishi and Ota Benga (though their full humanity was routinely questioned), not a chicken, but he's already halfway to Joann's cage or Edmund B. Ratner's career beginnings, the latter sold by his father into an "animal show" to ride an Irish wolfhound togged out as a cowboy. Only the ethnic component of this theme is newly emphatic—Portis had been putting both humans and animals on display in cages and circuses ever since the "alligator boy" in "Damn!" took a crowbar to Sanford T. McClerkin's leg in 1957. But in *Masters of Atlantis* both Maceo's time as Fahad Murad, selling Nation of Islam newspapers in Chicago, and Popper's imprisonment by the three "left-wing women" line up nicely with Golescu's treatment of Thomas as reminders of their shared subordinate place in the last spasms of the old European entrada into the New World.

All this is an unusually extended return to the world of Midge's plans for Webster Spooner's "small cart" snow-cone business in *The Dog of the South*, where Midge stands to Webster as Mrs. Symes to Elizabeth urged to recitation on effectual calling. Midge may be a gringo of goodwill, but his real and imagined works are hapless at best. His actual bequests to young Spooner are Mrs. Edge's silverware and "my own copy of Southey's *Life of Nelson*" as a Christmas gift, neither demonstrating the slightest awareness of young Mr. Spooner's needs or customs. Why, all these episodes in both novels ask with increasing insistence, do the surnames of the world, the Poppers and Jimmersons and Moalers and Midges, however clueless, end up giving orders to the given names of the world, the Elizabeths and Normas, the Maceos and Lázaros and Teresitas? In *Masters of Atlantis*, as in *The Dog of the South*, the deadpan funnyman is playing serious games under his slapstick surface. Midge can see Uranus, but his vision of Webster Spooner is a blinkered one. Portis thus sticks in *Masters of Atlantis* to the same sly strategies elaborated in *The Dog of the South*, developing his comic episodes explicitly and at length while keeping the dystopian counternarrative implicit, oblique, and above all brief. Heavy thematic lifts are accomplished by single words, offhand phrasings, indirect references.

"AMERICAN PYTHAGORAS" 117

It's not that Midge and Jimmerson are actual bad guys. They're not Dupree, or Symes, or even Popper. They're saints next to Fring and Chaney and Dan. They're actually a good bit alike, earnest, conflict averse, and eager to please, though rarely appreciative or even cognizant of the labors of others who sustain them. But a bedrock cluelessness and sense of entitlement swaddles the whole crowd— "Even the wretched hippies expected service." Midge's father, floating on his Alabama lake enjoying the fruits of his Midgestone successes, supports his son as Fanny Jimmerson supports her husband and brother, paying the one's printing bills and taxes and nursing the other through his Canadian illness. She also keeps her son, Jerome, afloat in his Greenwich Village life in "Japanese puppet theater." Every month she sends checks to all three, receiving only "spotty" responses.

It's a tough world they all live in, torn by Great Depressions and World Wars. The oldsters of Hogandale are "a dispirited lot of nesters and stragglers who had been beaten down by life," and the mean streets of Gary are roamed by a sorry biker gang that owns no bikes and is thus reduced to roaming "about on foot in a shambling troop." Abstracted goofs like Midge and Jimmerson, adrift in this hard land without Dad and Fanny sending checks, would soon hit hard FLORRs, think themselves lucky to own even Mr. Proctor's shed and TV setup. Fortunately for both, this doomsday arrives in neither work. *The Dog of the South* ends with Midge back in school with Dad still covering costs, while *Masters of Atlantis* closes on a truly upbeat, even exuberant note.

Once again, as with the Dante reference to *Paradiso*, canto 17, in *The Dog of the South*, the glancing allusions to Tiwanaku/Tihuanacu and the Chinese discovery of America in *Masters of Atlantis* might seem far-fetched until the reader encounters a sufficient number of equally arcane but more overt references. Here's another from the same novel: everywhere in Portis one notes Beckett echoes, only to reject them as overreading, more a consequence of familiarity with Beckett than deliberate reference. One becomes, over time, something of another mad Golescu, hearing Beckett as the Romanian hears "the poetry of Mu!" every time Thomas the Ute Christian opens his mouth. After all, they are never direct citations but mere tonal overlaps or structural similarities. Portis never makes it obvious, never names a character Hamm or Clov or Murphy or Malone; he never centers a play on a man alone in a room with a tape recorder. What he does do is stuff his works with characters with one-word names, center a story on a man alone in a room with a telephone, and write one-liner dialogues exposing the speakers as profoundly at sea, as in this one from Maurice Babcock and Ed, on their way from Indiana to Texas with a van full of Gnomon books and *Hoosier Wizard*. Ed leads off:

> Do you know what's going on?
>   Where?
>   Anywhere.
>   No.

Anybody with even one Beckett play in the cultural-literacy bank picks up a *Godot* note here, Gogo and Didi staving off panic with banality. Estragon leads off:

> ESTRAGON: (*anxious*) And we?
> VLADIMIR: I beg your pardon?
> ESTRAGON: I said, And we?
> VLADIMIR: I don't understand.
> ESTRAGON: Where do we come in?
> VLADIMIR: Come in?
> ESTRAGON: Take your time.
> VLADIMIR: Come in? On our hands and knees.

So, obvious tonal and structural consonance but no incontrovertible tie, no smoking-gun phrasal echo. So out the echo goes, with other similar instances, written off as reader-ascribed as opposed to writer-inscribed.

But then, right there on the page, two chapters earlier, is Popper's pitch to Mr. Jimmerson for a move to Texas, where Morehead Moaler has chosen the Gnomon Society over "the Sholto Business College of San Antonio" as beneficiary of his "sand and gravel" fortune. (Moaler, too, has grit and has monetized it.) But Sholto Business College? Sholto? A faint bell rings in memory's Beckett vault. Run to earth, it turns out to be from a work as minor in Beckett as *An Island in the Moon* is minor in Blake—a Dr. Sholto appears in "Fingal," the second story in his *More Pricks Than Kicks* collection, published almost two decades before *Godot* made him famous. The connection is hardly ironclad—a different Sholto or no Sholto at all may be intended—but it is at least direct and aligns very nicely with Portis's low-visibility style of allusive reference. With Sholto he flashes a Beckett card, just for an instant, in line with his earlier T.W.K. glimpse of Dante. And as with Dante all other Beckett echoes gain an increased plausibility based on one that seems at least slightly more explicit. More on Beckett later, when we get to "I Don't Talk Service No More."

RANCHO MOALER

As in *Norwood*, there's a very definite happy-ending uptick at the close of *Masters of Atlantis*. The Christmas holidays are approaching, and Portis seems to have contrived a "third time's the charm" narrative arc for his disaster-filled tale. Popper, twice reduced to headlong flight, in Colorado and Indiana, arrives in La Coma victorious in his encounter with Senator Churton's Texas tribunal, his deft mention of plans for a "hospital for poor children" having frustrated the designs of the "swaggering moron" Junior "Big Boy" Moaler on his father's properties and revenues. Hen, poisoned in his first stay in London and ignominiously rebuffed in his attempted return, is initially lured into Mr. Moaler's domino games out of courtesy to his host but soon enjoys them enough to decide that "Pythagoras would approve." And Mr. Jimmerson himself, disappointed first in his World War II mission to Washington and second in his aborted campaign for governor of Indiana, has just been described as the "American Pythagoras" to Lone Star congressmen. Their long-running bitter quarrels behind them at last, the now-reconciled savants lounge on the beach, marveling at the innocence of fishermen who pass by their "magisterial feet" unconscious of their "close brush with the two world Masters." The earlier "T.W.K." reference might resurface here, the amity of the old antagonists echoing the "*voci soave*" of the ancient philosophers in Dante's Limbo. Get Thales and Heraclitus comfortable in their "*prato di fresca verdure*," and their old disagreements might also fade into insignificance.

The big picture for the Gnomons has also markedly improved. Not long before this, things look very grim. The Temple in Gary is a ruin inhabited by tramps and warring armies of rats and roaches, the latter troop led by a comically repellent "big bull roach." The Council of Three is no more—Epps lost in the war, Bates dead, and Mapes off to a radio career in South Carolina. Popper is a dark-rum alcoholic living as an "urban tramp," while Hen, his New Croton Institute for Advanced Gnomonic Study long since shut down, is still in Mexico, living in Saltillo with Whit and Adele Gluter, Kinlow's replacement companions. And Mr. Jimmerson himself, the long-ago chosen apostle of Master Pletho Pappus, is holed up with Maceo, Ed, and the newly arrived Maurice Babcock in the Red Room ("red silk peeling from the walls"), where a still-operative fireplace offers the only heated space in the derelict and infested Temple.

Rescue arrives from a new trio as unlikely as the first modern Council of Three. First on the scene is Babcock, in Chicago, drawn to Gnomonism by its aura of occult profundity. Having purchased a bundle of "Gnomon pamphlets and books" for five dollars, he "read it through with wonder, lost in triangles for the weekend. *This is the stuff for me.* He knew it at once. *This is what I've been looking for.*" For Hen, half a century earlier, the experience had been no less immediate: "He turned in impatience to the English version and read hungrily. 'This is marvelous stuff!' he said, in a fairly loud voice. 'I can't make head or tail of it!' " Babcock soon moves into the Temple, bringing new energy to work on the Jimmerson Lag and new editions of *Gnomonism Today* and *Hoosier Wizard*.

Meanwhile, Popper, saved from the streets by doctors and AA meetings, newly aware of his gift for sales ("a gift for hopeful statement combined with short-term tenacity of purpose"), is back on his feet working in Texas oil and gas leases. The name Moaler, overheard at a businessman's luncheon in Corpus Christi, brings back memories: "Suddenly I remembered you, sir, and Maceo." A journey to La Coma follows. Popper's gifts come into play at this point—"I sounded Mr. Moaler out about the idea establishing a Gnomon retreat"—and before long he's on his way to Gary, determined to convince Mr. Jimmerson of a southward shift in the Telluric Currents.

Morehead Moaler, however, mentioned early but then mostly dropped from sight, is the crucial third party responsible for the Gnomon Society's survival. He's a longtime Gnomon, reported as joining before 1940 at the time of the Society's greatest success, though "little notice was taken of him at the time, or of his remote Texas Pillar." When he first appears at the La Coma estate, Popper encounters a disconsolate Moaler, convinced he's a South Texas Uncas, last of the Gnomons. "He thought we were extinct fauna, you and I," Popper later tells Mr. Jimmerson as part of his time-to-relocate pitch.

But the pitch—hopeful statement tenaciously pursued—is ultimately successful, and a substantial party eventually gathers in Texas around the now reassured and newly promoted Moaler. He's as avid of honorific titles as Hen and now wears a Poma himself, having made the awarding of the C.P. (Companion of Pythagoras) rank a condition of his bequest. Babcock, for his part, like some *Popol Vuh* court officer, has taken Keeper of the Plumes as his title. The newly consecrated Great Moaler Hall of Gnomons, a seventy-foot, three-bedroom mobile home, soon draws the other Gnomons and their attendants. Popper, Maceo, and Esteban (Popper's "security chief and director for press hospitality") chauffeur Mr. Jimmerson and the *Codex Pappus* from Gary in Popper's BIGG DIPPER ENERGY SYSTEMS camper van, leaving Babcock and Ed to manage the final harrowing retreat from the ruined Temple in a rental truck loaded with copies of *Hoosier Wizard* and other Gnomon publications. Hen and the Gluters arrive on a "second-class bus" from Saltillo, the tickets purchased with Fanny Jimmerson's Christmas check. Already in residence are Moaler himself; Lázaro, his cook and driver; and Teresita, his semiretired housekeeper.

Three trailers house this company—Moaler, Hen, and Jimmerson are in the Great Hall, with the late-returning Popper, back from Austin, on the couch beside the Christmas tree; the guest house is for the male staff (Babcock, Ed, Esteban, Lázaro, and Maceo), while Teresita's smaller trailer now also hosts Adele and Whit Gluter, who roll out their tatamis on her floor. Once the entire company is in place, conditions are sufficiently crowded for concerns about Mr. Moaler's long-term plans to arise among his many guests. He has promised an "announcement to make" for Christmas Day, convincing Babcock of their benefactor's plans for revealing his identity as the Lame One. But others think more of eviction notices. Whispered worries are exchanged, as this from Adele to Hen: "Ed told Whit that Mr. Moaler thinks there are too many people living here and that he's going to turn some of us out."

These worries prove unfounded. With "Big Boy" routed, Moaler Sr. is free to shower his philanthropy on the Gnomon Society he has served so devotedly for so long. And shower he does—he's Santa, not Scrooge. Christmas Day is celebrated with carefully planned festivity, everyone dressed in their best for a lavish dinner. There is both song and impressive ceremony—"the two Masters clasped hands across the burning bowl"—but the day's highlight comes with the arrival of a "rustling noise" outside, putting the apprehensive among the guests in mind of their ancient Atlantean ancestors "when they first heard the rumbling on their single day and night of misfortune." Everyone rushes to the windows, tilting the Great Hall, only to see Mr. Moaler's "interesting announcement" materialized in "a magnificent new mobile home," his holiday gift to his gratefully relieved guests.

It's a "top of the line" model too, he tells them, an "eighty-foot Cape Codder with cathedral roof and singles of incorruptible polystyrene," complete with "two master bedrooms for our two Masters." Ample new digs with room for all, a sumptuous feast for the apostolically resonant company of twelve, the long-running schism between the Jimmerson and Hen factions healed at last, thanks in part to the efforts of the Gluters—it's a stunningly harmonious close. "Another trailer!" thinks Popper, in a rare moment of happy laughter, and everything mobile, should there come an unanticipated day of additional Telluric Current shifts. All present are delighted, but none is so transported as Babcock, for whom the currents are at the moment flowing perceptibly in Texas and who in his turn is experiencing the same intuitive certainties that claimed Mr. Jimmerson so long ago: "He had often suppressed the thought but now he knew in his heart that he himself was a Master and that Maurice Babcock was to be Master of the New Cycle." Keeper of the Plumes is just a rung on a steeply ascendant ladder.

Sir Sydney is also thrilled, as he was numbered among the worried in the days leading up to the announcement. Saltillo with the Gluters, traveling by second-class bus on his sister's money—these were straitened circumstances after the opulence of the London Temple and Babette's lavish Cuernavaca villa. He's "exultant, foaming, almost weeping" at the news and tells Mr. Jimmerson of his plans to take up gardening: "I think I'll grow tomatoes by day, Lamar. The Better Boy variety for preference, in this sand. Yes, a little garden for me."

"AMERICAN PYTHAGORAS"   123

A little garden—here on the final page, after a narrative packed with far-flung and mishap-filled adventures—could this be another instance of Portis's fleeting but unusually direct quality lit references breaking the surface? It's Candide, after all, in Voltaire's savage satire, described on its opening page as a "simpleminded" (*avec l'esprit le plus simple*) young man entirely under the sway of his tutor Pangloss ("all talk"), who by its close has absorbed enough of the world's hard lessons to exit with his celebrated thanks-but-no-thanks response to yet another bit of Panglossian blather: " 'Nicely put,' Candide replied, 'but we must tend our own garden' " (*"Cela et bien dit," répondit Candide, "mais il faut cultiver note jardin"*). Does this happy Hen, with his plans for setting out Better Boy starts constituting something of a return to his pre–*Codex Pappus* days as a tender of botanicals, thus join Norwood and Midge among Portis's protagonists made marginally wiser by their adventures? Perhaps, but no chance Mr. Jimmerson makes this cut, developing an interest in something as useful as gardening—"It's study for me, Sydney," he replies. The pyromaniac Ed, one-time vinyl saboteur and would-be chloroformer of women, gets the novel's last words: "This is the best party I've ever been to!"

And isn't the entire Christmas Day episode a clear *Masters of Atlantis* analogue of *Norwood*'s happy gathering at the Reese residence, the impromptu hospitality of the fish fry amplified to carefully choreographed holiday scale (though under the festivities the old neocolonial hierarchies remain in place—the first names still tending to the surnames)? Rancho Moaler remains a paradise of bachelors, though the situation of the maids has improved slightly. If there's a touchstone scene in Portis's narratives, this one, hospitable sharing of food and shelter, lodges a strong claim. *Gringos* will feature a very different protagonist in a much shorter time frame, but even its versions of this scene will not be his last. Before he's through, he'll ring down the curtain on a dramatized and no less celebratory rendering.

6 —

THE HAUNTED MAN'S REPORT

GRINGOS

WHILE NOT AN ORNAMENT

Six years pass from the end of *Masters of Atlantis* to the beginning of *Gringos*, but it's still Christmas Day. Big changes, however, have been introduced on the protagonist front. Where Lamar Jimmerson begins and ends as a credulous simpleton requiring cradle-to-beach-chair maintenance by a host of caretakers, Jimmy Burns is a remarkably self-sufficient central figure. In this he stands out—he's the oldest primary character in a Portis novel (though younger than Mattie Ross remembering) and easily the most competent. From years of illegal digging and selling of Mayan antiquities, recently sworn off, Burns is also a practiced detector of fakes. He currently supports himself with hauling jobs, photographing tourists, and locating missing persons. He wouldn't be caught wearing Norwood's fancy stovepipe boots—he's happy in hand-me-down golf pants—but if he owned them, he would know how to keep them on his feet. Burns is even more competent than Mattie—his gun works.

These skills are immediately put to the test. Changing his truck's oil at the city dump, he avoids being robbed by a spaced-out group of American hippies led by a Manson wannabe named Dan only by producing his twelve-gauge shotgun instead of the promised Modelos. There's a moment in this episode where Burns also reveals a capacity for blind rage not previously encountered in Portis's fiction, though Norwood completely losing it in response to Fring's arson threat ("I'll bust your head open with a tar tool. I'll kill you.") might constitute a close approach. Burns is already wielding the gun, and the now-cowed

Dan is mouthing some inanity about "the correct path" when Burns nearly snaps: "Blood was roaring in my ears. I had to get away from these people before I did something." (Burns and Norwood—two Korean War vets invented by a third. Another "talk service" moment here, recollections of berserker loss of control? One more dispatch from "the bullet department"?) Finally, there is among the hippie crew a young woman called Red whose "rabbit face" jogs a memory from his "Blue Sheets" missing persons lists. Checking, he finds her listed as a Florida runaway named LaJoye Mishell Teeter, carrying a $2,000 dollar reward for safe return.

At the most basic plot level, all this adds up to an impressively streamlined opening. Twenty-five pages in and already we've got a semi-credible hero, a wholly credible bad guy, a vulnerable teenager in peril, and a straightforward narrative arc as centered on rescue as *True Grit*'s is centered on revenge. The following episode, a delivery of supplies to an archeological dig at a site in (fictional) Ektún, adds to the mix by including a visit to the family of Refugio Osorio, Burns's pal and one-time partner in the plundering business, and the rescue of extraterrestrials scholar Rudy Kurle's foundered taxi at the Tabí River crossing. The Tabí is also fictional, though the Usumacinta, also named, is a major Chiapas/Tabasco waterway. Introduced early, both Refugio and Rudy play substantial parts in the action. The comic critiques of the professions featured so prominently in earlier novels continue in *Gringos*, with archeologists and scholars in general getting their moments in Portis's send-up spotlight in place of the lawyers of *Masters of Atlantis* and the doctor of *The Dog of the South*. Writers of various kinds get pilloried across the board. Sales, however, comes in for spirited defense. We'll get to this later.

There is of course a subplot, now familiar. *The Dog of the South*, for all the time spent in Mexico and British Honduras and attention to historical and contemporary Anglo incursions, has next to nothing in the way of local presence, though Mexican auto-repair savvy is repeatedly praised: "A Mexican truck driver diagnosed the trouble as vapor lock. He draped a wet rag over the fuel pump to cool it down, to condense the vapor in the gas line." (You might pursue an analytic point along these lines—throughout *The Dog of the South* and "An Auto Odyssey through Darkest Baja" Anglos wreck vehicles and Mexicans fix them.) All major characters and most minor ones are Anglos. Take out the brothers at the Mayan ruin and the "Skraelings" who shoot up the Dupree ranch, and what's left are children (Webster, Elizabeth) and folks behind counters at hotels, pharmacies, and border posts.

Gringos is different. The novel is almost wholly set in Mexico, and while its Mérida hosts a substantial expatriate community, Mexican characters now play much more substantial roles. The subalterns begin to talk back. Notably obnoxious gringos occasionally get deported. Chief among the locals is the Osorio family—Refugio; Sula, his wife; and Manolo, their son. Sula is not only Mexican but also Mayan. Another revered figure is Soledad Bravo, a *curandera* respected by Burns on several counts: she "could deliver babies, remove warts and pull single-rooted teeth, no molars, and she could put her ear to your chest and look at your tongue and your eyes and feel around under your jaw, then tell you what was wrong and give you a remedy."

All this adds up to a general seal of approval: "Soledad had a gift. She got results. What more can you ask than to be healed? I wouldn't go to anyone else." Near the novel's end, at the opening of the final chapter, Soledad Bravo is called on once more on a matter not included in her already impressive list of competencies: "We went ahead with the marriage all the same. Soledad Bravo said the auspices were fair, good enough, *bastante*, if not entirely favorable." Burns also consults a lawyer named Nardo ("Nardo knew the ropes. He was well connected") and a funeral director named Huerta.

In short, he's that rare gringo who understands he's not in charge in Mexico. Midge, with his earnest if poorly thought-out plans to be a "*gringo of goodwill*" respectful of Mexican customs, could learn a great deal from him. Burns isn't dreaming a snow-cone-cart future for Refugio or drilling Soledad Bravo on effectual calling. He's still very much an imperfect specimen, no more an "ornament of our race" than the codger Portis conjures in "Combinations of Jacksons" as himself "just a few years from now," but Burns is working hard at his "program of moral improvement," determined, he reports in the novel's opening pages, "to be more considerate of other people in the coming year." His halo's rusted—his treasure hunting depredations have only very recently been curtailed, and he's still got a free drinks deal going with Cosme the bartender at Shep's-In-Between Club. Burns also cannot resist pocketing "a small Mixtec piece that caught my eye, a jaguar carved from some speckled stone" as he prepares Karl Kobold's "boxes of relics and photographs" for transfer to Camacho Puut, an "amateur Mayanist" regarded with "thorough contempt by Mexican and American scholars" and thus "just the man to get these goods." The climb to moral improvement is an uphill slope—even on the last page Burns confesses to missing "going out at night and putting my light in people's faces."

Burns, then, is a hardened man trained to violent worlds currently determined upon a change of life even as he recognizes his old life's appeal. There's a generous "talk service" component to *Gringos* in addition to the initial encounter with Dan—there's Burns's praise for Mormon fellow Marines and the encounter with the Guatemalan army patrol along the Usumacinta. Where Jimmerson is merely fortunate, dozing away on a Gulf Coast beach still imaging himself a Master of esoteric knowledge, Burns is capable in large matters as in small, eventually accomplishing in one shotgun's blast the rescue of a child and the removal from the landscape of one unusually virulent human stain. He will almost certainly continue to stand in Mattie Ross's shadow in the roster of Portis's characters, but he's as close as Portis was willing to go in the way of a hero.

BUT NOT ALL OF IT

In Burns's interactions with *Gringos*' large cast of varied characters (Soledad Bravo, Flandin, Rudy Kurle, and especially Louise) Portis also works out more fully the persistent epistemological issues he's been wrestling with at least since *True Grit*'s "faithful enough" court transcript. Burns's views, his sense of things known combined with respect for the limits of knowing, appear misleadingly simple as he states them. He's a "geocentric," he says: "In my cosmology men were here on earth and nowhere else, go as far as you like. There was us and the spirit world and that was it." This passage presents something of a minefield to the would-be close reader. In the first place, the second sentence does not simply restate the "humanity is found only on Earth" claim of the first, though Burns goes on to refer to both as a singular creedal statement: "It was a visceral belief or feeling so unshakable that I didn't even bother to defend it." There are actually multiple beliefs or feelings articulated. The first addresses the question of where humans are to be found. On Earth, it says, and nowhere else. The second goes on to address the question of what in addition to humans is to be found on Earth. A "spirit world," it says, and nothing else. There's a lot of connotative certitude suggested—"nowhere else, go as far as you like"—but the explicit claims are sharply delimited, leaving plenty of room for Rudy Kurle's space visitors so long as they're defined as "spirits." What's more, even the core assertion of the second sentence would seem to be spectacularly inadequate, failing as it does to account for anything beyond an "us" and "spirit world" binary. This is a bizarrely truncated taxonomy for a guy who keeps careful track of animals he's seen in Mexico: "Nor had I ever caught a glimpse of a jaguar here in the Petén forest. Pumas, ocelots, margays, but not one *tigre*." One freshwater spring at Likín is described as "a mystery under the whirling sand . . . a small shifting turbulence, nothing more, a spirit." Back in Mérida an old Mexican Mr. Proctor known as *El Obispo* who sleeps in a shed behind the church is said to change on certain nights into "a small reddish dog with a fox face." *Gringos* is chock full of animals, from tiny ants to deadly *palancas* to imagined Cape buffalo deployed to portray the suddenness of Dan's shotgun-effected collapse, but nowhere does Burns seem to class them as spirit beings.

As positional statement, then, this jumble falls pitifully short of coherence, a lack made more prominent by its emphatic endorsement. But the minefield of the "my cosmology" passage is additionally complicated in the larger context. Burns delivers it while he's pulling Rudy Kurle's taxi out of the Tabí. Rudy's convinced the Mayan sites he visits offer support to a narrative centered on ancient visits by "space dwarfs or 'manikins' . . . from a faraway planet." When Rudy visits the Ektún dig, he quickly perceives it as an "astroport." Given Burns's just-expressed skepticism, swift dismissal of Rudy might be anticipated. But no. "Still," he notes, "the flying saucer books were fun to read and there weren't nearly enough of them to suit me. I liked the belligerent ones best, that took no crap off the science establishment." Rudy himself is then stoutly defended against just this cohort: "Rudy was serious about his work. In the bars and cafés of Mérida I had heard anthropologists laughing at him, young hot shots who never left town themselves or who went out for a night or two and then scurried back."

This is something of a new note, perhaps a note present from the beginning but here made newly explicit. Burns is an amiable skeptic at once widely curious and remarkably welcoming to disbelieved views, the kind of man who might employ an "Odd Birds of Illinois and Indiana" to meet new friends. This, too, like the earlier statement of "geocentric" belief, might easily be misread. The investigations of Flandin, whose long-term study of Mayan glyphs Burns eagerly awaits, are nevertheless viewed with reservations analogous to those directed at Rudy. They differ, however, in being markedly more detailed and thus reveal more of Burns's tenor of mind: "Some of it would be nonsense and perhaps a lot of it but not all of it. Flandin was formidable in his way. . . . I knew he hadn't actually broken the code, but it was possible that he had hit on some useful new approach to the problem."

Burns thus brings a much more modest approach to the epistemological questions that attract him. "Nobody can do very much," he tells Flandin. He doesn't feel Telluric Currents underfoot or expect to be a Far-Seeing Arbiter or Companion of Pythagoras. He hopes only for "some useful new approach to the problem." But he also doesn't want Flandin or Rudy to be ignored or ridiculed any more than Rooster Cogburn, no ornament himself, wants mules to be mistreated. Portis opened his writing career attacking denigrators of his home state, and here in his final novel he sends Burns out swinging at the town-bound "hot shots" who ridicule Rudy and the academics who "didn't even take the trouble to dispute" Flandin's theories and "returned without comment" his submissions to professional journals. Burns's evaluation, evidently based on careful reading, is much less sweeping: "His crank claims and speculations made up only about twenty percent of his work but it was a fatal sufficiency. Or say thirty percent to be absolutely fair."

Near the end of the novel Portis comes full circle when Burns finds himself moved by LaJoye Mishell Teeter's earnest father, hopelessly out of his depth in Mexico but ready to face down any and every obstacle standing in the way of recovering his daughter. Here is their reunion at the Mérida airport: "I stood aside and looked away as he and his daughter came together in an embrace. He wept. 'Your mama and them thought you was dead but I never did give up.'" Dorsey Teeter is a logging contractor from Florida, a classic redneck:

> The back of his neck, a web of cracks, was burnt to the color and texture of red brick from much honest labor in the sun. A badge of honor, you might think, but no, it was the mark of the beast. The thanks Dorsey and his people got for all their noonday sweat was to be called a contemptuous name. . . . At least he had come here personally to pick up his lost child, which was more than his betters could find the time to do. Usually I had to turn these kids over to the protection officer at the embassy in Mexico City.

Dorsey's no "ornament of our race" either, any more than Rudy or Flandin or Burns himself. He's so xenophobic he won't leave the airport, and the only thing he'll drink is a Coke in its cafeteria. But neither is any of the four a "most depraved member" of the human gang, a Fring, Dupree, Symes, or Dan. Burns's portrait of Teeter, had Portis the student journalist mastered the voice he commanded thirty-four years later, would have made a much stronger response to *Time*'s clumsy sneer at the Natural State than the frontal assault on the Luces.

"BETTER THAN ANY PLAN OF MINE"

Overlaying Portis's dystopian portrayal of a New World despoiled by centuries-old and still-ongoing Europe-based invasions is the by-now-standard main plot centered on a primary character's responses to a novel challenge. Norwood and Midge get tangled up with a criminal and a con man in their respective attempts to collect a debt and recover a Torino and fleeing wife. Mattie Ross forges a lifelong relationship with an unlikely ally in her determination to avenge her father's death, and the hapless Lamar Jimmerson endures similarly extended struggles dealing with his unanticipated call to Gnomon apostleship. Things are a bit more complex in *Gringos*, where not one but two new challenges are present from the beginning. One is an overt threat who needs killing, and Jimmy Burns is quick to pick up on him. But the other is a blessing in disguise, and if he's

Illustration of figs from *Pomona Italiana* (1817–1839) by
Giorgio Gallesio (1772–1839).

slow to recognize her potential, it's not for lack of effort on her part. Louise Kurle is from the outset an insistent, even invasive presence. She dominates the opening chapter, flagging down his truck in the morning for a four-stop Christmas-errand route. She's something of a pain. Before the day ends, she's criticized Burns's "lack of delicacy" in running his truck over a dead snake and given him a "cold look" when the best he can do in the way of plans for future betterment is to "say that I hoped to be more considerate of other people in the coming year." Evening finds her delivering a gift of "green figs" to his hotel room, where she asks to use the bathroom even though, by her own report, she "didn't really have to go" but only wished to "check out your shaving things and your medicine cabinet." The day closes on sexual banter, with Burns replying to Louise's remark on his room's lack of a view by saying he once had a room fronting the street but had to move because of the women: "They were out there at all hours of the night throwing pebbles against my window."

"Don't you wish," says Louise.

"You say that but here you are," says Burns, eliciting a "Not for long" close from Louise.

Here we have something off-the-charts sexy, though the real eroticism is entirely implicit. Pebbles against the window? This is a nothing come-on, a throwaway line and obviously fictional into the bargain. But "green figs"? Burns is wholly oblivious. Louise is married to Rudy, or so Burns thinks, so he's stunned when fifteen chapters later she presents him with a sudden ultimatum—marry her or move out (and this from a newly acquired trailer to which he has legal title). "Here was another grenade, white phosphorus this time," he thinks. "Until this moment the thought of marrying into the Kurle family had not entered my head."

But back to the figs for a moment, to appreciate again Portis's combination of low-profile presentation with deeply traditional symbolic presence. The fig may be the top X-rated fruit on the botanical roster. Find a fig in a painting or poem, and you've demonstrated sex as a core subject. On the vine it's male, scrotal, a green or purple testicle. Halved on a plate, it's blatantly female, a fringed aperture. Check it out.

Any chance whatever the choice of fruit here is coincidental, or for that matter that almost any choice (bananas? apples?) could be free of erotic suggestion? None. Person A knocks on person B's door with fruit-basket gift, an invitation is getting delivered. The basket has figs, it's a frontal come-on.

So embedded in their traditional resonance are figs that any search across centuries and cultures for direct reference is a weirdly inverted haystack enterprise—modest haystack, overstock of needles. Millay's short, oblique "First Fig" and "Second Fig"? "Come and see my shining palace built upon the sand!" Lawrence's much longer, more explicit "Figs"? "The wonderful moist conductivity toward the centre." Plath's Esther "sitting in the crotch of this fig tree," pondering her choices?

Take your pick—all, one, two, three, none. My guess is Portis knew all four, but a more direct echo appears in Titania's instructions to her fairies in *A Midsummer Night's Dream*'s third act:

> Be kind and courteous to this gentleman.
> Hop in his walks and gambol in his eyes;
> Feed him with apricocks and dewberries,
> With purple grapes, green figs, and mulberries.

Here, like *Dusicyon australis*, is yet another finally unverifiable guess, though Burns as a Bottom with the head of an ass fits nicely to *Gringos*' narrative to come. Louise is start to finish courteous to her scruffy gentleman, though she tells him right off he looks worse close up than he does at a distance. "What was this weakness Louise had for older men with red faces?" he asks. "Or was it that she saw me as going with the trailer, like the butane bottle?"

There's next to zero sex in Portis's novels—Norwood's night-bus necking with Rita Lee and Golescu's sudden lunge at June Mack in Colorado are about it for steamy moments unless Adele Gluter's mention of Whit's sandal spankings counts. Midge's tepid reference to "weekly embraces" is par for Portis's course. And this pattern holds for *Gringos*, despite the figs. Louise and Burns have a lovely wedding, he moved to tears by a "crystal-pure" performance in English and Spanish of "Because God Made Me Thine," but they arrive at domestic felicity, complete with "Crock-Pot and our sectional plastic plates, trisected with little dividers to dam off the gravy from the peas," entirely without mention of the standard romantic/erotic preliminaries. No Golescu lunges or breathless Rita Lee wonderment for Jimmy and

Louise—not a single reported hug or kiss, though the groom does pay homage (three times) to his bride's "sandy ringlets."

This absence of ardor is as unremarked as it is obvious. These newlyweds have the essentials for long-term compatibility down: "We didn't get on each other's nerves in close confinement." Burns marvels at both the suddenness and the satisfactory outcome: "It was surprising how fast I moved on the thing, at my age, with so few reservations, how quickly I became a husband, and an indulgent one at that." This satisfaction holds, with the reformed treasure hunter contemplating at novel's end a future as co-owner with Louise and Refugio of the Posada Fausto where he lived as a bachelor and where Louise made her unrecognized "green figs" proposition not so long before. This, too, is Louise's idea: "She had thought it all out. A mom-and-pop hotel, with mom no doubt perched behind the cash register all day." Pop, however, on the novel's final page, is on board: "I feared debt and already I missed going out and putting my light in people's faces but it was a better plan than any plan of mine."

Before the hotel, however, as a counterpoint to the green figs of the beginning, Portis introduces another fruit with rich traditional resonances to ratify the newly rooted direction of Burns's life. His old treasure-hunting partner Eli Withering shows up at the trailer with Dan's old Jumping Jacks girlfriend Beany Girl in tow. Eli has found an undisturbed Mayan site in Belize, and he's offering a partnership deal: "We'll cut three quick trenches and see what we've got. Then a month's hard work and we'll skim the cream and be out. I'll split right down the middle with you." The appallingly evident pillager mind-set put aside for the moment, this sounds like a sweet deal, made sweeter by repayment with $40 extra—"Interest, he called it"—of a $500 loan Burns made to spring him from jail. But Eli is a ghost of the past, an old voice with old lies. "The fever was on him," Burns says. *Gringos'* single ******* usage issues from Eli's mouth. And it's a new time—Burns is married, out of the hotel and into the trailer. Withering senses the change:

But you ain't coming, are you, Budro?
No, I'm not.
I said I probably wouldn't be venturing out much anymore, into the *selva*. He opened the car door, and a pomegranate rolled

out. Neither of us made a move to pick it up. A sour and messy fruit. Somebody gives you one and you haul it around until it turns black or rolls away out of your life.

A sour and messy fruit, widely known as "the fruit of death" for its ties to the Adonis myth and Egyptian funerary practice, it stands here in stark if never directly stated opposition to Louise's "green figs." "Green, see, the color of life," says Refugio early on. Withering and Beany Girl depart, rolling away out of Burns's life "at a creep, lights out." "I ain't got paper one," he says, as they head for a selva tilted toward a Dantesque "dark wood" (*selva oscura*) by word choice alone. Burns, meantime, turns back to the Mobile Star trailer, the "only lighted box in the park." It's quite a stark contrast: "The coffee was made and so Louise and I sat up in our own kitchenette and had coffee and broken cookies from the Hoolywood bakery." Our own kitchenette. We're a page from the end, and Louise's plans for at long last taking down the "SE VENDE" sign at Posada Fausto are on the tip of her tongue—"a better plan than any plan of mine." Louise and Jimmy emerge by the close as Rita Lee and Norwood successfully grown older, made comfortable together in close quarters by their mutual accommodation and forbearance, the Crock-Pot and trailer the younger couple hope for already theirs. Here's Pauline charity yet again, straightforwardly enacted, stripped in *Gringos*' and *Norwood*'s primary narrative arcs of the savage ironies so subtly embodied in the sustained-through-three-novels subplot. Portis the artist presents again as a gringo with an Olmec aesthetic, burying his quality lit herbal allusions "twenty-five feet deep" under a deadpan comedy, the gifted "green figs" symbolizing a desired country, a calm domestic realm, the "sour and messy" pomegranate serving as emblem of its opposite, the dark wood of a scourged world.

SALES

Burns may be headed into the hospitality sector as *Gringos* ends, but he has long seen himself and his friend and partner Refugio as salesmen, and *Gringos* stands out in Portis's writing for its sustained positive portrayal of their occupation. This is itself a departure from his standard comic takedowns. Politicians, doctors (Soledad Bravo excepted), lawyers, archeologists, journalists, and writers of every sort are lampooned, but folks in sales get more than a pass. John Selmer Dix might seem to be an exception, given the incoherence of *With Wings as Eagles* as summarized by Midge, but Dix himself reportedly rejected the work as "nothing but trash," and only Symes regards it as gospel. Burns describes Refugio as "a good salesman, a natural closer," expressing special admiration for his mastery of "the No. 3 close" where the seller pretends "indifference to the sale" combined with impatience at protracted negotiation: "You put across that your patience is at an end, that you are just about to withdraw the offer." He ascribes his own insider knowledge to a three-day "salesmanship school at a Shreveport motel," but credits Refugio with possessing it "in his bones." Refugio is then seen in action sealing the deal on irrigation pipe with a Mennonite farmer named Winkel.

Earlier, witnessing a hostile exchange at Shep's In-Between Club between the proprietor and an unnamed hippie bumming a cigarette at his bar, Burns is moved to a more abstract review: "It was true that Shep didn't exert himself much these days, but I was thinking of a younger Shep, hopping from door to door selling term life insurance, and later, peddling badly worn furniture and carpeting from bankrupt motels. I wondered who bought those rugs. People make fun of salesmen, people with salaries or remittances, who don't have to produce. They have no idea of what a tough game it is."

A tough game, yes, but a thing of beauty when expertly played, as Burns notes when he records in detail a scene observed when he accompanies Nardo to return the boy Serafín to his family:

> Someone was haranguing a crowd behind the bus station. There were gasps and cheers and applause. . . . I shouldered my way in to get a look at this fellow who was inciting the people. What I found was a fast-talking young man in a T-shirt selling cake decorators. They were soft plastic tubes with adjustable nozzles. He squeezed pink icing onto white strips of cardboard, showing how you could make little rosettes and stars and hearts, and spell out birthday greetings. He was an artist with a sure hand, and a funny speaker, too, a fine salesman. "Add a personal touch to *all* your cakes!" he kept shouting at us, and he meant right down to our very smallest muffins.

An artist with a sure hand, certainly, like the character who notices him and the author who created both, both warmly appreciative of excellence in all its guises, and isn't it a deft shift that emphasizes the salesman's skills by so quickly including the newly arrived Burns among those captivated by his spiel? *Our* very smallest muffins. It's an altogether lovely scene, for all its brevity, a gentle comedy strong on warmth and emptied of mockery.

So central is sales to Burns's thinking that he has recourse to its language in narrating his story's climax scene, the twelve-gauge decapitation of Dan the false *El Mago* at the City of Dawn. Portis penned many a deadpan gem of black humor, but the close of this one might be his apex one-liner: "Yes, a strange business back there on that high terrace, and over so fast too. Shotgun blast or not at close range, I was still surprised at how fast and clean Dan had gone down. It was like dropping a Cape buffalo in his tracks at one go. I wasn't used to seeing my will so little resisted, having been in sales for so long."

The no. 4 close, you might call this, the last resort, deployed only with life itself at stake.

DAN

As the Falkland Islands wolf serves from *The Dog of the South* forward as a core emblem of a hemisphere ravaged and polluted by successive waves of colonialist exploitation, so Dan both appears in *Gringos* and echoes backward as the emblematic ravager of all ravagers. He thinks he's gone native with his intended blood sacrifice on Likín's stony altar, but he's much more adequately comprehended as an Aryan brother descendant of the killer Freydís Eiríksdóttir from *The Saga of the Greenlanders*, the first to turn the violence of the European entrada into the Western Hemisphere against her own. "Hand me an axe," she says when her two male henchmen hesitate to kill five women she wants dead. They called themselves Pilgrims and Puritans, spoke often of bringing salvation to savages, and soon learned to wrap their depredations in boilerplate like the 1629 "Great Seal" of the Massachusetts Bay Colony's hapless "Come over and help us" Indian, but the whole colonial enterprise was a bloodbath from the get-go, and few writers have called it out so persistently if so obliquely as laconic Charles Portis.

Dan thus stands as a crazed, homicidal apotheosis of the entire imperial project, totem beast of the apocalyptic European arrival.

Refugio divides the hippie infestation, the "birds without nests" ("*aves sin nidos*") as he describes them, into "*los tóxicos*" ("the dopers") and "*viciosos*" ("the hardened bums, kids gone feral"). But Dan not only embodies this entire rabble but also comes to represent the whole double-barreled *norteamericano* plague at the spent end of its devolutionary narrative arc. "We are weaker than our fathers," Midge tells Dupree. We're a full millennium in, counting from the Greenlanders' hassling of the Skraelings, and Dan has picked up a bit of Quiche lingo—"My true name is *Balam Akab*. I am the Jaguar of the Night"— along the way. But he's looking bad, with "sagging yellow pouches

First seal of the Massachusetts Bay Colony, used from 1629 to 1686 and from 1689 to 1692.

under his eyes like folds of chicken fat" and a "hairy white belly" visible under "the expando waistband of his pajamas." In Portis's larger scheme Dan is a degenerate conquistador, a pathetic but still murderous late spasm of the genocidal European entrada. "The *yanquis* took half my country in 1848," laments Nardo. Melt down to essence the subplot thematics of Portis's final trilogy, and you get Dan and *Dusicyon australis* left standing in the crucible. Dan has a club. At the City of Dawn, he's traded up to a knife.

The signature structural feature in all this is that Portis novels invariably highlight their generally upbeat protagonist-focused primary narratives, using them to disguise the bleak subplot. While the latter reveals in glimpses a fallen world ruled by knaves, the central narrative portrays in detail protagonists attempting to construct decent lives in its margins and fissures. In *Gringos* this protagonist is Burns, and his twelve-gauge, aimed at Dan since the novel's second chapter, outranks Dan's blade. "The password tonight is L. C. Smith," Burns says, and when plot meets subplot, Dan's head disappears. Too bad it didn't happen four centuries earlier—the Falkland Islands wolf might still be around. Too bad, that is, that "the great Cortez" and the *Mayflower* colonists were initially greeted by the more accommodating Montezuma and Tisquantum/Squanto instead of the fierce Skraelings whose armed resistance convinced the Greenlanders to abandon their settlement plans and thereby set back the European incursion by some four hundred years. That Squanto gets on-screen only as Austin Popper's talking blue jay is a typically oblique Portis move. His critique stops short of an Ibsenesque species erasure—"I'll gladly, myself, torpedo the Ark"—though a persistent-across-three-novels sense of the Euro-American entrada as an unwelcome arrival comes through clearly.

(The very word "entrada" carries this pejorative sense in New World usage—"a Spanish exploring or conquering expedition in America," says Merriam-Webster. When Flandin dramatizes the trip to Likín as his "last *entrada*," he thus unwittingly presents himself as a latter-day conquistador armed not with a sword but with a pen, bullying his companions into signing scribbled affidavits of their acceptance "without reservation of Dr. Richard Flandin's theory of direct Trans-Pacific Chinese settlement of Meso-America.")

There's also a neat reversal of malevolent intent in Dan's exit episode. Back at the beginning, in the Mérida dump, Dan's Jumping Jack subordinates excitedly pursue a goat at his order. "I want that animal," Dan cries. "Get him! His name is Azazel! He's carrying off all the sins of the people! I must lay my hands on him and say some words!" "And cut his throat!" adds Beany Girl. (Dan has scrambled his scripture—Azazel is a demon or a place, never a named goat.) By the time they meet again at Likín, there's no goat at all, only Dan with a knife leading the boy Serafín and the girl LaJoye Mishell on a rope, the two linked at the wrist with baling wire and with red threads around their necks. But thanks to Refugio and Burns, his murderous sacrificial design fails. Dan, not the children, ends up tumbling headless off the cliff. He's the goat for Azazel.

An elegant diagram might jazz up a scholarly journal article at this point. Picture three separate line segments as an upper tier with a solid lower line of equal length below; label the upper segments left to right with the titles of the last three novels written above them and place "Midge," "Jimmerson," and "Burns" over both titles and segments. Meanwhile, label the single extended bottom line with the phrase "Euro-American Entrada" underneath. At the top, in bold, center "**PLOTS**" with a matching "**SUBPLOT**" below. This would make an impressive visual, suggesting both precision of thought and reduction to essentials—the cleverness of the critic foregrounded and every signature of authorial presence erased. Some of it would be nonsense and perhaps a lot of it but not all of it.

PLOTS

Midge	Jimmerson	Burns
The Dog of the South	*Masters of Atlantis*	*Gringos*

Euro-American Entrada
SUBPLOT

Enough of the diagram.

ORNAMENT AFTER ALL

The fact that *Gringos*' subplot focuses attention on Jimmy Burns's SWAT-team and search-and-rescue skills—somebody has to shoot Dan, retrieve LaJoye Mishell and Serafín, and rescue Rudy—should not obscure the primary arc of his story. He's a man of forty-one determined to redirect his life. He's "out of the game," he tells Emmett at the Christmas Day pancake feast, the "game" being digging for and trading in Mayan antiquities. Burns has been a treasure hunter, among other things, a *"schatzgraber,"* as the dying Alma Kobold puts it when she asks him to see to the disposition of her late husband's photo archive. From the perspective of Portis's sustained subplot critique Burns thus appears first as yet another mop-up agent in the senescent stages of colonialist assault. In the first phase, drunk on your accidental technical and epidemiological advantages, you ravage the surface—torch the villages; subdue, enslave, and exterminate the "Skraelings"; and turn the Jesuit and Dominican and Calvinist ancestors of Mrs. Symes and Mrs. Blaney loose to stuff effectual calling, English conversation, and ballroom dancing into their children. You then invade the depths, sluice out the gold from the Andes north to Hogandale and beyond. Finally, with all this behind you, the natives either extinct or demoralized and their landscape reduced to toxic tailings, you "cut three quick trenches . . . skim the cream and be out."

Burns has done other work in Mexico—there was a prosperous interval spent selling "long tan coats," and more recently he's been using his truck for hauling jobs and his flashlight working for a missing persons bureau. He even takes Polaroid pictures of tourists. But it's the treasure-hunting "game," with its clear echoes of the gold-rush ravages of Spanish conquistadors and American forty-niners, he's decided to flee, and a central function of the final scene in the trailer park is to demonstrate his resolution in the face of temptation. At its end Eli and Beany Girl are leaving, and Burns is headed back into the trailer for coffee and cookies with Louise.

What might easily be missed or underappreciated in this episode is his generosity toward his old partner in pillage: "I told him I wouldn't be needing my three-burner stove and he could take the thing along if he wanted it." Eli does want it, and he repays the kindness by also pilfering a Coleman lantern and a box of mantles. They're a bad pair, Eli and Beany Girl, but if Burns's choice of companions is newly improved, his openhandedness has been conspicuous from the start. Louise Kurle's Christmas Day "cold look" at his avowed intention to "be more considerate of other people in the coming year" is spectacularly misdirected—from Christmas Day through the following spring he gives her a run for her money as the most considerate expat in Mérida. And she's very good. Her Christmas is filled with errands of mercy, for which she enlists Burns and his truck. "Louise was a good girl," he allows. "Some days she went out into the countryside plucking bits of blowing plastic from bushes so the goats could get at the leaves. She truly wished everyone well."

But it's Burns himself the novel follows most closely, and his list of good deeds extends over its whole length. Planning to change the oil in his truck as the second chapter opens, he pauses to thread a needle for Alma Kobold, is rebuked for forgetting "my cakes," and ends up leaving money at the front desk for their delivery. A day or two later, off to Chiapas with supplies for the Ektún archeological dig, he stops on the way to buy "two buckets of fresh shrimp, one for Refugio and one for the college diggers." He already has gifts for Refugio's family—soccer magazines for Manolo, a hair dryer and a box of iodized salt for Sula. Before Burns makes it to Ektún, he pulls Rudy Kurle's taxi out at the Tabí River ford—for this he gets no thanks, only Rudy pointing out a "nick" in the bumper. "That's what your strap did," he says. No good deed unpunished.

Things only get worse at Ektún. Dr. Ritchie dies suddenly just after refusing Burns's offer of a ride to a hospital, and his loathsome second-in-command, Skinner, quarrels so heatedly over prices that Burns ends up charging him thirty dollars, paid in advance before the supplies are unloaded, for the bucket of shrimp intended as a gift. The dig falls apart, with Skinner and a colleague driving Dr. Ritchie's body to Villahermosa to record the death and Burns returning to Mérida with two female graduate students in tow. Even here, in all the upheaval, he thinks to purchase a bag of cacao beans from two Lacandón crew members as a gift for Louise.

He's no sooner home than the calls on his time and money resume. Alma Kobold needs more cakes, and a near stranger named Beavers hits him up for a ten-dollar loan "so fast I couldn't think of a way to say no." An old girlfriend named Beth needs some furniture hauled to her home and set up in her courtyard. Burns gets Alma's cakes, hands Beavers the loan, and transports Beth's furniture. He even remembers to bring treats for her cat. This section also offers a glimpse into the community's wider support network. In addition to his duties with the cakes, Burns is responsible for Frau Kobold's hair appointments: "Once a month I rolled her down to the *sala de belleza* to get her hair done, and air her out a bit." Alma still pays the *sala*'s staff only five pesos, "having no idea of what the peso was worth these days," so "Fausto and Doc and I made up the difference behind her back, as we did with her other creditors."

Gringos is almost as rich in these community-wide episodes of support and accommodation as it is in the good works of Louise and Burns. The comic element in their presentation—"air her out a bit"—is par for the Portis course. When a man named Harlan Shrader dies in his hotel room, Huerta the mortician hammers together a narrow coffin and buries him with cowboy boots on his feet, making him in death "a member of the equestrian class" for only forty dollars, grave plot included. "I think they must have belonged to some former occupant," Burns observes, since the living Harlan "tramped around town in threadbare canvas shoes with his toes poking out." This send-off is also a community effort: "Mott and I paid Huerta. Shep applied to the Veterans Administration for the $250 burial allowance but said he never got it." These ongoing episodes of consideration and accommodation bring a bit of Reese-residence vibe to Yucatán, enlarged from family-homestead to urban-community scale. Burns emerges from all this as a unique figure in the Portis cast of characters. He's got grit aplenty, and Serafín and LaJoye Mishell need every bit of it, but at forty-one he's more sharply aspirant to something like goodness. Lucky for him, Louise has been knocking on his door with green figs all the while, just waiting for him to notice.

THE HAUNTED MAN'S REPORT

Wade Watson is "a government clerk from Jefferson City, Missouri" whose plans for a meeting with *El Mago* and journey to the City of Dawn are interrupted when he's arrested by mistake on the day of his arrival in Mérida. Burns sees him sweeping the streets as a jailbird, gives him a few pesos for food, and asks Louise to see to his release before leaving for Chiapas and his own unplanned appointment with Dan in Likín. Burns is surprised to encounter Watson again at Shep's bar after his return, lecturing the other barflies about UFOs and setting small fires in small piles of torn-up napkins. The police turned him over to Louise for transport to the airport, but he missed the flight "and had been hanging about town ever since."

Almost as surprising as the miniature arsons is Watson's formal request to Burns: "May I relate a personal experience?" he asks. Burns, generous as ever, on this occasion with his time, not only agrees to listen but also formulates a striking general policy: "It seems to me you must let a haunted man make his report." What a line! It fits nicely into the immediate situation—Watson recounts the tale of a visit to his Missouri apartment by two "shining androids"—but there's just enough lyric lift and singular wording in the phrase to suggest a more general statement. A "haunted man"? This is pretty strong, though Watson's "experience" would certainly unsettle anyone. And the barely noticeable shift to second person—what of this? At a social level such listening is a matter of ordinary etiquette—*Norwood*'s Rita Lee listened gracefully, addressing her repeatedly as "ma'am," as Mrs. Whichcoat filled her "in on the judge and told her all about the Butterfields."

The line thus jumps out just enough to first slow and later arrest a reader's pace and at last prompt the notion that one function of the "you" could be direct address. Perhaps the reader, any reader, might be construed as asked to permit a writer construed as "haunted" to make his at once blistering and affectionate report. We're winding up a chapter in Portis's final novel here, with only one chapter to go, centered on a play and one especially strong short story, so here's an opportunity to lay out whatever summary assessment the journey has generated. It occurs to the Portishead who copped at the outset to plural biographies but has thus far eschewed biographical intrusion that Portis himself, like his importunate character, might be understood as possessing "personal experience" leading to elevated levels of long-term haunting.

A small-town Ark-La-Tex teenager goes directly from high school to a frontline Marine trench in the final months of the Korean War. From this special hell, following a stint at the University of Arkansas, he moves to a journalistic career, which throws him into the frontline violence of resistance to the civil rights movement. He sees telephone operators blown up in New York and Medgar Evers assassinated in Mississippi. He speaks with the martyred man's wife and surely sees the heartbreaking funeral photo of her comforting her son at his father's funeral that ran on the cover of the next week's *Life*. He witnesses and describes atrocities for which the victims had no words. Words are his job, and the thousands he produces chronicle a wide range of our species's worst behaviors.

This young man's mature successor, busy with a chosen career as a fiction writer, assiduously avoids interviews and other limelight moments while producing a series of novels heavily laded with mustered-out soldiers and pronounced "talk service" elements, the long arc of whose persistent if low-profile subplots constitute a whisper-level indictment of American exceptionalist thinking as sweeping as anything in Twain or even Melville. Perhaps he's haunted; perhaps he isn't, but his novels, taken together, are reasonably construed as the closest approach to a "report" a remarkably private man was willing to make. Each individual title, meanwhile, occludes its scorching if deeply interred critique by highlighting its protagonist's search within this violently desecrated natural and social world for Reese-residence, Rancho Moaler, and Mobile Star–trailer havens. As *Gringos* ends, a Posada Fausto analogue may be on the horizon.

Here then is the central claim, unsuspected at the outset, worked out in our class and in the writing. There's a lovely, hilarious, and greatly underrated play and a masterful short story still to come, but Portis ended his novel-writing run with *Gringos*, and it is the novels, especially the final three, that build the frame used here to read him, for better or worse. Not a hint of Telluric Currents—just a gathering confidence in the solid case made by the works themselves. Quality lit? We barely sensed the half of it. Next up, *Delray's New Moon*.

7 –

"A BRIEF REPRIEVE"

DELRAY'S NEW MOON

TALKING SERVICE COAST TO COAST

"I Don't Talk Service No More" appeared in the May 1996 issue of the *Atlantic Monthly*. It's a brevity, but it concentrates a persistently recurrent component of Portis's larger body of fiction into three pages. You could do worse than to read it as a fictional version of "That New Sound from Nashville," published in the *Saturday Evening Post* thirty years earlier: both are sketches of often-glamorized occupational niches with high mortality rates. Neither soldiers nor country music stars die on the job at rates challenging loggers or commercial fishermen, but both professions are dangerous gigs, and even for survivors the nonfatal wounds can fester. "Mostly they're glad to hear from me and we'll sit in the dark and talk service for a long time," Portis's unnamed narrator says of the Fox Company recipients of his nocturnal calls. He's up front about his obsessive focus—"I told Neap service was the only thing I did talk"— and only a vague sense of conversational proprieties sustains his attentiveness to Neap's account of his current condition. It's not good. "My house is sinking. I live in a bog now," Neap tells him. His wife "had something wrong with her too," but the caller has little interest in this: "His wife wasn't on the Fox Company Raid." The bigger picture in "I Don't Talk Service No More" is also bleak. Of sixteen soldiers in the Fox Company Raid party, Dill and Gott are dead, Sipe is "a fugitive from justice," the Neaps "were going all the way down," and the chronicler of it all, "talking service coast to coast every night," is calling from "a nut ward."

"That New Sound from Nashville," for its part, is also chock full of bad news. Life on the road is hazardous, with cars and planes smashing into each other and the ground. "We were burying 'em around here like animals for a while," Roy Acuff says of a recent spate of early 1960s crashes (and one house trailer fire) that took the lives of seven stars. "Disaster and sudden death," the author concludes, "have come to be a part of the country-music scene."

You might also do worse than to read "I Don't Talk Service No More" as a short-story redo of Samuel Beckett's *Krapp's Last Tape*: both are retrospective monologues by codger loners mediated by audio technologies. Neap, awakened by telephone in (actual) Orange, Texas, responds to the memory-lane invite negatively: "I told him I had been thinking about the Fox Company Raid and thought I would give him a ring," the narrator says. "I don't talk service no more," Neap replies, but he ends up doing just that, first by not hanging up, second by coming up when challenged with the names of five fellow raid participants, and finally by going all in with questions about the justice of the awards handed out in its aftermath: "Neap said it was Dill and Sipe who grabbed those prisoners and that Zim had nothing to do with it. I told him Zim had something to do with getting us over there and back. He said yeah, Zim was all right, but he didn't do no more in that stinking trench line than we did, and so how come he got meritorious R and R in Hong Kong and we didn't?"

Krapp's interactions with his ledger and tapes follow a similar arc. He converses with no one but himself, but he also repeatedly renounces his "retrospect" even as he returns obsessively to its single focus. That his ruminations center on one man's failed love affair instead of an infantry company's successful raid on enemy positions should not occlude the two pieces' fundamental similarity—in both instances a stoppage in interior life is portrayed; a mind stays behind, locked in a vanished moment, while the body it inhabits ages on. For Krapp as for Neap and his caller an incident more than thirty years in the past is repeatedly made present. "Be again, be again," says Krapp. "(*Pause.*) All that old misery. (*Pause.*) Once wasn't enough for you." For the two vets, too, yesteryear's event is, in their conversation, reanimated as today's grievance: "How come he got meritorious R and R in Hong Kong and we didn't? I couldn't answer that question. I can't find anyone who knows the answer to that." Once isn't enough for them either.

There's a sense, too, in which Neap, along with the others who "sit in the dark and talk service for a long time," is living up to Jimmy Burns's code, his sense that "you must let a haunted man make his report." The single word "report" is a thin reed in support of an argument, but the old soldier on the line every night from the D-3 ward hasn't yet called Sergeant Zim, because "I wanted to have the squad pretty much accounted for before I made my report to him." Good man, Neap, for not hanging up, for lending your midnight ear to a barely remembered Fox Company buddy from forty years back. You've clearly got a full plate of your own worries, what with the sick wife and needing a stepladder to get in your front door, but next to the man on the line you're in clover, free in the world with a house and wife to worry about. Props, Neap—Jimmy Burns and the whole Private Slovik American Legion post salute you (Bolus with his feet in Korea, Mott all the way crazy half the time or half way crazy all the time).

Humor is a near omnipresence in Portis's writing—even "I Don't Talk Service No More" has its laugh-out-loud moments. The sinking house with the improvised stepladder entrance has a crazy humor to it, as does the image of Sipe the septuagenarian fugitive from justice tottering through the world with lawmen hot on his trail. But even these laughs are rooted in the dark, life-as-long-pratfall world of silent film comedy. And suddenly here's Buster again—Neap's house is built in the same universe as Keaton's boat, sliding smoothly from launching pier to the bottom in the 1921 short *The Boat* with its captain stoically at attention at the stern, or the more celebrated collapsing house in the 1928 feature *Steamboat Bill, Jr.* The whole country is overrun by con men—Neap no doubt purchased his "mud flat" house and lot from an Orange County Symes, a League of Leaders brother in commerce to the peddler of ranchettes in Colorado, his ailing spouse prescribed some newly minted (and addictive into the bargain) nuxated zinc or Omni-Balsamic-Reinvigorator by today's Big Pharma herb doctor. The Fox Company boys, along with Cogburn and LaBoeuf and Norwood and Burns and *The Dog of the South*'s Flying Tiger and the *Masters of Atlantis* expats, mustered out with their wartime wounds and traumas into a land of the free overrun by Fring and Symes and Popper. Speckled yellow ties everywhere. Portis may have written no darker line than this story's close: "For a long time I didn't have the keys." This is cold—the pathos of such a claim!—a life sentence on the "nut ward" holding tight to keys that unlock no door back to the world, both story and closing line the late work of an author who "talked service" to the end.

To the very end—check out the grave marker down in Hamburg. Name, dates, and "SGT US MARINE CORPS KOREA." Service talk, every word. Nothing more, not even the standard cross for Christian vets. The nearby epitaphs of his parents are downright fulsome in comparison, if almost as brief: "A CHRISTIAN SOUTHERN GENTLEMAN" for Dad, "BELOVED WIFE AND MOTHER" for Mom. Here's a no-frills sign-off! Not a trace of cutup; "laconic" has worked well to describe Portis's humor throughout, but here it falls short of capturing the austerity of the old Marine's final, lapidary report.

THE SPECIAL VALUE PACKAGE

Portis's single play, the three-act *Delray's New Moon*, was given its only performances in a two-week run in April 1996, a month before the publication of "I Don't Talk Service No More." The two works are strikingly different, the play being a rare Portis work lacking both a character identified as a veteran in its cast and prominent "talk service" elements in its dialogue (though Mrs. Vetch speaks with pride of her son, killed in Korea, as "a brave and handsome captain in the paratroopers"). It closes, more unreservedly than *Masters of Atlantis* or even *Gringos*, on an upbeat, downright jubilant note, but at bottom the standard Portis double perspective is sustained.

But here the narrative order is different. Where the havens of Rancho Moaler and the Mobile Star trailer in *Masters of Atlantis* and *Gringos* are achieved after long struggle near each tale's end, in *Delray's New Moon* the long-established southern-Arkansas refuge of Miss Eula's Sunnyside Hotel is disrupted at the outset by the owner's decision to sell her property to Delray Scantling. Despite his structural centrality as the serpent in the Sunnyside's garden, Scantling has a subordinate role in the play. A figure of fun from the beginning, he's eventually a physical punching bag in a brutal comedy

Portis's grave marker. *Photo by author.*

of slapstick violence. Portis doesn't explicitly date the action, but the stage directions locate Miss Eula's establishment *"just off the highway—Interstate 30—about halfway between Little Rock and Texarkana."* Interstate 30 opened in Arkansas in 1957; Texarkana is just over 140 miles southwest of Little Rock, so Miss Eula's hotel operated in the general vicinity of Arkadelphia, in Clark County, sometime in the latter decades of the twentieth century.

The stage directions go on to specify an *"outdoor sign, not yet hung,"* urging passersby to *"DINE AND DANCE AT DELRAY'S NEW MOON,"* leaning against a wall. There's also a *"life-size cardboard cutout"* of two dancers, who *"have a 1930s look."*

This is more than enough, isn't it, before a line is spoken, to reveal Scantling's dream of "night club history" being made by his "very smart supper club" as sheer folly? "My vision is national," he says, illustrating his point with a comparison to Wall Drug in South Dakota, where thousands even now line up daily for the roarings and gnashings of an animatronic T. rex. They're not "highly select guests"—founding druggist Ted Hustead aimed at a broader market when he opened up with little more than "Free Ice Water" back in the Great Depression. Nobody dines and dances, but everybody eats donuts and buys souvenirs. Delray's New Moon, with its *"1930s look,"* is clearly doomed—not even Mrs. Edge, back in Little Rock, expects dining with her dancing, and Scantling himself (appropriately named) is a negligible figure.

(As with *Norwood*'s educated chicken and Hot Springs' IQ Zoo, Portis may here be offhandedly dropping another Arkansas reference. Delray's New Moon bears more than a passing resemblance to the Vapors, also in Hot Springs, a lavishly appointed nightclub "where diners could sit and eat their expensive steaks while watching entertainers from all over the world." At show's end the "hydraulic stage" pulled back to make room for a house orchestra and a "polished mahogany dance floor.")

The play's central villain is Dr. Lloyd Mole, never seen or heard but forcefully represented onstage by his self-proclaimed "love child" Mae Buttress, charged with "Receiving and Interrogation" at Avalon, his retirement home, purveyor of the widely advertised "Special Value Package." "There's always room for you—at Avalon," say the TV ads. "No waiting list ever." Mole's establishment has somehow signed up four longtime residents of Miss Eula's just-shuttered hotel, and the curtain opens on a dining room in transition. Ms. Buttress has not yet arrived—she'll be delayed and so shaken by the Avalon van's wreck on a rain-slicked highway that she faints away before she can register her new residents—but Mr. Niblis is already downstairs, packed and ready to go, when Mr. Palfrey enters with his elder daughter, Fern. They're regular visitors who use Miss Eula's as a handoff point in Dad's moves back and forth between stays with Fern in Texarkana and his younger daughter, Lenore, in Little Rock. He's agitated to discover he's left his police scanner behind—"That won't do me any good tonight," he grouses when Fern offers to send it up the next day on the bus—but he orders breakfast and discusses purchasing a pecan log from Marguerite, an entrepreneurial nine-year-old planning on a dance career as "the radiant Miss Annabel" but meanwhile raising money for new band uniforms.

They're soon joined by Mrs. Vetch and Mr. Mingo, also bound for Avalon, escorted downstairs by Duvall, Delray's assistant. Mr. Ramp, a fourth Sunnyside resident known to Mr. Palfrey from prior visits, has mysteriously disappeared. He, too, is scheduled to move to Avalon. Mr. Ramp, like Dr. Mole, is another of *Delray's New Moon*'s very large cast of offstage characters.

"A BRIEF REPRIEVE" 153

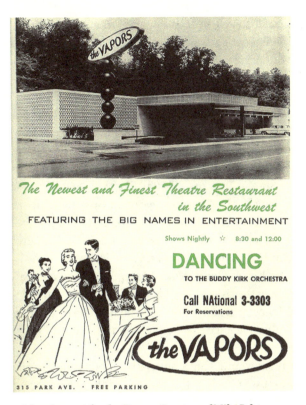

Advertisement for the Vapors. *Courtesy of Mike Polston, Museum of American History, Cabot Public Schools (Cabot, AR).*

All this may be the laconic cutup yet again, at play this time in a visual medium. The sometimes-casual handling of characters and events noted in the fiction surfaces here in the cast list, which includes thirteen roles—Mae Buttress, Delray, Duvall, Fern, Kate, Lenore, Marguerite, Mr. Mingo, Mr. Niblis, Mr. Palfrey, Tonya, Mrs. Vetch, and an unnamed "Police Detective." All these appear onstage, balanced by another thirteen (or fourteen) who do not—Boyce; Ruth Buttress, R.N.; Miss Eula; Garland; Jerry; Dr. Lloyd Mole; Prentice; Mr. Ramp; Sammy; and "four or five morons" who turn out to be sons of a drunken painter searching for their father. But what about this drunken painter? He fits in neither category—absent from the cast list, he nevertheless appears in a brief cameo.

Under all this clown-car slapstick, the world outside Miss Eula's Sunnyside is Portis's standard dystopian nightmare presented via a rhetoric of darkest comedy, the poisoned mine tailings of Hogandale and the burning sofa at the derelict Burnette Temple moved east and south to Arkansas. Families in the Arkadelphia area are evidently warehousing their oldsters in record numbers, as Dr. Mole's Avalon operation has at least two area competitors to worry about—Mrs. Vetch has heard that the staff at Gathering Shade "hang a placard from your neck if you misbehave, and you must wear it in shame for a week. 'I Spread Rumors.' Things like that. 'I Talked Back to Staff.' 'I am a TV Hog.'" Mr. Mingo's report on Sinking Embers is similarly dismaying: "They sometimes wake you in the night," he says. "Some orderly on the night shift. Some young fellow like Duvall there. He sits by your bed in the dark and asks difficult questions in a soft voice."

Next to this, Avalon's "New Concept in Twilight Care" comes off as Dr. Symes's arthritis clinic or City of Life dream refined to Auschwitz-level efficiency. "I wonder how they do it at the price," asks Fern of the Special Value Package's "One flat fee up front and no more worries" promise.

"Fast turnaround, that's how," Mr. Niblis replies. "Accelerated disposal. When we check in the front door they're dragging corpses out the back door. Out the door, into the dumpster and off the books."

Fern can't take this in. "Who would do such a thing?" she asks.

"A foul lump of grease named Lloyd Mole, that's who," Mr. Niblis continues. "It's the vital organs racket. They're bootlegging vital organs out of Avalon. Dr. Mole and his accomplice Ruth Buttress."

Dr. Mole, by his love child's report, "likes to have a little one-on-one chat with each new guest. About their allergies, you know, and their medications and their unencumbered assets." A special feature of these interviews is "the great advantages of giving him power of attorney and of having all their checks deposited directly to the Avalon account." Mr. Palfrey is, in the play's first act, serenely confident of his own security—"Don't you have any chirren to look after you?" he asks, obtusely, given his interlocutors—but he's soon rattled when Lenore arrives bearing an Avalon brochure recommended by his son-in-law Boyce. "See?" she says. "The days are full at Avalon and before you know it, it's bedtime." He's downright shocked ("*Stunned*" is the stage direction) when Fern later lets slip that Boyce has euthanized his father-in-law's favorite hunting dog, Blanche. "Poor old Blanche," he mourns. "I was hoping she had found a good home with a dry bed to sleep in." Lenore is unmoved: "She was all wore out, Daddy. Her time had come. We have to face up to these things."

A MIRACLE OF THE LIGHTS AT THE SUNNYSIDE HOTEL

Well, maybe not, at least not yet, though as act 3 opens things are looking grim in the shuttered hotel. Mae Buttress is still passed out offstage, but a lightning strike has triggered a power outage, and the evictees are sitting around like children wearing Avalon caps and holding balloons, with *"shipping tags"* tied to their clothes. The conversation around the candlelit tables has turned to varieties of "stale air." Mr. Palfrey, again inconsiderately, given the situation faced by the others, provides an opening category: "People don't know what stale air is until they've been in an old folks home." He's immediately countered by Mr. Niblis, who opts for "veterans' hospital" air: "A good long whiff of that and your knees will buckle, Mr. Palfrey." Following brief digressions into the causes of such bad air (Mr. Palfrey and Mrs. Vetch concur on "bathrobe vapors") and the acceptability of "shorty pajamas" at Avalon (rejected by both Fern and Mrs. Vetch), Mr. Palfrey returns to the "stale air" topic with a third candidate: "Bus station air is pretty bad air." This in turn reminds Mr. Niblis of "the air in your flop-house hotel across the street from your bus station" before Mr. Mingo alleges that the "stagnant" air in the Mingo family home "stunted our development in so many ways." Red curtains, he adds, "never parted or drawn," contributed "a reddish, infernal tone."

"Infernal" gets this whole scene pretty well, doesn't it? Power out, flaming candles the only light, stale air the dominant topic of conversation, the oldsters awaiting transport to Avalon, "over there in . . . that great swamp called the Chinkypin Bottoms"—it's a second or third coming of Portis's countrified Dantesque, Acheron just off Interstate 30, Charon at the wheel of the Avalon backup van.

As it turns out, however, Mr. Palfrey is spared his Avalon conversation with Boyce, at least for the time being. He doesn't, quite yet, have to "face up to these things." Good things begin to happen. Barbecue sandwiches come first—always a good omen—followed by the appearance from the back of Mae Buttress, stripped of her Nurse Ratched authority, bleeding from a scalp wound (she's resisted arrest) and handcuffed to the drunken painter by a police detective who has mistaken her for the waitress Kate and him for her criminal boyfriend, Prentice. Things are clearly looking up.

It gets better. Delray's protests of his painter's arrest get him his own beating—"He's got Delray laid out like a starfish in the handicap parking space and he's beating the daylights out of him!" Marguerite reports. Like a starfish? In the handicap space? The Portis details! At this point the policeman leaves with his misidentified prisoners, the bloodied Delray staggers back inside for treatment, and Mr. Palfrey returns briefly to the spotlight.

Fern has seen enough. Boyce's interest in Avalon's Special Value Package is the last straw—let Daddy return to Little Rock, and he could soon be gone as suddenly as Blanche. The voice of Lenore, channeling Boyce, is in her head. A car pulls up outside. "This must be Garland," says Fern. "Are you ready, Daddy? It's Garland. We're going home."

"I don't know about this," Mr. Palfrey says. "What will Garland say?"

"Garland will do the right thing," Fern replies, and when Lenore speaks up for her husband ("And Boyce won't?"), Fern has a ready response: "It's not in him, Lenore. Garland could teach you both some manners." She even puts his hat on his head and reminds him to remember his flashlight. He could be huddled over his police scanner by sundown. Emboldened by Fern's resolve, Mr. Palfrey has his own answer when Lenore asks what she should tell Boyce about Avalon: "Tell him I'd rather live in a crawdad hole."

Fortunate Mr. Palfrey, in his life-saving elder daughter, like fortunate Jimmy Burns (in Louise Kurle) and fortunate Lamar Jimmerson (in Fanny) and perhaps also fortunate Norwood Pratt (in Rita Lee, who knows?). And as it happens, the arriving car is neither Garland's nor the Avalon van. Miss Eula herself is at the wheel, though she's a Mrs. now. "She's with Mr. Ramp!" Marguerite exclaims. "They ran off and got married and have just got back from their honeymoon in Antlers, Oklahoma!" Add fortunate Mr. Ramp to the list.

This unsuspected groom, his earlier disappearance now explained, is asleep in the back seat, and Miss Eula herself is initially self-conscious, worried, reports Marguerite, that "y'all will laugh at 'em and make fun of 'em for getting married when they're so old like that." But Mrs. Vetch rises to the occasion with fulsome welcome: "Tell Eula we all love her and we've missed her so much, and we want to see her. Nobody's going to laugh." "You have my promise," adds Mr. Mingo.

There's a lot of back-and-forth with Marguerite, who operates throughout the third act as the modern-stage equivalent of a *kēryx*, the herald/messenger of classical theater whose announcement of offstage events is by convention regarded as accurate. Through her Miss Eula reports (twice) that Mr. Ramp is a "wonderful companion," though "he can't see to drive good anymore," making it necessary for Eula to "do all the driving to Antlers and back." She also, through Marguerite again, tells Delray his payments are two months behind and gives him one month to get them current. But now the battered Delray, frustrated from the beginning by the inertia of the hapless Duvall, senses the bedrock impossibility of his project. "The dance floor isn't nearly big enough," he notes. "I knew that all along." He surrenders. "Tell her I accept foreclosure," he informs Marguerite. "I relinquish all claims. . . . Tell her the New Moon didn't work out," he says, handing her the keys.

As Marguerite departs with Delray's keys and capitulation, the lights suddenly come back on, and even the three Avalon consignees sense a sharply changed atmosphere. First the threat of immediate banishment to Avalon removed by the sight of Mae Buttress hustled out in handcuffs and now the saving return of Miss Eula—Mrs. Vetch at once attributes her unexpected rescue to supernatural intervention. "It's the miracle of the lights at the Sunnyside Hotel!" she exclaims. Mr. Niblis is more restrained. "I don't know about that," he says. "A reprieve anyway." But he takes off his Avalon cap and immediately rolls a cigarette. Later he'll pop his balloon with it. Smoking is once again most definitely allowed. Mr. Mingo is the last to speak. "Executive clemency, Mr. Niblis," he says. "And not to be scorned. A brief reprieve is all anybody ever had."

Mae Buttress gone; Mr. Palfrey ready to go; Mrs. Vetch, Mr. Niblis, and Mr. Mingo ready to stay—we've reached the drama's end, and Marguerite makes a final headlong entry to announce the play's small-bore resurrection in a blizzard of exclamation points. "He's up!" she cries. "Mr. Ramp is up!" (Mrs. Vetch, already alert to miracle, would hear this as "He is risen!" Add a rainbow to the thunderstorm's end, and she'll be on her knees.) Mr. Ramp needs his shirt tucked in, but Eula is there to tend to this. "Now she's taken his arm!" Marguerite adds. "She's got all her keys in her other hand!"

"Is she radiant?" asks Mrs. Vetch.

"Her cheeks are rosy!" Marguerite reports. "Mr. Ramp's face is red, too!" By this description Mr. Mingo recognizes a well-mated pair: "Already they're beginning to look alike!"

"Here they come, everybody!" cries Marguerite at the curtain. "Here they are! Mr. and Mrs. Ramp!"

A BRIEF REPRIEVE

So much has been left out—whole stories and nonfiction pieces omitted or barely mentioned ("Your Action Line," "Nights Can Turn Cool in Viborra," "The Forgotten River," "The Wind Bloweth Where It Listeth"), high-visibility themes noted only in passing. But here is nevertheless the spot to end, with *Delray's New Moon* appreciated as something of a minor-key reprise of Portis's signature narrative moves and thematic preoccupations. Mr. Palfrey, just for starters, would be understood as a threatened protagonist from the moment he appears by audience members familiar with Norwood Pratt, Mattie Ross, Ray Midge, Lamar Jimmerson, or Jimmy Burns. He has no idea, confident as he is in the solicitude of his "chirren," but Boyce is back in Little Rock with plans in his head, a brochure in Lenore's hand.

And behind Boyce is Dr. Lloyd Mole, his Avalon facility down in the Chinkypin Bottoms an up-and-running version of Reo Symes's plans for a "City of Life" on his mother's Mississippi River island. Mole's checkered past includes clashes with Florida authorities over "his red vinegar therapy" and the "big Fungometrics scandal," but he's blanketing the Ark-La-Tex with "Special Value Package" ads, and his methods of geriatric "horde control" are developed far beyond Guy Dupree's pathetic outline thanks to his experiments with his mistress/rat manager Ruth Buttress. The Mole-Buttress operation comes across as Bedlam South, Last Breath Farm. Think of the Avedon photographs, East Louisiana State Mental Hospital. Mr. Mingo, despite the orientalist slur, gets it close to right: "We'll just be sitting around all day in a big room. That's all. Day after day we'll sit there in Asiatic resignation. . . . We'll sit there slumped and gaping as we're being methodically dried out. . . . They'll draw all the moisture out of our bodies, all the volatile components, until we're reduced to living mummies. Little stick figures, just bits of bone and hair and leather. Until we're not much bigger than spider monkeys. That's how these places work."

But threats to Portis protagonists are overcome, almost always, and by predictable, time-honored means. It's the women, Mattie Ross, Fanny Hen, and Louise Kurle, who mostly save the Portis day, though Jimmy Burns saves LaJoye Mishell Teeter from Dan's fumbled *Balam Akab* sacrifice. "No way these old folks end up at Avalon," a knowing Portis reader in the audience might whisper to her companion midway through, "but meanwhile, this Mr. Mingo's tale of pestilent editorials is the funniest thing I've heard since Symes's riff on Rod Garza's El Tigre dentures." Fern and Miss Eula, as we've seen, will prove her right.

Something of a model for Miss Eula may have appeared in the author's life back in the 1960s if the "Motel #1" section of "Motel Life, Lower Reaches" may be read as straightforward reportage (though it wasn't published until 2003). She is not named, and she oversees "an old 'tourist court,' a horseshoe arrangement of ramshackle cabins." But she spares him the "sharp practice" of listing a rock-bottom rate on a highway billboard only to have them taken just before the customer arrived, and then wins him over completely in the morning by the "unprecedented gesture" of delivering breakfast to his door "with some buttered toast and a little china jug of honey." Miss Eula, by Mrs. Vetch's account, also set a good table: "We did have some awfully good puddings and pies here at the Sunnyside."

It's especially good to have "Motel Life, Lower Reaches" on the screen here at the sign-off. It comes across as a briefer exercise in the "Combinations of Jacksons" vein, though more tightly focused on Portis himself than on his family background. Along with the nicely modulated warmth of the "Motel #1" portrait of its honey-bearing hostess there's the moment earlier in the same sketch where the narrator decides to "go for price alone" in making his choice from the rich and widely advertised menu of lodging options in Truth or Consequences, New Mexico. This choice gets him the old lady and her three-dollar room with the nice breakfast included, but it was rooted in a final inability to factor in the numerous "frills" listed on the highway signs.

"How could you reckon in cash," he asks, "the delight value of a miniature golf course with its little plaster windmills, tiny waterfalls, and bearded elves perched impudently on plaster toadstools?"

The "bearded elves" are funny, a worthy detail of miniature golf course description. But "delight value"? You get exactly this nowhere else, close maybe in DeLillo—the earnest idiocy of monetized delight. The closest parallels are other Portis moments—Midge covering "every square inch" of his apartment table with savings bonds or struggling in vain to make sense of Dix's contradictory sales maxims or the California radio preacher's sonic mix of the "very persuasive" with "a Satanic note." "I couldn't work it out," he says. The deep comedy here lies not in the failure but in even constructing the terms of the attempt.

There's pathos too, mixed in with the laughs, and here the throttled ex-biographer surfaces again, muttering through his gag. Look, he insists, this author of yours repeatedly projects, in essay, fiction, and drama, a rich variety of appealing last-act scenarios. The "Combinations of Jacksons" piece from 1999 presents near its close a solitary coot on the move in a junker car with the standard Portis male accessories (flashlight, jumper cables, gun) on board. "I could see myself all too clearly," he writes, behind the wheel of "that old butterscotch Pontiac, roaring flat out across the Mexican desert and laying down a streamer of smoke like a crop duster."

Earlier, with *Gringos* and *Delray's New Moon*, he'd imagined two very different golden-years arrangements, neither including roaring across anywhere. Mr. Palfrey lives with his two daughters, while Burns and Mr. Ramp marry women who come to the altar equipped with lodgings of their own. Pros and cons are getting figured out here—the "delight value" of mobility and self-sufficiency balanced against the appeal of security and companionship.

(The reference is oblique, but might there be a final suggestion of such plans for companionship in "The Wind Bloweth Where It Listeth," where Portis's final published line hints at a "little announcement"? Any chance Frankie and the protagonist contemplate making their break in the now-defunct *Blade*'s "pick of the litter" blue Gremlin? That would be an upbeat end to a markedly downbeat story, its final loyalties tipping toward the novels' main plots. A sharply alternative reading, aligning this last sign-off with the earlier subplots, would sense in the same close not a hint of a last-minute connubial elopement in the manner of Mr. Ramp and Miss Eula but rather a return to *Norwood*'s use of Melville's *The Confidence-Man*, as bleak as any vision ever penned of the American landscape. Here's Melville's close, the final sentence in his final published novel: "Something further may follow of this Masquerade." Here's Portis's: "We may have another little announcement quite soon.")

But here's the point, before we sedate the would-be bio man again: Mr. Portis mostly gets dealt none of these happy hands, though it's good to see at least some enactment of the solitary-traveler vision in "The Forgotten River" and "Motel Life, Lower Reaches" pieces. In retrospect, both the dream of the oldster on the pedal-to-the-metal loose and the vision of a cozy-trailer last chapter as the "indulgent" husband of a good-hearted Louise stand revealed as vain hopes. The worries about nursing home life, however—present from beginning to end—seem eerily prescient. Norwood's parting words to the hobo Eugene end with the threat of geriatric confinement: "They'll put you in a home somewhere if you don't watch out." There it is.

DESERT VIEW

Four motels are visited in "Motel Life, Lower Reaches." The last one is described very briefly—only two paragraphs—but it's the one that matters. The day begins with departure from the third and a return visit to Truth or Consequences, where "I could find no trace of the old yellow cabins" of the first motel, "nor even locate the site." "Things disappear, too, utterly," he says. He ends up at the Desert View, locale unspecified, which stands out not for its shortcomings but for its unsettling perfections. The place is "clean, new, modern, all those things, with a gleaming white bathroom." There are no guests "of sly or rat-like appearance," a far cry from the estimated up to 10 percent "genuine felons on the lam, some with their molls" who sign the register at the Ominato on a given night. "The Desert View," he concludes, is "pretty close to that ideal in my head of the cheap and shipshape roadside dormitory, what I kept looking for all those years."

It gives him the creeps. "Something felt wrong. Everything, more or less, but something bizarre in particular that I couldn't put my finger on." He eventually singles out the carpet—"The very *carpet* was clean. *Motel carpet!*"—though the real malaise runs deeper and reaches much wider. "I didn't get it. Who were these Desert View people?" He finds no answer: "I cleared out of there at dawn and still don't know."

There's a deft mix of time and space in this whole piece, a sense of vast disorienting shifts with a fundamental entropy masquerading as progress at the helm. Portis was a 1940s and 1950s youngster who went off as a teenager to a war never formally ended and came home to a world in upheaval. He forged a career in print journalism just as newspapers were ceding their breaking-news role to television (the *Herald Tribune* folded in 1966, only eighteen months after he left). Rock and roll left him cold—he was a big Lawrence Welk fan—and both beat and hippie culture held zero appeal for him. The Desert View is to the motels he's familiar with as "news matter" is to the "lively asides" of the rural correspondents he was paid to edit out. He succeeded spectacularly at everything he tried, but there seems more than a little of Ray Midge ("I had to get on with my reading!") and quite a lot of Jimmy Burns ("Hard worker. Solitary as a snake.") in his makeup.

It's a reach to call him a casualty of war. He's no "fugitive from justice" like Sipe or a bughouse resident like the unnamed narrator of "I Don't Talk Service No More" (though a ten-minute film version names him "Buddy"). But the prominence of the "talk service" element in Portis's fiction (if anything underestimated here) does come across as suggesting a persistent presence verging on haunting. It's present in the whole of his "report," crafted over nearly half a century, from Elvis Presley's army leave in 1958 and the funeral of Lieutenant Train in 1962 to the American Legion bar in the Ominato Motel section of "Motel Life, Lower Reaches" in 2003. Something feels wrong. Everything, more or less. Portis endings tend toward comity, but something fundamental is very often off, as in Rancho Moaler's reification of neocolonial hierarchies. Very often but not always, and only an ideologically committed Malvolio or Mrs. Grundy could dredge up much to carp at in the Reese-residence scene, the achieved satisfactions of Louise and Jimmy in their Mobile Star trailer, or the welcome reopening of Miss Eula's Sunnyside Hotel.

Portis's "report" is thus built into his fiction at a structural level, in the nearly omnipresent tension between plot and subplot stressed throughout this exploration. It's not so easy to fathom. His method embodies at bottom an Olmec aesthetic as he describes it—first he buries his dots, and then he places them at great remove from one another, though once in a great while he puts the haunting out in the open for just an instant, as in Jimmy Burns's momentary surge of rage ("Blood was roaring in my ears") at Dan and his Jumping Jack crew. But his dots do connect, and eventually they weave a subterranean take on Dante's "narrow plot where we behave so savagely." Telluric Currents! In journalism, fiction, memoir, and drama Charles Portis constructed a sustained portrait, strikingly coherent, savagely comic, of a despoiled world recognizably ours, not so new and conspicuously not brave, overrun by knaves. They often get theirs in the end—blown up in cars, run down by semis, beheaded by shotgun blasts. Meanwhile, other people want what most people have always wanted. These are Portis's protagonists. They're comic figures too, but their creator is on their side, and almost always they eventually find some form of the "brief reprieve" achieved when grit joins hands with charity's day-to-day gestures of consideration and accommodation.

ACKNOWLEDGMENTS

John Pickerill and Jeff Gordon, best of friends since high school and college, critiqued individual chapters as I wrote. Portis was new to both—a big plus. Mike Bieker, director of the University of Arkansas Press, had both read the novels and met the author. He was first to read a complete draft. I benefited greatly from the insights of all three.

Haunted Man's Report is not a biography, so I made less sustained use than usual of the University of Arkansas Libraries' interlibrary loan staff. But I did make some, especially in searching out early journalistic efforts, and I'm grateful for the skilled assistance of Robin Roggio in particular. I also benefited again from the local history expertise of Fayetteville historian Charlie Allison, who filled me in on Portis's work for the *Arkansas Traveler* student newspaper.

In the earliest stages of both research and writing I learned much from twelve University of Arkansas graduate students in a Portis seminar in the spring semester of 2022. Specific insights originating with individual students are listed in the notes, but we learned as a group, and everybody contributed. Thanks go to Morgan Akers, Tate Aldrich, Heathermarie Brown, Bethany Cole, David Eichelberger, Conor Flannery, Joaquín Gavilano, Scott Hendry, Tyler Houston, Taylor Pike, Abigail Ross, and Eden Shulman.

I vowed early on to respect Mr. Portis's determined resistance to celebrity's intrusions by refraining from pestering family members and friends, but when Eichelberger's student research gained him a luncheon engagement at the Faded Rose in Little Rock with Jonathan Portis, Charles's younger brother, I happily accepted the invitation to join them. A picture of the author still displayed behind the bar (it's modest in size—I wouldn't have noticed it without help) was only one of that afternoon's pleasures. I was also assisted in acquiring the wartime photo of Portis the young Marine by Jay Jennings, the number one hero in anybody's Charles Portis rescue story.

At the other end of the project, with the manuscript taken ably in hand by the UA Press production team, I was greatly aided in the tedious business of securing permissions to reprint photographs and illustrations by the happy accident of having a daughter experienced in the process. Masie Cochran, editorial director at Tin House, guided me over those hurdles with unprecedented dispatch. Over nearly three decades I've watched UA Press editors, designers, copy editors, and publicists turn at least fifteen manuscripts I've been a part of into handsome books. It has been a particular pleasure to serve as editor for the Arkansas Character series volumes (another Mike Bieker idea). Even at eighty I dare to plan for more of those. *Haunted Man's Report* belongs to no larger series, but like its predecessors it owes its existence between hard covers to the talents and efforts of the UA Press staff—in this case, Daniel Bertalotto, Mike Bieker, David Manuel Cajias Calvet, David Scott Cunningham, Janet Foxman, Katie Herman, Joelle Kidd, Melissa King, Sam Ridge, and Charlie Shields.

Final thanks, as always, go to our family, who over more than four decades have shared in every enthusiasm leading to articles and books and documentary videos and museum exhibits. So: for Bobby and Jannet and Mark, Shannon and Sam and Robin and Davy and Sol, Masie and Aaron and Luke and Everett and Milo, Jesse and Sarah, Taylor and Madison and Kai. And once more for Suzanne—darling companion, Mom, Mo—who keeps us all close.

NOTES

PREFACE

VII **quality lit game:** Cited as spoken by Portis (who credited the phrase to Terry Southern) in a telephone conversation in Donna Tartt, "Charles Portis: A Remembrance," afterword to *Escape Velocity: A Charles Portis Miscellany*, by Charles Portis, rev. ed., ed. Jay Jennings (Little Rock: Butler Center for Arkansas Studies, 2021), 361. The phrase is also credited to Southern in Nile Southern, "Now Dig the Archive," afterword to *Now Dig This: The Unspeakable Writings of Terry Southern, 1950–1995*, by Terry Southern, ed. Nile Southern and Josh Alan Friedman (New York: Grove Press, 2001), 261, where it is described by Nile Southern (Terry's son) as "a phrase Terry facetiously coined around 1962."

VII **Comparisons:** The comparisons listed are from: Twain: Ron Rosenbaum, "Our Least-Known Great Novelist," *Esquire*, January 1998, pp. 30, 32–33. DeLillo and Pynchon: Ron Rosenbaum, "Of Gnats and Men: A New Reading of Portis," *Observer*, May 24, 1999, https://observer.com/1999/05/of-gnats-and-men-a-new-reading-of-portis/. Robinson: Tobias Carroll, "Charles Portis Was One of the Great American Novelists," *InsideHook*, February 18, 2020, https://www.insidehook.com/article/books/charles-portis-literary-legacy. García Márquez: Nora Ephron, cited in Charles McGrath, "True Grit, Odd Wit: And Fame? No Thanks," *New York Times*, December 20, 2010, sec. C. Melville: McGrath, "True Grit, Odd Wit." Gogol: Paul Theroux, in "The Man with the Keys," *Oxford American*, February 20, 2020, https://main.oxfordamerican.org/item/1903-man-with-the-keys. Cervantes: Jack Goodstein, "Book Review: The Dog of the South by Charles Portis," *Seattlepi.com*, January 28, 2011, https://www.seattlepi.com/lifestyle/blogcritics/article/Book-Review-The-Dog-of-the-South-by-Charles-985953.php.

VII **One scholar:** John L. Idol, "Charles McColl Portis," in *Contemporary Fiction Writers of the South: A Bio-Biographical Sourcebook*, ed. Joseph M. Flora and Robert M. Bain (Westport, CT: Greenwood

Press, 1993), 360–70. The thirty-one are Hugh Henry Brackenridge, Thomas Browne, John Bunyan, Miguel de Cervantes, Dante, Charles Dickens, William Faulkner, Henry Fielding, Barry Hannah, George Washington Harris, Homer, Johnson J. Hooper, Samuel Johnson, Jack Kerouac, Ring Lardner, Sinclair Lewis, Herman Melville, H. L. Mencken, Vladimir Nabokov, Thomas Nashe, Edwin Newman, Flannery O'Connor, William Safire, Edmund Spenser, Jonathan Swift, Torquato Tasso, Mark Twain, Voltaire, Eudora Welty, Thomas Wolfe, and the author of the *Epic of Gilgamesh*.

VII **It is a crime:** Rosenbaum, "Our Least-Known Great Novelist," 33.

VII **The author of classics:** Rosenbaum, "Our Least-Known Great Novelist," 32.

VII **disturbance:** Charles Portis, *The Dog of the South* (1979; repr., New York: Overlook Press, 1999), 47, quoted in Roy Blount Jr., "Comedy in Earnest," in Portis, *Escape Velocity*, 315.

VII **It was nothing:** Portis, *Dog of the South*, 48, quoted in Blount, "Comedy in Earnest," 315.

VII **ranchettes in Colorado:** Portis, *Dog of the South*, 63, quoted in Blount, "Comedy in Earnest," 314.

VIII **hail-damaged pears:** Portis, *Dog of the South*, 63, quoted in Blount, "Comedy in Earnest," 313.

VIII **A GUY YOU'VE:** Ed Park, "Like Cormac McCarthy, but Funny," *Believer* (March 1, 2003), https://www.thebeliever.net/like-cormac-mccarthy-but-funny/#fnref:10.

VIII **He hardly spoke:** Portis, *Dog of the South*, 14, quoted in Park, "Like Cormac McCarthy," 325.

VIII **weekly embraces:** Portis, *Dog of the South*, 24.

VIII **to return to school:** Portis, *Dog of the South*, 12.

IX **A long, relaxed:** Donna Tartt, "On *True Grit*," in Portis, *Escape Velocity*, 357.

IX **Naw, Portis said:** Tartt, "On *True Grit*," 358.

IX **miscellany:** See the full title: *Escape Velocity: A Charles Portis Miscellany*.

X **neither help nor:** Samuel Beckett, quoted in Deirdre Bair, *Samuel Beckett: A Biography* (New York: Harcourt Brace Jovanovich, 1980), xi.

X **obliquely expressed:** At least one profile reports his antipathy directly: "He's made it very clear that he doesn't want anyone writing his biography." Alex Heard, "Portishead: The Literary Genius of

Charles Portis," *New Republic*, October 7, 2012, https://newrepublic.com/article/108232/charles-portis-escape-velocity-true-grit.

X **professional burglar:** Janet Malcolm, *The Silent Woman: Sylvia Plath & Ted Hughes* (New York: Alfred A. Knopf, 1994), 9.

X **biografiend:** James Joyce, *Finnegans Wake* (New York: Viking Press, 1965), 55.

X **Elvis got two:** Peter Guralnick, *Last Train to Memphis: The Rise of Elvis Presley* (New York: Little, Brown, 1995); and Peter Guralnicick, *Careless Love: The Unmaking of Elvis Presley* (New York: Little, Brown, 1999).

X **Freeman's four-volume:** Douglas Southall Freeman, *R. E. Lee: A Biography*, 4 vols. (New York: Charles Scribner's Sons, 1934–1945).

X **Malone's six-volume:** Dumas Malone, *Jefferson and His Time*, 6 vols. (New York: Little, Brown, 1948–1981).

X **I'm not even the best:** Charles Portis, quoted in "Man with the Keys," *Oxford American*. One caveat: the source for this modesty is Paul Theroux, himself a prolific, widely successful, not conspicuously modest writer. His Portis tribute blurbs not one but two of his own books. He's canny in regard to his own presence for the remark—a first-person report would raise the possibility of a deft Portis compliment less deftly received. This caveat registered, everything Theroux says about Portis seems astute.

XI **Critics are the words:** Roger Kahn, "Fiddler on the Shelf," *Life* (October 31, 1969), quoted in Richard Brody, "Childlike Stars," *New Yorker* (April 21, 2015), https://www.newyorker.com/culture/richard-brody/childlike-stars.

XI **spiffy:** Berryman's Dream Song for Stevens is number 219 ("So Long? Stevens"), where "He mutter spiffy." John Berryman, *The Dream Songs* (New York: Farrar, Straus and Giroux, 1965) 238.

XII **most fashionable suburb:** Charles Portis, *Masters of Atlantis* (1985; repr., New York: Overlook Press, 2000), 24.

XIII **custodian of almanacs:** Portis, *Masters of Atlantis*, 49.

XIII **Master of the New Cycle:** Portis, *Masters of Atlantis*, 313.

1. "WORDS FAILED HER": JOURNALISM

1 **Wide Acclaim:** "Wide Acclaim Given *Traveler* Feature Writer Portis," *Arkansas Traveler*, October 23, 1957.

1–2	**ugly; about as feminine:**	Buddy Portis, "Of *TIME* and the River and Greasy Creek, Etc.," *Arkansas Traveler*, September 24, 1957.
2	**for people who can't:**	Portis, "Of *TIME* and the River."
2	**A source not at all:**	Portis, "Of *TIME* and the River."
2	**my smartass response:**	Charles Portis, "*Gazette* Project Interview with Charles Portis," interview by Roy Reed, in *Escape Velocity*, 296.
2	**ever worked for:**	Portis, "*Gazette* Project Interview," 295.
2	**Cretin P. Slime:**	Buddy Portis, "Imaginary Poll Divulges Opinions on Integration," *Arkansas Traveler*, October 1, 1957.
2	**a parody:**	Editor's note to Buddy Portis, "Who, What, When Where," *Arkansas Traveler*, September 17, 1957.
2	**reported to be doing:**	Portis, "Who, What, When, Where."
2	**Busy Bee Circle:**	Portis, "Who, What, When, Where."
3	**beautiful satin-covered:**	Portis, "Who, What, When, Where."
3	**golden wedding:**	Portis, "Who, What, When, Where."
3	**Their theme was:**	Charles Portis, *Norwood* (Woodstock, NY: Overlook Press, 1999), 36.
3	**like Stonewall Jackson:**	Portis, *Norwood*, 37.
3	**very exclusive lawyers':**	Portis, *Masters of Atlantis*, 166.
3	**I edited the:**	Portis, "*Gazette* Project Interview," 294–95.
3	**relaxed conversation:**	Tartt, "On *True Grit*," 357.
3	**indefatigable writer:**	Tartt, "On *True Grit*," 359.
3	**Those are just:**	Tartt, "On *True Grit*," 359.
4	**I like to do:**	Elvis Presley, quoted in Charles Portis, "Mrs. Presley's Spirits Raised; Elvis Tells of His Devotion," *Commercial Appeal*, August 14, 1958, in *Escape Velocity*, 6.
4	**shaken and limp:**	Charles Portis, "Elvis Presley Tells Mother, 'Goodbye, Darling,' at Grave," *Commercial Appeal*, August 16, 1958, in *Escape Velocity*, 7.
4	**I came over:**	Portis, "*Gazette* Project Interview," 286.
4	**Judge Ptak's:**	Portis, "*Gazette* Project Interview," 294.
4	**Clumsy, half-baked:**	Portis, "*Gazette* Project Interview with Charles Portis," 289.
4	**high-rollers in dusty:**	Portis, "*Gazette* Project Interview," 289. The article Portis recalls is Charles Portis, "Cockfighting," Our Town, *Arkansas Gazette Sunday Magazine*, March 20, 1960, 43.
4	**drag pit:**	Portis, "Cockfighting," 43.
5	**writing about:**	Charles Portis, "Rare Specimen," *Arkansas Gazette*, February 3, 1960, in *Escape Velocity*, 17.

NOTES

5   **I was the only one:** Charles Portis, "As Confidently Predicted, He Puffed First," *New York Herald Tribune*, June 22, 1962, in *Escape Velocity*, 30.

6   **its little red:** Charles Portis, "The Shattered Scene of Blast," *New York Herald Tribune*, October 4, 1962, in *Escape Velocity*, 35.

6   **other reporters:** David Anderson, "Sunny Calm of Accounting Office Collapses in Smoke and Tragedy," *New York Times*, October 4, 1962.

6   **referred to as "girls":** Portis, "Shattered Scene." "Girls" is the default term for the telephone operators throughout the article.

6   **tweedy, well-shod:** Charles Portis, "2 Men—1,700 Women, Peace Train to Capital," *New York Herald Tribune*, January 16, 1962, in *Escape Velocity*, 21.

6   **exemplary:** Charles Portis, "Court Rules: Lion Is a Wild Animal," *New York Herald Tribune*, November 24, 1960, in *Escape Velocity*, 19.

6   **Mrs. Ruth Gage-Colby:** Portis, "2 Men—1,700 Women," 23.

6   **I recognized why:** Portis, "2 Men—1,700 Women," 23.

6   **I understood what:** Portis, "2 Men—1,700 Women," 23.

6   **on a women's peace:** Portis, "2 Men—1,700 Women," 23.

7   **Fifty years I'm:** Portis, "2 Men—1,700 Women," 22.

7   **relented under:** Portis, "2 Men—1,700 Women," 22.

7   **asking him about:** Portis, "*Gazette* Project Interview," 301.

7   **Good point:** Portis, "*Gazette* Project Interview," 301.

7   **with a little less:** Portis, "*Gazette* Project Interview," 301.

7–8   **He had a presence:** Portis, "*Gazette* Project Interview," 301.

8   **But what can you:** Portis, "*Gazette* Project Interview," 301.

8   **furious: He was climbing:** Tom Wolfe, *The New Journalism* (New York: Harper and Row, 1973), 5.

8   **middle of the night:** Ernest Dumas, quoted in Roy Reed, ed., *Looking Back at the "Arkansas Gazette": An Oral History* (Fayetteville: University of Arkansas Press, 2009), 67.

8   **As it happens:** I was led to the recording of the Malcolm X interview by student Eden Shulman, who unearthed it during his research for our class.

9   **clip with the Portis tale:** It's available online at Mike Fleming Jr., "Hot Video: Tom Wolfe, J. D. Salinger and Charles Portis from 'Salinger,'" *Deadline*, January 24, 2014, https://deadline.com/2014/01/hot-video-tom-wolfe-j-d-salinger-and-charles-portis-from-salinger-669031/.

9	**throttling back:** Portis, *Norwood*, 140.	
9	**embarrass Norma:** Portis, *Dog of the South*, 23.	
10	**summer of 1962:** Portis's earliest filing from Georgia that I located (my survey was neither cursory nor exhaustive) was Charles Portis, "In Georgia—Conscience and the Law," *New York Herald Tribune*, August 3, 1962.	
10	**fall of 1963:** I found nothing from Portis on the subject of civil rights later than Charles Portis, "Rolling Down from N.Y.: Hopes, Fears and Holiday," *New York Herald Tribune*, August 29, 1963.	
10	**wilted Dacron:** Charles Portis, "Biggest Spectacle," *Arkansas Gazette*, August 13, 1959, in *Escape Velocity*, 11.	
11	**he would talk:** Portis, "*Gazette* Project Interview," 286.	
11	**If them rabbis:** Eugene "Bull" Connor, quoted in Charles Portis, "Birmingham Bargaining before Watchful World," *New York Herald Tribune*, May 10, 1963, in *Escape Velocity*, 41.	
11	**I been waitin':** Eugene "Bull" Connor, quoted in Charles Portis, "Birmingham's Trigger Tension," *New York Herald Tribune*, May 8, 1963, in *Escape Velocity*, 37.	
11	**frightening development:** Charles Portis, "How the Night Exploded into Terror," *New York Herald Tribune*, May 13, 1963, in *Escape Velocity*, 45.	
11	**I'll stop those:** Portis, "How the Night Exploded," 45.	
11	**jabbing a couple:** Portis, "How the Night Exploded," 45.	
11	**It was pretty:** Portis, "How the Night Exploded," 47.	
12	**warning individual:** Portis, "How the Night Exploded," 47.	
12	**But someone put:** Portis, "How the Night Exploded," 48.	
12	**It was a sparkling:** Portis, "How the Night Exploded," 48.	
12	**Negro civil defense:** Portis, "How the Night Exploded," 44.	
12	**moves "fearlessly":** Portis, "How the Night Exploded," 45.	
12	**aided and comforted:** Charles Portis, "How the Night Exploded into Terror," *New York Herald Tribune*, May 13, 1963. This photo and caption do not appear in the reprint of the article in *Escape Velocity*.	
13	**was booed:** Charles Portis, "Call for a White Boycott Menaces Racial Accord," *New York Herald Tribune*, May 12, 1963.	
13	**Camp Ginger:** I'm with Midge in liking maps. I found Camp Ginger on one labeled "1st and 5th Marines Sector, 26 March, 1953" in Bernard C. Nalty, *Outpost War: US Marines from the Nevada Battles to the Armistice* (Washington, DC: US Marine Corps Historical Center, 2002), 12.	

NOTES

13 **three hours:** Charles Portis, "Klan Rally—Just Talk," in *Escape Velocity*, 48.

13 **huge crosses:** Portis, "Klan Rally," in *Escape Velocity*, 48.

13 **messianic status:** Student Abigail Ross brought the rich ironies of Dr. King's unwitting veneration to our class's attention.

13 **If so much as:** Portis, "Klan Rally," in *Escape Velocity*, 49. This passage is one where Portis was overruled somewhere up the editorial chain. It did not appear in the street edition, but, according to editor Jay Jennings, "in a version distributed by the *Herald Tribune* News Service."

13–14 **By 10:30:** Charles Portis, "Klan Rally—Just Talk," *New York Herald Tribune*, May 13, 1963, 8.

14 **Everyone drifted:** Portis, "Klan Rally," *New York Herald Tribune*, 8.

14 ***Life* ran a photo:** The photo appeared in the January 27, 1958, issue. The event, now best known as the Battle of Hayes Pond, remains a popular topic online. Of particular interest may be a site posted by the University of North Carolina, Pembroke. See https://www.uncp.edu/resources/museum-southeast-american-indian/museum-exhibits/battle-hayes-pond-routing-kkk.

14 **After a month:** Charles Portis, "Birmingham Peace: An Omen," *New York Herald Tribune*, May 11, 1963, 1.

15 **ballet; a moral drama; final act:** Charles Portis, "A Long Day of Defiance," *New York Herald Tribune*, June 12, 1963, in *Escape Velocity*, 50.

15 **final moves of:** Portis, "A Long Day of Defiance," 51.

15 **pageant; solemn proclamation:** Portis, "A Long Day of Defiance," 53.

15 **got into his car:** Portis, "A Long Day of Defiance," 51.

15 **Governor, I'm not...; They will register:** Portis, "A Long Day of Defiance," 53.

15 **respected:** Charles Portis, "A Murder in Mississippi," *New York Herald Tribune*, June 13, 1963, in *Escape Velocity*, 54.

15 **man in a beer joint:** Portis, "A Murder in Mississippi," 55.

15 **plea that all of you:** Portis, "A Murder in Mississippi," 56.

16 **tired and ... frustrated:** Charles Portis, "Fires of Hate in Jackson," *New York Herald Tribune*, June 14, 1963, in *Escape Velocity*, 57.

16 **there being no one:** Portis, "Fires of Hate," 58.

16 **The Jackson police:** Portis, "Fires of Hate," 58.

16 **Later in the afternoon:** Portis, "Fires of Hate," 59.

16 **Negro woman:** Portis, "Fires of Hate," 57.

16	**When the dust:**	Portis, "Fires of Hate," 58.
17	**Debbie Reynolds:**	Charles Portis, "The Marchers: Blueprint for Protest," *New York Herald Tribune,* August 25, 1963, sec. 2.
17	**Still, the spectre:**	Portis, "Marchers."
18	**hundred or so:**	Portis, "Marchers."
19	**We were young:**	Charles Portis, "From West Point to Far East—Taps," *New York Herald Tribune,* July 10, 1962. The portion of the eulogy quoted in Portis's article is a slightly altered version of a quotation from the Archibald MacLeish poem "The Young Dead Soldiers Do Not Speak. [Washington, 194.]," 1940, Printed Ephemera Collection, Library of Congress, Washington, DC, https://www.loc.gov/item/2020783928/.
19	**Since he came here:**	Charles Portis, "New Englander on Mission in Georgia," *New York Herald Tribune,* August 5, 1962.
20	**a population of:**	Portis, "New Englander."
20	**not a big talker:**	Portis, "New Englander."
20	**I'm here because:**	Portis, "New Englander."
20	**sequence of verb:**	Portis, "*Gazette* Project Interview," 291.

2. "CHARITY ENDURETH ALL THINGS": *NORWOOD*

21	**I liked it:**	Portis, "*Gazette* Project Interview," 305–6.
21	**pitiful bust:**	Portis, "*Gazette* Project Interview," 306.
21	**try my hand:**	Portis, "*Gazette* Project Interview," 307.
21	**"cold" and "rough":**	Portis, "*Gazette* Project Interview," 308.
22	**Bethel Liver Emulsifier:**	Charles Portis, "Damn!," in *Escape Velocity: A Charles Portis Miscellany*, ed. Jay Jennings, paperback ed. (New York: Overlook Duckworth, 2013), 152. All other citations of *Escape Velocity* refer to the Charles Portis, *Escape Velocity: A Charles Portis Miscellany*, by Charles Portis, rev. ed., ed. Jay Jennings (Little Rock: Butler Center for Arkansas Studies, 2021). "Damn!" was first published in *Nugget*, October 1957, 70.
22	**church folks:**	Portis, "Damn!," 155.
22	**hillbilly singer:**	Portis, "Damn!," 155.
22	**No population:**	*Handbook of Texas*, s.v. "Ogg, TX," by H. Allen Anderson, last modified May 1, 1995, https://www.tshaonline.org/handbook/entries/ogg-tx.
22	**back and forth along:**	Portis, *Norwood*, 10–11.

NOTES

23	**alcoholic auto mechanic:** Portis, *Norwood*, 10.
23	**"banks" of Highway 82:** Portis, *Norwood*, 11.
23	**did all his best work:** Portis, *Dog of the South*, 71.
23	**sessile:** Portis, *Masters of Atlantis*, 116.
23	**free-lance travel writer:** Portis, *Norwood*, 102.
23	**the *Trib*:** Portis, *Norwood*, 103.
23	**from handouts:** Portis, *Norwood*, 102.
23	**distress:** Portis, *Norwood*, 8.
23	**Mr. Pratt's old:** Portis, *Norwood*, 10.
23	**sleeping porch bedroom:** Portis, *Norwood*, 43.
23–24	**new from Sears:** Portis, *Norwood*, 12.
24	**and said so:** Portis, *Norwood*, 12.
24	**big new Buick:** Portis, *Norwood*, 37.
24	**stopped and started:** Portis, *Norwood*, 79.
24	**house shoes:** Portis, *Norwood*, 84.
24	**commuter special:** Portis, *Norwood*, 86.
24	**That fog was there:** Portis, *Masters of Atlantis*, 29.
25	**not in active practice:** Portis, *Dog of the South*, 63.
25	**a gift for hopeful:** Portis, *Masters of Atlantis*, 211.
25	**number eight on Herr:** Portis, *Masters of Atlantis*, 38–39.
25	**I certified many:** Portis, *Dog of the South*, 75.
25	**the most depraved:** Charles Portis, "Combinations of Jacksons," in *Escape Velocity*, 200. First published in the *Atlantic Monthly*, May 1999.
26	**a good many:** Portis, *Norwood*, 33.
26	**New Orleans talent:** Portis, *Norwood*, 34–35.
26	**lovely young girls:** Portis, *Norwood*, 35.
26	**I've had my eye:** Portis, *Norwood*, 35.
26	**She's a dandy:** Portis, *Norwood*, 35.
26	**And sweet too:** Portis, *Norwood*, 35.
26	**about seventeen:** Portis, *Norwood*, 35.
26	**I think she:** Portis, *Norwood*, 35.
26	**I'd rather not:** Portis, *Norwood*, 35.
26	**skating fast:** Portis, *Norwood*, 31.
26	**Cresswell girl:** Portis, *Norwood*, 35.
26	**Make those profligate:** Portis, *Norwood*, 39.
26	**surplus:** Portis, *Norwood*, 40.
26	**big 98 Oldsmobile:** Portis, *Norwood*, 51.

26	**We always give:**	Portis, *Norwood*, 51.
27	**going up on:**	Portis, *Norwood*, 54.
27	**You are not:**	Portis, *Norwood*, 55.
27	**coal-black 14-inchers:**	Portis, *Norwood*, 45.
27	***peckerwood*:**	Portis, *Norwood*, 55.
27	**without a word:**	Portis, *Norwood*, 68.
27	**can press two hundred:**	Portis, *Norwood*, 60.
27	**what looked like:**	Portis, *Norwood*, 68.
27	**official bread hat:**	Portis, *Norwood*, 70.
27	**old timers' high-tops:**	Portis, *Norwood*, 84.
27	**He *was* a mess:**	Portis, *Norwood*, 87.
27	**Grady told me:**	Portis, *Norwood*, 62.
27	**You are the:**	Portis, *Norwood*, 62.
27	**any woman or girl:**	Mann Act of 1910, Pub. L. No. 61–277, 36 Stat. 825 (1910).
27	**Now they can send:**	Portis, *Norwood*, 61.
28	**Oh fer Chrissakes:**	Portis, *Norwood*, 88.
28	**Go bother Mayor:**	Portis, *Norwood*, 93.
28	**stretched out on:**	Portis, *Norwood*, 93.
28	**dope fiend:**	Portis, *Norwood*, 89.
28	**What did they think:**	Portis, *Norwood*, 89.
28	**any beatnik girls:**	Portis, *Norwood*, 107.
28	**always wearing:**	Portis, *Norwood*, 109.
28–29	**Once on the boat:**	Portis, *Norwood*, 109.
29	**agreeable in many:**	Portis, *Norwood*, 109.
29	**nothing ever got:**	Portis, *Norwood*, 109.
29	**hateful town:**	Portis, *Norwood*, 112.
29	**with white gravy:**	Portis, *Dog of the South*, 32.
29	**What I want:**	Charles Portis, *Delray's New Moon*, in *Escape Velocity*, 210.
29	**He slept for 335 miles:**	Portis, *Norwood*, 8.
29	***What a honey!*:**	Portis, *Norwood*, 118.
30	**Norwood, I think:**	Portis, *Norwood*, 126.
30	**Some powerful Noxema:**	Portis, *Norwood*, 127.
30	**Beat it:**	Portis, *Norwood*, 92.
30	**draw up some:**	Portis, *Norwood*, 130.
30	**Man can't have:**	Portis, *Norwood*, 130.
30	**We closed, hat man:**	Portis, *Norwood*, 131.

30	**midget of inestimable:** Portis, *Norwood*, 132.	
30	**on the way down:** Portis, *Norwood*, 134.	
30	**Pizzas, thick pastramis:** Portis, *Norwood*, 136.	
30	**curious pair:** Portis, *Norwood*, 140.	
30	**getting some television:** Portis, *Norwood*, 138.	
30	**I'm just a bit:** Portis, *Norwood*, 141–42.	
30	**Glad to have you:** Portis, *Norwood*, 142.	
30	**diverted:** Portis, *Norwood*, 143.	
30	**imprisoned:** Portis, *Norwood*, 144.	
30	**Dominecker:** Portis, *Norwood*, 148.	
30	**circus-looking cage:** Portis, *Norwood*, 144.	
30–31	**JOANN THE:** Portis, *Norwood*, 144.	
31	***Charity Endureth*:** Portis, *Norwood*, 145.	
31	**searching mind:** Portis, *Norwood*, 24.	
33	**writer Calvin Trillin:** See Calvin Trillin, "The Chicken Vanishes," *New Yorker*, February 8, 1999, 38–41.	
33	**throttling back:** Portis, *Norwood*, 140.	
33	**I thought you'd:** Portis, *Norwood*, 145.	
33	**out in the Mediterranean:** Portis, *Norwood*, 145.	
33	**But I didn't care:** Portis, *Norwood*, 145.	
33	**with so many:** Portis, *Norwood*, 145.	
33	**She looked up:** Portis, *Norwood*, 145.	
33	**just wherever you:** Portis, *Norwood*, 156.	
33	**poolroom clown:** Portis, *Norwood*, 163.	
33	**Norwood, how very:** Portis, *Norwood*, 149.	
34	**family fish fry:** Portis, *Norwood*, 154.	
34	**Is there anybody:** Portis, *Norwood*, 156.	
34	**a sprawling:** Portis, *Norwood*, 159.	
34	**twenty acres or so:** Portis, *Norwood*, 158.	
34	**knew his business:** Portis, *Norwood*, 158.	
34	**eighty paper-shell:** Portis, *Norwood*, 158.	
35	**I hope don't nobody:** Portis, *Norwood*, 76.	
35	**rocks and clinkers:** Portis, *Norwood*, 80.	
35	**house shoes:** Portis, *Norwood*, 84.	
35	**a little talk:** Portis, *Norwood*, 171.	
35	**humane:** Portis, *Norwood*, 173.	
36	**satin-covered pillow:** Portis, "Who, What, When, Where."	
36	**a picture of the post:** Portis, *Norwood*, 179.	

36	**like a bobcat:** Portis, *Norwood*, 185.	
36	**Just stay away:** Portis, *Norwood*, 186.	
36	**with his feet up:** Portis, *Norwood*, 188.	
36	**pea gravel driveway:** Portis, *Norwood*, 189.	
36	*Entwicklungsroman*: R. Baird Shuman, "Portis' *True Grit*: Adventure Story or *Entwicklungsroman*?," *English Journal* 59, no. 3 (March 1970): 367–70.	
36	**Mind your own:** Portis, *Norwood*, 190.	
37	**woman in the:** Portis, *Norwood*, 91.	
37	**about forty:** Portis, *Norwood*, 91.	
37	**powerful Noxema:** Portis, *Norwood*, 127.	
37	**Confederate Daughters:** Portis, *Norwood*, 163.	
37	**She often managed:** Portis, *Norwood*, 164	
37	**a sharper and a tramp:** Portis, *Dog of the South*, 105.	
37	**sanguinary ambuscade:** Charles Portis, *True Grit* (New York: Overlook Press, 2010), 33.	
38	**winged Pegasus:** Portis, *True Grit*, 37.	
38	**Richer than the fabled Croesus:** Portis, *Norwood*, 36.	
38	**like Stonewall Jackson:** Portis, *Norwood*, 37.	
38	**altogether too kind:** Portis, *Norwood*, 146.	
38	**You *functionary*:** Portis, *Norwood*, 143.	
38	**jugged hare at Rule's:** Portis, *Norwood*, 141.	
38	**Here was another grenade:** Charles Portis, *Gringos* (1991; repr., New York: Overlook Press, 2020), 285.	
39	**I let the matter:** Portis, *Dog of the South*, 14.	
39	**to be more considerate:** Portis, *Gringos*, 15.	
39	**I let it go:** Portis, *Gringos*, 92, 172.	
39	**We will let it go:** Portis, *True Grit*, 24.	
39	**nothing to be gained:** Portis, *True Grit*, 29.	
39	**Somebody else said:** Portis, "Biggest Spectacle," 10.	
39	**I thought we'd *never*:** Charles Portis, "An Auto Odyssey through Darkest Baja," in *Escape Velocity*, 107. Originally published in *Los Angeles Times*, February 26, 1967.	
39	**We let that one slide:** Portis, "Auto Odyssey," 107.	
39–40	**While not an ornament:** Portis, "Combinations of Jacksons," 200.	
40	**best friend:** Portis, *Norwood*, 123.	
40	**I'll say this:** Portis, *Norwood*, 124.	
40	**famous athlete:** Portis, *Norwood*, 113.	

40	**They don't know how:** Portis, *Norwood*, 113.
40	**white town:** Portis, *Norwood*, 131.
40	**a long tall redbone:** Portis, *Norwood*, 53.
40	**He told her fifteen:** Portis, *Norwood*, 57.
41	**picked up his old:** Portis, *Norwood*, 12.
41	**Every time you:** Portis, *Norwood*, 15.
41	**choice downtown:** Portis, *Norwood*, 21.
41	**No one you could:** Portis, *Norwood*, 21.
42	**everybody on the:** Portis, *Norwood*, 48.
42	**hateful town:** Portis, *Norwood*, 112.
42	**beautician school:** Portis, *Norwood*, 124.
42	**play records:** Portis, *Norwood*, 170.
42	**I'm twenty-three:** Portis, *Norwood*, 170.
42	**junkyard:** Portis, *Norwood*, 179.
42	**We didn't get on:** Portis, *Gringos*, 287.
43	**confession magazines:** Portis, *Norwood*, 147.
43	**Lewisville, Kentucky:** Portis, *Norwood*, 125.
43	**Right here, he says:** Portis, *Norwood*, 126.
43	**crawfish:** Portis, *True Grit*, 23.
43	**true grit:** Portis, *True Grit*, 59.
43	**Yall will have to:** Portis, *Norwood*, 175.

3. "HARD, ISOLATE, STOIC": *TRUE GRIT*

45	**hard to dress:** Portis, "*Gazette* Project Interview," 290.
45	**I had to get on:** Portis, *Dog of the South*, 11.
46	**Well, Rooster:** Portis, *True Grit*, 202.
46	**Here is what happened:** Portis, *True Grit*, 11, 15; also 155, 168.
46	**credence:** Portis, *True Grit*, 1.
46	**When we locate:** Portis, *True Grit*, 111.
46	**Would you two like:** Portis, *True Grit*, 120.
47	**It is good enough:** Portis, *True Grit*, 115.
47	**My thought was:** Portis, *True Grit*, 40, 105, 133, 148, 196, 198, 205, 221.
47	**We reached:** Portis, *True Grit*, 160.
47	**Our course was:** Portis, *True Grit*, 108.
47	**Now I will:** Portis, *True Grit*, 41, 109.
47	**true account:** Portis, *True Grit*, 224.

47	**a gallant knight:**	Portis, *True Grit*, 14.
47	**plunging steed:**	Portis, *True Grit*, 201.
47	**nor would he ever:**	Portis, *True Grit*, 15.
47	**I must own:**	Portis, *True Grit*, 71.
47	**true and interesting:**	Portis, *True Grit*, 43.
47	**discursive:**	Portis, *True Grit*, 43.
47–48	**cut some platters:**	Portis, *Norwood*, 118.
48	***Cut some platters?:***	Portis, *Norwood*, 118.
48	**to write it down:**	Portis, *Dog of the South*, 254.
48	**This ends my true:**	Portis, *True Grit*, 224.
48	**I can see that I have given:**	Portis, *Dog of the South*, 254.
48	**She has got the best:**	Portis, *True Grit*, 110.
48	**She has won her spurs:**	Portis, *True Grit*, 167.
48	**pearl of great price:**	Portis, *True Grit*, 79.
48–49	**the weather sharp:**	T. S. Eliot, "Journey of the Magi," lines 4–5.
49	**bloody, and unnatural:**	William Shakespeare, *Hamlet*, act 5, sc. 2, lines 381–83.
49	**Louisiana cur:**	Portis, *True Grit*, 24.
49	**the Katy**:	Augustus J. Veenendaal Jr., *Smoke Over Oklahoma: The Railroad Photographs of Preston George* (Norman: University of Oklahoma Press, 2017), 4.
49	**Thus we had:**	Portis, *True Grit*, 154.
49	**traveling east:**	Portis, *True Grit*, 167.
49	**well after midnight:**	Portis, *True Grit*, 174.
50	**alternately intense:**	Charles Portis, quoted in Jay Jennings, "On the Trail of 'True Grit': A Tale Comes to Life," *New York Times*, June 16, 2014, https://www.nytimes.com/2014/07/20/travel/on-the-trail-of-true-grit-a-tale-comes-to-life.html. Student Tyler Houston's term paper and in-class presentation made helpful discoveries about Portis's historical research for *True Grit*.
52	**two long pistols:**	Portis, *True Grit*, 21.
52	**rifle fire:**	Glenn Shirley, *Law West of Fort Smith: A History of Frontier Justice in the Indian Territory, 1834–1896* (1957; repr., Lincoln: University of Nebraska Press, 1968), 35.
52	**now this was all:**	Portis, *True Grit*, 222.
52	**black murder:**	Portis, *True Grit*, 58.
52	**a mixture of Creek:**	Shirley, *Law West of Fort Smith*, 159.

52	**Creeks are good:** Portis, *True Grit*, 58.
52	**letters every:** Portis, *True Grit*, 13.
53	***pit*:** Portis, *True Grit*, 204.
53	**the corpse of a man!:** Portis, *True Grit*, 207.
53	***ball of snakes!*:** Portis, *True Grit*, 208.
53	**a deep crevice:** Shirley, *Law West of Fort Smith*, 56.
53	**What Spencer didn't:** Shirley, *Law West of Fort Smith*, 56.
53	**the skeletons crawling:** Shirley, *Law West of Fort Smith*, 56.
53	**his nerves soon:** Shirley, *Law West of Fort Smith*, 57.
53	**two rattlers struck:** Portis, *True Grit*, 212. The snakes swarming Cheney may suggest those of *Inferno* 25, where the thief Vanni Fucci is swarmed by serpents following his gestured curse of God. Dante the pilgrim cheers them. Mattie doesn't go quite so far.
53	**Those serpents:** Dante, *Inferno*, 25:4. References are to canto and line; my translation.
54	**Sunlight and blue sky:** Portis, *True Grit*, 214.
54	**things of beauty:** Dante, *Inferno*, 34:137–38.
54	**did not raise:** Shirley, *Law West of Fort Smith*, 182.
54	**had mistaken:** Portis, *True Grit*, 17.
54	**notorious desperado:** Shirley, *Law West of Fort Smith*, 175.
54	**I've robbed:** Kathy Weiser, "Henry Starr—the Cherokee Bad Boy," Legends of America, updated November 2019, https://www.legendsofamerica.com/we-henrystarr/.
55	**Come back when:** Portis, *Norwood*, 175.
55	**I'll see you:** Portis, *Norwood*, 175.
55	**I am in your debt:** Portis, *True Grit*, 215.
55	**tail end:** Portis, *Norwood*, 121.
55	**the slacker's friend:** Portis, *Dog of the South*, 75.
55	**more than four hundred:** Portis, *Dog of the South*, 69.
55	**desert rainstorm:** Portis, *Dog of the South*, 43.
56	**Pollard was his man:** Portis, *Dog of the South*, 68.
56	**Private Slovik Post:** Portis, *Gringos*, 86.
56	**I Don't Talk Service:** Charles Portis, "I Don't Talk Service No More," in *Escape Velocity*, 166. Originally published in the *Atlantic Monthly*, May 1996, 90–92.
56	**almost sick:** Portis, *True Grit*, 157.
56	**I have always regretted:** Portis, *True Grit*, 157.

56	**It's just as well to step:** Portis, *Gringos*, 197.	
56	**the Ominato Inn:** Charles Portis, "Motel Life, Lower Reaches," in *Escape Velocity*, 140. First published in *Oxford American*, January/February 2003, https://oxfordamerican.org/magazine/issue-43-january-february-2003/motel-life-lower-reaches.	
56–57	**came to know:** Portis, "Motel Life, Lower Reaches," 141.	
57	**Ominato was both:** Student Heathermarie Brown made Portis's military references a subject of her class presentation; she called my attention to this one.	
57	**Vietnam is conspicuous:** Student Scott Hendry was first to point out the absence of references to the Vietnamese conflict in Portis's work.	
57	**Better put the boots:** Portis, *Norwood*, 78.	
57	**Like getting caught:** Portis, *Norwood*, 78.	
57	**Bolus had lost:** Portis, *Gringos*, 126.	
57	**They tell me:** Portis, *True Grit*, 59.	
58	**sand:** Portis, *True Grit*, 34.	
58	**I would see:** Portis, *True Grit*, 23.	
58	**Game? I was born:** Portis, *True Grit*, 85.	
58	**killed where he stood:** Portis, *True Grit*, 150.	
58	**He was tough:** Portis, *True Grit*, 188.	
58	**I don't say:** Portis, *True Grit*, 189.	
58	**Quincy was always:** Portis, *True Grit*, 135.	
58	**criminal trash:** Portis, *True Grit*, 185.	
58	**not altogether rotten:** Portis, *True Grit*, 185.	
59	**criticized:** Portis, *True Grit*, 219.	
59	**lovelorn:** Lloyd M. Daigrepont, "The Protestant Ethic and the Spirit of Capitalism in *True Grit*: The Lovelorn Character of Mattie Ross," *Western American Literature* 50, no. 2 (Summer 2015): 105.	
59	**her incredible:** Daigrepont, "Protestant Ethic," 107.	
59	**scarred for life:** Kenneth Millard, "History, Fiction, and Ethics: The Search for the True West in *True Grit*," *Philological Quarterly* 90, no. 4 (Fall 2011): 476.	
59	**descriptions of Chaney:** Daigrepont, "Protestant Ethic," 111.	
59	**He was a half-breed:** Portis, *True Grit*, 58.	
59	**I am Mattie Ross:** Portis, *True Grit*, 183	
59	**I need a good judge:** Portis, *True Grit*, 188.	
59	**faculty lounge:** After half a century's happy residence in the faculty lounge it's a bad look for me to scoff at it. They really are not wrong,	

but the omnipresent note of arraignment is more a signature of the cultural moment than an indicator of personal outrage. The scholars cited wrote at a time (still ongoing) when prosecutorial "interrogation" of "texts" was standard and thus universal practice. The lemming is the scholar's totem. Exposure of shortcoming in both author and character was requisite. Each cultural moment makes its contribution, but the scholar who fails to conform to the mode courts rejection.

59–60 **since I was a child:** Donna Tartt, afterword to Portis, *True Grit*, 226.
60 **implacable stoniness:** Tartt, afterword to Portis, *True Grit*, 232.
60 **official bread hat:** Portis, *Norwood*, 70.
60 **ranchettes in Colorado:** Portis, *Dog of the South*, 63.
60 **I have never held:** Portis, *True Grit*, 221.
60 **essential American soul:** D. H. Lawrence, "Fenimore Cooper's Leatherstocking Novels," in *Studies in Classic American Literature* (1923; repr., New York: Penguin, 1977), 68.
60 **tough littleness:** William Carlos Williams, "Voyage of the Mayflower," in *In the American Grain* (1925; repr., New York: New Directions, 1956), 65.
60 **jargon of God:** Williams, "Voyage of the Mayflower," 64.
60 **roasting and screaming:** Portis, *True Grit*, 24.
60 **We cheer and cheer:** I cheer too, despite my faculty-lounge sympathy for the scholars' critiques registered above. I also cheer Ahab's Promethean defiance (to steal Tartt's example). Mattie Ross's stiff-necked Calvinism is reminiscent of Alice Munro's fierce Cameronians (see especially "Friend of My Youth").
61 **lovely young girls:** Portis, *Norwood*, 35.
61 **suicidal owl:** Portis, *Norwood*, 151.
61 **maybe dead:** Portis, *Norwood*, 177.
61 **No grit?:** Portis, *True Grit*, 201.
61 **throttling back:** Portis, *Norwood*, 140.
61 **I got to give her:** Portis, *Norwood*, 148.
61 **Norwood, how very:** Portis, *Norwood*, 149.
62 **bad part:** Portis, *True Grit*, 23.
62 **Perhaps you can:** Portis, *True Grit*, 23.
62 **Nevertheless it had:** Portis, *True Grit*, 23.
62 **I have never been:** Portis, *True Grit*, 23.
62 **Yarnell wanted:** Portis, *True Grit*, 20.
62 **Miss Mattie:** Portis, *True Grit*, 24.
62 **We will not haggle:** Portis, *True Grit*, 24

62	**We will let it go:** Portis, *True Grit*, 24.
62	**bandit chieftain:** Portis, *True Grit*, 152, 182, 183, 191, 195, 196.
62	**If I see:** Portis, *True Grit*, 182–83.
62	**Help yourself:** Portis, *True Grit*, 186.
62	**Five minutes is well:** Portis, *True Grit*, 187.
62	**I will do:** Portis, *True Grit*, 183.
62	**Very well then:** Portis, *True Grit*, 192.
62	**meetinghouse:** Portis, *True Grit*, 191.
63	**Make yourself:** Portis, *True Grit*, 196.
63	**If any harm comes:** Portis, *True Grit*, 191.
63	**People do not give:** Portis, *True Grit*, 11.
63	**Here is what happened:** Portis, *True Grit*, 11, 15, 155, 168.
63	**This ends my true:** Portis, *True Grit*, 224.
63	**I cannot say:** Portis, *True Grit*, 16.
63	**There is no knowing:** Portis, *True Grit*, 23.
63	**Marshal Cogburn and:** Portis, *True Grit*, 182.
63	**A RESOLUTE OFFICER:** Portis, *True Grit*, 223.
63–64	**newspaper record:** Portis, *True Grit*, 42.
64	**sanguinary ambuscade:** Portis, *True Grit*, 33.
64	**not in active practice:** Portis, *Dog of the South*, 63.

4. "HORDE CONTROL" AND "THE ANCIENT FEAR": *THE DOG OF THE SOUTH*

65	**shamefully neglected:** Portis, *Dog of the South*, 12.
65	**floating somewhere:** Portis, *Dog of the South*, 20.
65	**I love nothing:** Portis, *Dog of the South*, 9.
65	**The last position:** Portis, *Dog of the South*, 11.
66	**sat easily upon him:** Samuel Beckett, "What a Misfortune," in *More Pricks Than Kicks* (1934; repr. New York: Grove Press, 1972), 120.
66	**Any man who:** Beckett, "What a Misfortune," 120.
66	**I should have paid:** Portis, *Dog of the South*, 11.
66	**I had to get on:** Portis, *Dog of the South*, 11.
66	**play a more active:** Portis, *Dog of the South*, 11.
66	**crazy about dancing:** Portis, *Dog of the South*, 26.
66	**I mean smoking soles!:** Portis, *Dog of the South*, 26.
66	**more than four hundred:** Portis, *Dog of the South*, 69.
66	**sixty-six lineal:** Portis, *Dog of the South*, 69.

NOTES

66   **drawer full of pistols:** Portis, *Dog of the South*, 20.
66   **the great captains:** Portis, *Dog of the South*, 10.
66   **rock-and-roll twerp:** Portis, *Dog of the South*, 24.
66   **Noise was his joy:** Portis, *Dog of the South*, 24.
66   **pill:** Portis, *Dog of the South*, 26.
66   **I was biding my time:** Portis, *Dog of the South*, 9.
66   **at least two bachelor's:** Portis, *Dog of the South*, 13.
66   **some pre-law:** Portis, *Dog of the South*, 13.
66   **where I studied:** Portis, *Dog of the South*, 13.
67   **I thought about:** Portis, *Dog of the South*, 149.
67   **I once looked into:** Portis, *Dog of the South*, 63.
67   **She would thank me:** Portis, *Dog of the South*, 24.
67   **sort of youth congress:** Portis, *Dog of the South*, 21.
67   **Junior Bankers or:** Portis, *Dog of the South*, 25.
67   **ranchettes in Colorado:** Portis, *Dog of the South*, 63.
67   **What is the burgling:** Bertolt Brecht, *The Threepenny Opera*, book trans. Desmond Vesey, lyrics trans. Eric Bentley (New York: Grove Press, 1964), 92.
67   **League of Leaders:** Portis, *Gringos*, 157.
67   **The paper didn't run:** Portis, *Dog of the South*, 23.
67   **wildly back and forth:** Portis, *Dog of the South*, 12.
67   **When the beer came:** Portis, *Dog of the South*, 33.
68   **She was afraid:** Portis, *Dog of the South*, 31.
68   **famous lecture:** Portis, *Dog of the South*, 13.
68   **bravura:** Portis, *Dog of the South*, 13.
68   **I had heard the tape:** Portis, *Dog of the South*, 13.
68   **Dr. Bud:** Portis, *Dog of the South*, 13.
68   **great captains of:** Portis, *Dog of the South*, 10.
68   **With nothing more than:** Portis, *Dog of the South*, 13.
69   **aslant the brook:** Charles Portis, "The Forgotten River," in *Escape Velocity*, 121. First published in *Arkansas Times*, September 1991. The *Hamlet* reference is to act 4, sc. 7, line 190.
69   **sturdy bricks:** Portis, "The Forgotten River," 121.
69   **excellent workhorse:** Portis, "The Forgotten River," 121.
69   **girdled the shade:** Portis, "The Forgotten River," 121. "Tie a Yellow Ribbon Round the Ole Oak Tree" was a hit for Tony Orlando and Dawn in 1973. Portis, in one of the most unobtrusive of the omnipresent "talk service" elements in his work, reports the practice as

still going strong in southern Arkansas in 1991 to welcome Desert Storm troops home.
- 69 **city obstruction:** Portis, *Dog of the South*, 26.
- 69 **tiny James Madison:** Portis, *Dog of the South*, 17.
- 69 **Tiny things take on:** Portis, *Dog of the South*, 40.
- 69 **three interesting things:** Portis, *Dog of the South*, 29.
- 69 **piled high with loose watermelons:** Portis, *Dog of the South*, 29.
- 69 **Topology!:** Portis, *Dog of the South*, 30.
- 69 **better motel:** Portis, *Dog of the South*, 31.
- 69 **an old man wearing clown shoes:** Portis, *Dog of the South*, 34.
- 69 **I'm a party:** Portis, *Dog of the South*, 35.
- 70 **Phone call for:** Portis, *Dog of the South*, 35. *The Sheriff of Cochise* was a 1950s television crime show.
- 70 **looks like a:** Portis, *Dog of the South*, 40.
- 70 **bad eye:** Portis, *Dog of the South*, 39.
- 70 **I'm just fooling:** Portis, *Dog of the South*, 39.
- 70 **shopping-cart lady:** Portis, *Dog of the South*, 39.
- 70 **She picks up bottles:** Portis, *Dog of the South*, 39.
- 70 **so the cars and trucks:** Portis, *Dog of the South*, 39.
- 70 **the ever-popular:** Portis, *Dog of the South*, 40.
- 70 **adios AMIGO:** Portis, *Dog of the South*, 40.
- 70 **I couldn't make:** Portis, *Dog of the South*, 40.
- 70 **Watch out for the:** Portis, *Dog of the South*, 146.
- 70 **I was heavy:** Portis, *Dog of the South*, 146.
- 70 **What a piddler!:** Portis, *Dog of the South*, 146.
- 70 **big rock the size:** Portis, *Dog of the South*, 207.
- 71 **a resentful drunk:** Portis, *Dog of the South*, 56.
- 71 **suitable place for their:** Portis, *Dog of the South*, 46.
- 71 **hippie wagon:** Portis, *Dog of the South*, 47.
- 71 ***¡Misión cumplida!*:** Portis, *Dog of the South*, 52.
- 71 **the hateful town:** Portis, *Norwood*, 112.
- 71 **a curious mix:** Portis, *Dog of the South*, 52.
- 72 **Class B irritant:** Portis, *Dog of the South*, 178.
- 72 **disturbing divine:** Portis, *Dog of the South*, 63.
- 72 **There was generally:** Jack Meriwether, quoted in Reed, *Looking Back*, 55; brackets in original.
- 72 **This makes thirty:** Portis, *Dog of the South*, 175.
- 72 **Your mother will:** Portis, *Dog of the South*, 175.

NOTES

72	**I remember you:** Portis, *Dog of the South*, 144.
72	**Are you with:** Portis, *Dog of the South*, 99.
72	**Has he got:** Portis, *Dog of the South*, 99.
72	**fruity breath:** Portis, *Dog of the South*, 82.
73	**the greatest writer:** Portis, *Dog of the South*, 70.
73	**bits of gray:** Portis, *Dog of the South*, 87.
73	**amber nose:** Portis, *Dog of the South*, 131.
73	**The old man:** Portis, *Dog of the South*, 131.
73	**How about a theme:** Portis, *Dog of the South*, 66.
73	**just like David and Jonathan:** Portis, *Dog of the South*, 183.
74	**Rod had an interest:** Portis, *Dog of the South*, 183.
74	**Put a halfgrain:** Portis, *Dog of the South*, 126–27.
74	**Those pimps:** Portis, *Dog of the South*, 182.
74	**gold salts:** Portis, *Dog of the South*, 177.
74	**Double Chloride of Gold:** See Felix V. Rinehart [Vance Randolph], *Confessions of a Booze-Fighter* (Girard, KS: Haldeman-Julius Publications, 1943), 8.
74	**Samaritan Pain:** Herman Melville, *The Confidence-Man: His Masquerade* (Evanston, IL: Northwestern University Press, 1984), 84.
74	**Omni-Balsamic Reinvigorator:** Melville, *The Confidence-Man*, 79.
74	**You can't talk:** Portis, *Dog of the South*, 182.
74	**I was a bigger:** Portis, *Dog of the South*, 130.
74	**It's time for plain:** Portis, *Dog of the South*, 140.
75	**entire estate:** Portis, *Dog of the South*, 140.
75	**If I did have:** Portis, *Dog of the South*, 140.
75	**low companions:** Portis, *Dog of the South*, 141.
75	**I had a massive:** Portis, *Dog of the South*, 141
76	**I was always afraid:** Portis, *Dog of the South*, 141.
76	**Just as I am, without:** Portis, *Dog of the South*, 144.
76	**Just as I am, though:** Portis, *Dog of the South*, 144.
76	**My face is now turned:** Portis, *Dog of the South*, 141.
76	**I paid particular:** Portis, *Dog of the South*, 115–16.
77	**judge it too:** Portis, *Dog of the South*, 72.
77	**Do you know that:** Portis, *Dog of the South*, 71.
77	**Dix puts William:** Portis, *Dog of the South*, 70.
77	**nothing but trash:** Portis, *Dog of the South*, 184.
77	**watch out for the:** Portis, *Dog of the South*, 40.
77	**Find the missing:** Portis, *Dog of the South*, 184.

NOTES

77	**warranty deed:** Portis, *Dog of the South*, 66.
78	**foul grunting:** Portis, *Dog of the South*, 72.
78	**for being a man:** Portis, *Dog of the South*, 22.
78	**became solemn:** Portis, *Dog of the South*, 254.
78	**some thought:** Portis, *Dog of the South*, 254.
78	**a good job of work:** Portis, *Dog of the South*, 255.
78	**radical photographers:** Portis, *Dog of the South*, 243.
78	**a third party:** Portis, *Dog of the South*, 243.
78	**a shopping center:** Portis, *Dog of the South*, 243.
79	**famous speech:** Portis, *Dog of the South*, 247.
79	**artist from Arizona:** Portis, *Dog of the South*, 167.
79	**in the confident:** Portis, *Dog of the South*, 238.
79	**Wayne was in fact:** For the booing of Wayne, see William Manchester, "The Bloodiest Battle of All," *New York Times Magazine*, June 14, 1987, 84.
79	**a week or ten:** Portis, *Dog of the South*, 240.
79	**church is out:** Portis, *Dog of the South*, 220.
79	**Let me tell you:** Portis, *Dog of the South*, 218.
80	**father-and-son rape**: Portis, *Dog of the South*, 137.
80	**new Christmas carols:** Portis, *Dog of the South*, 134.
80	**outline; almost complete:** Portis, *Dog of the South*, 156.
80	**horde control:** Portis, *Dog of the South*, 156.
80	**Shaping up:** Portis, *Dog of the South*, 156.
80	**low-voltage strobe:** Portis, *Dog of the South*, 156.
80	**What you have to:** Portis, *Dog of the South*, 155.
80	**Terrible things went:** Portis, *Dog of the South*, 248.
80	**wily and vicious:** Portis, *Dog of the South*, 247.
80	**effectual calling:** Portis, *Dog of the South*, 132.
81	**Effectual calling:** Portis, *Dog of the South*, 132–33.
81	**I didn't see why:** Portis, *Dog of the South*, 194.
81	**Tarzan action:** Portis, *Dog of the South*, 195.
82	**They're running wild:** Portis, *Dog of the South*, 64.
82	**They're water-skiing:** Portis, *Dog of the South*, 64.
82	**hi-lo shag:** Portis, *Dog of the South*, 63.
82	**vibrating jowl straps:** Portis, *Dog of the South*, 83.
82	**life spared:** Portis, *Dog of the South*, 237.
82	**the ancient fear:** Portis, *Dog of the South*, 236.
82	***gringo of goodwill***: Portis, *Dog of the South*, 42.

83	**queer:** Portis, *Dog of the South*, 48.	
83	**Creeps! Nuts!:** Portis, *Dog of the South*, 79.	
83	**bell captain:** Portis, *Dog of the South*, 196.	
83	**snow-cone business:** Portis, *Dog of the South*, 204.	
83	**A small cart:** Portis, *Dog of the South*, 204.	
83	**three columns:** Portis, *Dog of the South*, 187.	
83	**House of Leet:** Portis, *Dog of the South*, 192.	
83	**Arizona art:** Portis, *Dog of the South*, 167.	
83	**guys and chicks:** Portis, *Dog of the South*, 221.	
83	**Indian men:** Portis, *Dog of the South*, 149.	
83	**always hiding:** Portis, *Dog of the South*, 159.	
84	**as merry as ever:** Portis, *Dog of the South*, 210	
84	**strange birds:** Portis, *Dog of the South*, 79.	
84	**make ******* work:** *Dog of the South*, 155.	
84	**tossing him about:** Portis, *Dog of the South*, 220.	
84	**biding my time:** Portis, *Dog of the South*, 9.	
85	**make my move:** Portis, *Dog of the South*, 19–20.	
85	**rules:** Portis, *Dog of the South*, 14.	
85	**my reading:** Portis, *Dog of the South*, 11.	
85	**at least forty:** Portis, *Dog of the South*, 25.	
85	**It wasn't my car:** Portis, *Dog of the South*, 25.	
85	**because at that:** Portis, *Dog of the South*, 28.	
85	**around ninety:** Portis, *Dog of the South*, 44.	
85	**Candy wrappers:** Portis, *Dog of the South*, 44.	
85	**If some burglar:** Portis, *Dog of the South*, 26.	
85	***I will be out*:** Portis, *Dog of the South*, 24.	
85	**good job with:** Portis, *Dog of the South*, 26.	
85	**I was furious:** Portis, *Dog of the South*, 27.	
85	**knocked around in:** Portis, *Dog of the South*, 179.	
86	**Why would I want:** Portis, *Dog of the South*, 180–81.	
86	**happy domestic:** Portis, *Dog of the South*, 252.	
86	**world's number one:** Portis, *Dog of the South*, 208.	
86	**I can read:** Portis, *Dog of the South*, 15.	
86	**prodigies of:** Portis, *Dog of the South*, 115.	
86	**I was always good:** Portis, *Dog of the South*, 165.	
86	**keep an eye:** Portis, *Dog of the South*, 228.	
87	**look after:** Portis, *Dog of the South*, 195.	
87	**lie down, against:** Portis, *Dog of the South*, 207.	

87	**I was lying:** Portis, *Dog of the South*, 208.	
87	**Send him to Dean:** Portis, *Dog of the South*, 193.	
87	**Two of my rules:** Portis, *Dog of the South*, 14.	
87	**weekly embraces:** Portis, *Dog of the South*, 24.	
88	**Then I saw:** Portis, *Dog of the South*, 244.	
88	**cuties:** Portis, *Dog of the South*, 54.	
88	**squeezing:** Portis, *Dog of the South*, 193.	
88	**to football games:** Portis, *Dog of the South*, 256.	
88	**We reaffirmed our:** Portis, *Dog of the South*, 254.	
88	**very exciting:** Portis, *Dog of the South*, 256.	
88	**well worth looking:** Portis, *Dog of the South*, 149.	
88	**when I withdrew:** Portis, *Dog of the South*, 30.	
88	**great captains:** Portis, *Dog of the South*, 10.	
88	**nature's tricks:** Portis, *Dog of the South*, 30.	
88	**Topology!:** Portis, *Dog of the South*, 30.	
88	**Strength of materials!:** Portis, *Dog of the South*, 50, 89.	
89	**very exciting and:** Portis, *Dog of the South*, 256.	
89	**plate tectonics:** Portis, *Dog of the South*, 256.	
89	**city obstruction:** Portis, *Dog of the South*, 26.	
89	**big red-faced men:** Portis, *Dog of the South*, 26.	
89	**I didn't go after:** Portis, *Dog of the South*, 256.	
89	**biding my time:** Portis, *Dog of the South*, 9.	
89	**great Cortez:** Portis, *Dog of the South*, 42.	
89	**get up and walk:** Portis, *Dog of the South*, 10.	
89	**the great captains:** Portis, *Dog of the South*, 10.	
89	**the most depraved:** Portis, "Combinations of Jacksons," 200.	
90	**Then I saw:** Portis, *Dog of the South*, 244.	
91	**the Gauchos also:** Charles Darwin, *The Voyage of the Beagle*, in *"The Origin of Species" and "The Voyage of the Beagle"* (New York: Everyman's Library, 2003), 206. *The Voyage of the Beagle* was first published in 1839.	
91	*Dusicyon australis*: Barry Holstun Lopez, *Of Wolves and Men* (New York: Charles Scribner's Sons, 1978), 18.	
91	**great Humboldt:** Portis, *Dog of the South*, 117.	
92	**strange birds:** Portis, *Dog of the South*, 79.	
92	**What a life!:** Portis, *Dog of the South*, 47.	
92	**shot the cows:** Portis, *Dog of the South*, 248.	
92	**Motor Ranch:** Portis, *Dog of the South*, 187.	

92	**squealed and buzzed:**	Portis, *Dog of the South*, 144.
92	**some shell-pocked:**	Portis, *Dog of the South*, 60.
93	**the great Cortez:**	Portis, *Dog of the South*, 42.
93	**the orchidean beauty:**	William Carlos Williams, "The Destruction of Tenochtitlan," in *In the American Grain*, 27.
93	**superbly suited:**	Williams, "The Destruction of Tenochtitlan," 27.
93	**full of gentleness:**	Portis, "The Destruction of Tenochtitlan" 31.
93	**suave personality:**	Portis, "The Destruction of Tenochtitlan," 35.
93	**tact:**	Portis, "The Destruction of Tenochtitlan," 34.
93	**declare himself:**	Portis, "The Destruction of Tenochtitlan," 31.

5. "AMERICAN PYTHAGORAS": MASTERS OF ATLANTIS

95	**a little gray book:**	Portis, *Masters of Atlantis*, 2.
95	**the secret wisdom:**	Portis, *Masters of Atlantis*, 2.
95	**the first modern Master:**	Portis, *Masters of Atlantis*, 2.
96	**Entered Apprentice:**	Portis, *Masters of Atlantis*, 2.
96	**Night of Figs:**	Portis, *Masters of Atlantis*, 3.
96	**Night of Utter Silence:**	Portis, *Masters of Atlantis*, 3–4.
96	**ancient words:**	Portis, *Masters of Atlantis*, 4.
96	**secret books:**	Portis, *Masters of Atlantis*, 4.
96	**torpedoed or lost:**	Portis, *Masters of Atlantis*, 4.
96	**because he, Lamar:**	Portis, *Masters of Atlantis*, 4.
96	**read strange books:**	Portis, *Masters of Atlantis*, 6.
96	**apt pupil:**	Portis, *Masters of Atlantis*, 11.
96	**Villa Hen:**	Portis, *Masters of Atlantis*, 11.
96	**talked far into:**	Portis, *Masters of Atlantis*, 6.
97	**faithful enough:**	Portis, *True Grit*, 42.
97	**true account:**	Portis, *True Grit*, 224.
97	**marvelous stuff:**	Portis, *Masters of Atlantis*, 10.
97	**I can't make:**	Portis, *Masters of Atlantis*, 10.
97	**Keeper of the Botanical:**	Portis, *Masters of Atlantis*, 6. Portis the voracious reader shows signs here of having done some homework, though he plays very loose with its results. The Argotti Botanical Gardens in Floriana, just outside Valletta, originated in the eighteenth century as the private gardens of Manuel Pinto da Fonseca, grand master of the Order of Saint John from 1741 until his death in 1773. Another grand master! Pinto also crossed paths

with Giuseppe Balsamo (1743–1795), the alchemical con artist better known as Cagliostro. Portis tosses all these titles and orders and aliases into his Malta scene, listing Balsamo/Cagliostro with Pythagoras and Cornelius Agrippa (1486–1535) as Masters of the nonexistent Gnomon Society. Finally, Jimmerson's meeting with the secretary of the "Grand Master of the Knights of St. John of Jerusalem" (Portis, *Masters of Atlantis*, 5) would have been with an underling of one of several revived Saint John orders (the Sovereign Military Order of Malta, the Order of Saint John, the Most Venerable Order of Saint John, and perhaps others), as the original "of Jerusalem" outfit was evicted by Napoléon following his conquest of Malta in 1798.

97 **behind the giant:** Portis, *Masters of Atlantis*, 10.
97 **he was under:** Portis, *Masters of Atlantis*, 12.
97 **knew in his heart:** Portis, *Masters of Atlantis*, 13.
97 **Can't you see it**: Portis, *Masters of Atlantis*, 13.
97 **Hierophant of Atlantis:** Portis, *Masters of Atlantis*, 13.
98 **his Gnomon Temple:** Portis, *Masters of Atlantis*, 16.
98 **very famous members:** Portis, *Masters of Atlantis*, 18. Portis alters the society's name from Hermetic Order of the Golden Dawn to Golden Order of the Hermetic Dawn.
98 **working out of Chicago:** Portis, *Masters of Atlantis*, 17.
98 **make a good:** Portis, *Masters of Atlantis*, 16.
98 **Odd Birds of Illinois:** Portis, *Masters of Atlantis*, 19.
98 **worthy few:** Portis, *Masters of Atlantis*, 19.
98 **even bagged a new:** Portis, *Masters of Atlantis*, 20.
98 **courses in accounting:** Portis, *Masters of Atlantis*, 22.
99 **now had time:** Portis, *Masters of Atlantis*, 22.
99 **By the summer:** Portis, *Masters of Atlantis*, 22.
99 **a mansion:** Portis, *Masters of Atlantis*, 24.
99 **private secretary:** Portis, *Masters of Atlantis*, 127.
99 **in his sly mode:** Portis, *Masters of Atlantis*, 133.
99–100 **a prose narrative:** Randall Jarrell, "An Unread Book," introduction to *The Man Who Loved Children*, by Christina Stead (New York: Picador, 2001), xl. Jarrell's introduction originally appeared in the 1965 reissue edition of Stead's 1940 novel.
100 **I can see Uranus:** Portis, *Dog of the South*, 15.
100 **unfortunate name:** Portis, *Masters of Atlantis*, 213.

100	**gateway claims:** Portis, *Dog of the South*, 22.
100	**approaches to this:** Portis, *Masters of Atlantis*, 260.
100	**tell us of his:** Portis, *Masters of Atlantis*, 260–61.
100	**fraternal:** Portis, *Masters of Atlantis*, 25.
100	**T.W.K.:** Portis, *Masters of Atlantis*, 29.
100	**Those Who Know:** Portis, *Masters of Atlantis*, 29.
101	**The Olmecs didn't:** Portis, *Gringos*, 115.
101	***'l maestro di color:*** Dante, *Inferno*, 4:131.
101	**Dante the exile:** *"Tu proverai sì come sa di sale / lo pane altrui, e come è duro calle / lo scendere e 'l salir per l'altrui scale."* (You will taste the salt / in others' bread, and know hard / ups and downs on others' stairs.) Dante, *Paradiso*, 17:58–60; my translation. References are to canto and line.
101	**I've always had:** Portis, *Gringos*, 95.
102	**mucous track:** Portis, *Dog of the South*, 131.
102	**fresh, green breast:** F. Scott Fitzgerald, *The Great Gatsby* (1925; repr., New York: Collier Books / Macmillan, 1992), 189.
102	**smoldering mattress:** Portis, *Norwood*, 96.
102	**hippie wagon:** Portis, *Dog of the South*, 47.
102	**utterly lifeless:** Portis, *Masters of Atlantis*, 69.
102	**bog:** Portis, "I Don't Talk Service," 166.
103	**deadpan manner:** Tartt, "On *True Grit*," 347.
103	**cosmos:** Dana Stevens, *Camera Man: Buster Keaton, the Dawn of Cinema, and the Invention of the Twentieth Century* (New York: Atria Books, 2022), 136.
103	**essential solitude:** Stevens, *Camera Man*, 104.
103	**solitary as a snake:** Portis, *Gringos*, 126.
104	***Even Animals near:*** Sir Thomas Browne, *The Garden of Cyrus, or the Quincunciall, Lozenge, or Net-work Planations of the Ancients, Artificially, Naturally, Mystically Considered*, in *Hydriotaphia* [. . .] *Together with The Garden of Cyrus* [. . .] (London, 1658), chap. 3, para. 61, https://penelope.uchicago.edu/gardennoframes/garden3.xhtml.
104	**Quincuncial order:** Browne, *Garden of Cyrus*, chap. 3, para. 12.
104	**The way the study:** Rosenbaum, "Of Gnats and Men."
106	**the way the mind:** Rosenbaum, "Of Gnats and Men."
106	**three-wheel motorcycle:** Portis, *Dog of the South*, 158.
106	**aimless trek:** Portis, *Dog of the South*, 10.

106	**be on the ground:** Portis, *Dog of the South*, 218.
106	**tiny girl:** Portis, *Dog of the South*, 29.
106	**narrow plot where we:** Dante, *Paradiso*, 22:151; my translation.
107	**I could be content:** Sir Thomas Browne, *Religio Medici and Urne-Burial*, ed. Stephen Greenblatt and Ramie Targoff (New York: New York Review Books, 2012), 78.
107	**Lo the bat:** William Blake, "An Island in the Moon," in *The Complete Writings of William Blake*, ed. Geoffrey Keynes (London: Oxford University Press, 1966), 54.
107	**Kiss my Roman Anus:** Blake, "Island in the Moon," 54.
107–8	**Hawking and spitting:** Portis, *Dog of the South*, 125.
108	**The sun came up:** Portis, *Dog of the South*, 84.
108	**an ordinary turd:** Portis, *Dog of the South*, 58.
108	**Hen furioso:** Portis, *Masters of Atlantis*, 41.
108	**It's the House:** Portis, *Masters of Atlantis*, 206.
108	**the only begetter:** Portis, *Masters of Atlantis*, 262.
108	**Professors Duncan:** The faculty at the time featured other pedagogical stalwarts, but Eaves and Kimpel were true stars, the former a world-class madcap raconteur and the latter still the most deeply learned human I've encountered. There are good entries for both Eaves and Kimpel in the online CALS Encyclopedia of Arkansas. For Eaves, see https://encyclopediaofarkansas.net/entries/thomas-cary-duncan-eaves-8730/. For Kimpel, see https://encyclopediaofarkansas.net/entries/ben-drew-kimpel-1688/.
108	**mail boy:** Portis, *Masters of Atlantis*, 26.
108	**new probationary:** Portis, *Masters of Atlantis*, 29.
108	**simplified version:** Portis, *Masters of Atlantis*, 28.
108	**in comic dialogues:** Portis, *Masters of Atlantis*, 31.
108	**thousands of new members:** Portis, *Masters of Atlantis*, 31.
108	**paid companion:** Portis, *Masters of Atlantis*, 33.
109	**rocked the Gnomon:** Portis, *Masters of Atlantis*, 34.
109	**Grand Prior of World:** Portis, *Masters of Atlantis*, 34.
109	**charter:** Portis, *Masters of Atlantis*, 35.
109	**strong stuff too:** Portis, *Masters of Atlantis*, 35.
109	**Jimmerson school:** Portis, *Masters of Atlantis*, 36.
109	**First came the Gnomon:** Portis, *Masters of Atlantis*, 38.
109	**rallied to the colors:** Portis, *Masters of Atlantis*, 38.

109	**winning the war:** Portis, *Masters of Atlantis*, 39.
109	**courtesy call:** Portis, *Masters of Atlantis*, 39.
109	**cut the ground:** Portis, *Masters of Atlantis*, 41.
109	**Rod of Correction:** Porits, *Masters of Atlantis*, 45.
110	**three-day Gnomonic:** Portis, *Masters of Atlantis*, 60.
110	**completed the triangle:** Portis, *Masters of Atlantis*, 60.
110	**New Croton:** Portis, *Masters of Atlantis*, 61.
110	**thirty push-ups:** Portis, *Dog of the South*, 177.
110	**an imperial quart:** Portis, *Masters of Atlantis*, 61.
110	**the joys of:** Portis, *Masters of Atlantis*, 121.
110	**He had prepared:** Portis, *Masters of Atlantis*, 121.
110	**ignored, written off:** Portis, *Masters of Atlantis*, 122.
110	**You're a back number:** Portis, *Masters of Atlantis*, 122.
110	**current male:** Portis, *Masters of Atlantis*, 62.
110	**heroic bust:** Portis, *Masters of Atlantis*, 125.
111	**Public service:** Portis, *Masters of Atlantis*, 148.
111	***boktos*:** Portis, *Masters of Atlantis*, 39.
111	**Banco Plan:** Portis, *Masters of Atlantis*, 74.
111	**writer "Dub" Polton:** The fictional Polton bears a striking resemblance to folklorist and hack writer Vance Randolph (1892–1980), who turned out scores of books and booklets for everything from university presses to Haldeman-Julius's Little Blue Books series under at least twelve names other than his own. Star Portis champion and editor Jay Jennings may be right to observe that Arkansas is "not a fundamental part of the imaginative world" (introduction to Portis, *Escape Velocity*, xiv) of Portis's novels, but the Olmec aesthetic at the heart of his practice is worth recalling. He buries his art, and Arkansas is often a barely subterranean presence. There's Hot Springs' IQ Zoo in *Norwood*, T. Texas Tyler of Mena in *The Dog of the South*, Texarkana's Grim Hotel in *Delray's New Moon* (it's in Texas but right off State Line Avenue), and perhaps Vance Randolph of Eureka Springs and Fayetteville in *Masters of Atlantis*. Perhaps. Like the one to *Dusicyon australis*, this reference can't be nailed down. Portis sometimes kept company in Little Rock with fellow author Dee Brown, a great admirer of Randolph's hack-writing virtuosity. The biographer itches to go looking, but he's staying cuffed. I'm like Keats, content with half knowledge, the blessing

of every "fine isolated verisimilitude." (This from the deservedly famed 1817 "Negative Capability" letter to his brothers.) John Keats, *Selected Letters* (Oxford: Oxford University Press, 2002), 42.

111 **very exclusive lawyers':** Portis, *Masters of Atlantis*, 166.
111 **family memoir:** Portis, *Masters of Atlantis*, 149.
111 **rejected all suggestions:** Portis, *Masters of Atlantis*, 158
112 **sacred macaws:** Portis, *Masters of Atlantis*, 161.
112 **widely accepted:** Portis, *Masters of Atlantis*, 162.
112 **campaign biography:** Portis, *Masters of Atlantis*, 150.
112 **far too many:** Portis, *Masters of Atlantis*, 182.
112 **drowsy:** Portis, *Masters of Atlantis*, 178.
112 **unexpected guest:** Portis, *Masters of Atlantis*, 181.
112 **U.S. Attorney:** Portis, *Masters of Atlantis*, 181.
112 **glee club:** Portis, *Masters of Atlantis*, 182.
112 **good many stanzas:** Portis, *Masters of Atlantis*, 183.
112 **long line of beaters:** Portis, *Masters of Atlantis*, 185.
112 **burrow:** Portis, *Masters of Atlantis*, 186.
113 **Hen, an envious:** Portis, *Masters of Atlantis*, 263.
113–14 **Don't you recall:** Portis, *Masters of Atlantis*, 40.
114 **the first modern Master:** Portis, *Masters of Atlantis*, 2.
114 **keen interest:** Portis, *Masters of Atlantis*, 2.
115 **Go to Bucharest:** Portis, *Masters of Atlantis*, 53.
115 **Tiwanaku or Tihuanacu:** Student Joaquín Gavilano made the Tiwanaku site the subject of his in-class presentation. My subsequent investigations were prompted by his research.
115 **the one who claims:** Portis, *Masters of Atlantis*, 254.
115 **Fu-Sang theory:** For a readable if somewhat dated survey of these controversies, see Robert Wauchope, *Lost Tribes and Sunken Continents* (Chicago: University of Chicago Press, 1962). For the Fu-Sang theory and the French conference, see pp. 29, 90–91, and 97–102.
115 **Dr. Richard Flandin's:** Portis, *Gringos*, 205.
115 **Where are you from:** Portis, *Masters of Atlantis*, 104.
116 **routinely questioned:** For Ota Benga, see Pamela Newkirk, *Spectacle: The Astonishing Life of Ota Benga* (New York: Amistad, 2016). For Ishi, see *Ishi: The Last Yahi*, produced and directed by Jed Riffe (Jed Riffe Films, 1992).
116 **animal show:** Portis, *Norwood*, 136.
116 **alligator boy:** Portis, "Damn!," 151.

116	**left-wing women:** Portis, *Masters of Atlantis*, 270.	
116	**small cart:** Portis, *Masters of Atlantis*, 204.	
116	**my own copy:** Portis, *Dog of the South*, 256.	
117	**Even the wretched:** Portis, *Dog of the South*, 115.	
117	**Japanese puppet theater:** Portis, *Masters of Atlantis*, 190.	
117	**spotty:** Portis, *Masters of Atlantis*, 190.	
117	**a dispirited lot:** Portis, *Masters of Atlantis*, 75.	
117	**about on foot:** Portis, *Masters of Atlantis*, 232.	
117	**the poetry of Mu!:** Portis, *Masters of Atlantis*, 104.	
118	**Do you know what's:** Portis, *Masters of Atlantis*, 237.	
118	**ESTRAGON: *(anxious)*:** Samuel Beckett, *Waiting for Godot* (New York: Grove Press, 1954), 13a–13b.	
118	**the Sholto Business:** Portis, *Masters of Atlantis*, 219.	
118	**sand and gravel:** Portis, *Masters of Atlantis*, 220.	
119	**hospital for poor:** Portis, *Masters of Atlantis*, 252.	
119	**swaggering moron:** Portis, *Masters of Atlantis*, 216.	
119	**Pythagoras would:** Portis, *Masters of Atlantis*, 290.	
119	**American Pythagoras:** Portis, *Masters of Atlantis*, 253.	
119	**magisterial feet:** Portis, *Masters of Atlantis*, 289.	
119	***voci soave*:** Dante, *Inferno* 4:114. The phrase translates as "soothing voices."	
119	***prato di fresca verdure*:** Dante, *Inferno* 4:111. The phrase translates as "fresh green meadow."	
120	**big bull roach:** Portis, *Masters of Atlantis*, 231.	
120	**urban tramp:** Portis, *Masters of Atlantis*, 269.	
120	**red silk peeling:** Portis, *Masters of Atlantis*, 209.	
120	**Gnomon pamphlets:** Portis, *Masters of Atlantis*, 195.	
120	**He turned in impatience:** Portis, *Masters of Atlantis*, 10.	
120	**a gift for hopeful:** Portis, *Masters of Atlantis*, 211.	
120	**Suddenly I remembered:** Portis, *Masters of Atlantis*, 214.	
120	**I sounded Mr. Moaler:** Portis, *Masters of Atlantis*, 217.	
121	**little notice was taken:** Portis, *Masters of Atlantis*, 30.	
121	**He thought we were:** Portis, *Masters of Atlantis*, 215.	
121	**security chief:** Portis, *Masters of Atlantis*, 251.	
121	**second-class bus:** Portis, *Masters of Atlantis*, 287.	
121	**announcement to make:** Portis, *Masters of Atlantis*, 304.	
121	**Ed told Whit:** Portis, *Masters of Atlantis*, 307.	
122	**the two Masters:** Portis, *Masters of Atlantis*, 309.	

122	**rustling noise:** Portis, *Masters of Atlantis*, 312.
122	**interesting announcement:** Portis, *Masters of Atlantis*, 304.
122	**a magnificent new:** Portis, *Masters of Atlantis*, 312.
122	**top of the line:** Portis, *Masters of Atlantis*, 312.
122	**Another trailer!:** Portis, *Masters of Atlantis*, 312.
122	**He had often:** Portis, *Masters of Atlantis*, 313.
122	**exultant, foaming:** Portis, *Masters of Atlantis*, 313.
123	*avec l'esprit le plus*: Voltaire, *Candide et autres contes, II* (Paris: Gallimard, 1992), 9.
123	*Cela et bien dit*: Voltaire, *Candide*, 108.
123	**It's study for me:** Portis, *Masters of Atlantis*, 313.
123	**This is the best:** Portis, *Masters of Atlantis*, 313.

6. THE HAUNTED MAN'S REPORT: *GRINGOS*

125	**I'll bust your head:** Portis, *Norwood*, 186.
126	**the correct path:** Portis, *Gringos*, 30.
126	**the bullet department:** Portis, *True Grit*, 157.
126	**rabbit face:** Portis, *Gringos*, 31.
126	**Blue Sheets:** Portis, *Gringos*, 30.
126	**A Mexican truck driver:** Portis, *Dog of the South*, 86.
127	**could deliver babies:** Portis, *Gringos*, 96–97.
127	**Soledad had a gift:** Portis, *Gringos*, 97.
127	**We went ahead:** Portis, *Gringos*, 305.
127	**Nardo knew the ropes:** Portis, *Gringos*, 266.
127	*gringo of goodwill*: Portis, *Dog of the South*, 42.
127	**ornament of our:** Portis, "Combinations of Jacksons," 200.
127	**program of moral:** Portis, *Gringos*, 13.
127	**to be more considerate:** Portis, *Gringos*, 15.
128	**a small Mixtec:** Portis, *Gringos*, 278.
128	**boxes of relics:** Portis, *Gringos*, 277.
128	**amateur Mayanist:** Portis, *Gringos*, 278.
128	**going out at night:** Portis, *Gringos*, 320.
128	**faithful enough:** Portis, *True Grit*, 42.
128	**geocentric:** Portis, *Gringos*, 52.
128	**In my cosmology:** Portis, *Gringos*, 52.
128–29	**It was a visceral:** Portis, *Gringos*, 52.
129	**nowhere else:** Portis, *Gringos*, 52.

129	**Nor had I ever:** Portis, *Gringos*, 54.
129	**a mystery under:** Portis, *Gringos*, 223.
129	**a small reddish dog:** Portis, *Gringos*, 140.
129	**space dwarfs:** Portis, *Gringos*, 51.
129	**astroport:** Portis, *Gringos*, 60.
129	**Still:** Portis, *Gringos*, 52.
129–30	**Rudy was serious:** Portis, *Gringos*, 53.
130	**Some of it would:** Portis, *Gringos*, 88–89.
130	**Nobody can do:** Portis, *Gringos*, 95.
130	**some useful new:** Portis, *Gringos*, 89.
130	**hot shots:** Portis, *Gringos*, 53.
130	**didn't even take:** Portis, *Gringos*, 98.
130	**His crank claims:** Portis, *Gringos*, 99.
130–31	**I stood aside:** Portis, *Gringos*, 269.
131	**The back of his neck:** Portis, *Gringos*, 271.
133	**lack of delicacy:** Portis, *Gringos*, 13.
133	**cold look:** Portis, *Gringos*, 15.
133	**green figs:** Portis, *Gringos*, 19.
133	**They were out there:** Portis, *Gringos*, 20.
133	**Don't you wish:** Portis, *Gringos*, 20.
133	**You say that:** Portis, *Gringos*, 20.
133	**Here was another:** Portis, *Gringos*, 285.
134	**Come and see my:** Edna St. Vincent Millay, "Second Fig," line 2, in *The Selected Poetry of Edna St. Vincent Millay*, ed. Nancy Milford (New York: Modern Library, 2002), 49.
134	**The wonderful moist:** D. H. Lawrence, "Figs," line 16, in *The Works of D. H. Lawrence* (Hertfordshire, UK: Wordsworth Editions, 1994), 222.
134	**sitting in the crotch:** Sylvia Plath, *The Bell Jar* (New York: Harper Perennial, 2005), 77.
134	**Be kind and courteous:** William Shakespeare, *A Midsummer Night's Dream*, act 3, sc. 1, line 170.
134	**What was this weakness:** Portis, *Gringos*, 285.
134	**weekly embraces:** Portis, *Dog of the South*, 24.
134	**crystal-pure:** Portis, *Gringos*, 306.
134	**Crock-Pot and:** Portis, *Gringos*, 285.
135	**sandy ringlets:** Portis, *Gringos*, 284. The ringlets are "blond" on p. 75 and unmodified on p. 273.

135	**We didn't get:**	Portis, *Gringos*, 287.
135	**It was surprising:**	Portis, *Gringos*, 305.
135	**She had thought:**	Portis, *Gringos*, 320.
135	**I feared debt:**	Portis, *Gringos*, 320.
135	**We'll cut three:**	Portis, *Gringos*, 312.
135	**Interest, he called it:**	Portis, *Gringos*, 311.
135	**The fever:**	Portis, *Gringos*, 311.
135–36	**But you ain't coming:**	Portis, *Gringos*, 315–16.
136	**Green, see, the color:**	Portis, *Gringos*, 41.
136	**at a creep:**	Portis, *Gringos*, 319.
136	**I ain't got paper:**	Portis, *Gringos*, 314.
136	**only lighted box:**	Portis, *Gringos*, 319.
136	**The coffee:**	Portis, *Gringos*, 319.
136	**a better plan:**	Portis, *Gringos*, 320.
136	**twenty-five feet deep:**	Portis, *Gringos*, 115.
137	**nothing but trash:**	Portis, *Dog of the South*, 184.
137	**a good salesman:**	Portis, *Gringos*, 157.
137	**salesmanship school:**	Portis, *Gringos*, 157.
137	**It was true:**	Portis, *Gringos*, 117.
137	**Someone was:**	Portis, *Gringos*, 268.
138	**Yes, a strange:**	Portis, *Gringos*, 255.
138	**Hand me an axe:**	Keneva Kunz, ed. and trans., *The Saga of the Greenlanders*, in *The Vinland Sagas* (New York: Penguin, 1997), 19.
139	**birds without nests:**	Portis, *Gringos*, 35.
139	**We are weaker:**	Portis, *Dog of the South*, 157.
139	**My true name is *Balam*:**	Portis, *Gringos*, 246. Portis's prodigious reading had by this time managed to include the *Popol Vuh* or at least one of the Chilam Balam books. A much-praised translation of the former by Dennis Tedlock was published in 1985, and Munro S. Edmundson produced translations of *The Book Chilam Balam of Tizimin* in 1982 (published as *The Ancient Future of the Itza*) and *The Book of Chilam Balam of Chumayel* (published as *Heaven Born Merida and Its Destiny*) in 1986. *Gringos* was published in 1991.
139–40	**sagging yellow pouches:**	Portis, *Gringos*, 244.
140	**hairy white belly:**	Portis, *Gringos*, 245.
140	**The *yanquis* took:**	Portis, *Gringos*, 128.
140	**The password tonight:**	Portis, *Gringos*, 237.
140	**the great Cortez:**	Portis, *Dog of the South*, 42.

NOTES

140   **I'll gladly, myself:** Henrik Ibsen, "To My Friend the Revolutionary Orator," in *Ibsen's Poems*, trans. John Northam (Oslo: Norwegian University Press, 1986), 95.
140   **last *entrada*:** Portis, *Gringos*, 179.
140   **without reservation:** Portis, *Gringos*, 205.
141   **I want that animal:** Portis, *Gringos*, 26.
141   **And cut his throat!:** Portis, *Gringos*, 26.
142   **out of the game:** Portis, *Gringos*, 17.
142   ***schatzgraber*:** Portis, *Gringos*, 276.
142   **cut three quick:** Portis, *Gringos*, 312.
142   **long tan coats:** Portis, *Gringos*, 153.
142   **I told him I wouldn't:** Portis, *Gringos*, 316.
143   **Louise was a good:** Portis, *Gringos*, 13.
143   **my cakes:** Portis, *Gringos*, 21.
143   **two buckets of fresh:** Portis, *Gringos*, 35.
143   **nick:** Portis, *Gringos*, 50.
143   **That's what your strap:** Portis, *Gringos*, 50.
143   **so fast I couldn't:** Portis, *Gringos*, 78.
144   **Once a month:** Portis, *Gringos*, 82.
144   **having no idea:** Portis, *Gringos*, 82.
144   **a member of:** Portis, *Gringos*, 103.
144   **I think they must:** Portis, *Gringos*, 103.
144   **Mott and I paid:** Portis, *Gringos*, 103.
144   **a government clerk:** Portis, *Gringos*, 118.
145   **and had been hanging:** *Gringos*, 294.
145   **May I relate:** Portis, *Gringos*, 294.
145   **It seems to me:** Portis, *Gringos*, 294.
145   **shining androids:** Portis, *Gringos*, 295.
145   **in on the judge:** Portis, *Norwood*, 161.

7. "A BRIEF REPRIEVE": *DELRAY'S NEW MOON*

147   **Mostly they're glad:** Portis, "I Don't Talk Service," 167.
147   **I told Neap:** Portis, "I Don't Talk Service," 167.
147   **My house is sinking:** Portis, "I Don't Talk Service," 166.
147   **had something wrong:** Portis, "I Don't Talk Service," 167.
147   **a fugitive from:** Portis, "I Don't Talk Service," 168.
147   **were going all the way:** Portis, "I Don't Talk Service," 169.

147	**talking service coast:** Portis, "I Don't Talk Service," 167.
147	**a nut ward:** Portis, "I Don't Talk Service," 168.
148	**We were burying:** Charles Portis, "That New Sound from Nashville," in *Escape Velocity*, 85.
148	**Disaster and sudden:** Portis, "That New Sound," 85.
148	**Orange, Texas:** Orange is the county seat of Orange County, Texas.
148	**I told him I had:** Portis, "I Don't Talk Service," 166.
148	**I don't talk service:** Portis, "I Don't Talk Service," 166.
148	**Neap said it was Dill:** Portis, "I Don't Talk Service," 168–69.
148	**retrospect:** Samuel Beckett, *Krapp's Last Tape and Other Dramatic Pieces* (New York: Grove Press, 1960), 16.
148	**Be again, be again:** Beckett, *Krapp's Last Tape*, 26–27.
148	**How come he got:** Portis, "I Don't Talk Service," 169.
149	**sit in the dark:** Portis, "I Don't Talk Service," 167.
149	**you must let:** Portis, *Gringos*, 294.
149	**I wanted to have:** Portis, "I Don't Talk Service," 169.
149	**mud flat:** Portis, "I Don't Talk Service," 169.
150	**For a long time:** Portis, "I Don't Talk Service," 169.
150	**a brave and handsome:** Portis, *Delray's New Moon*, 218.
151	*just off the highway*: Portis, *Delray's New Moon*, 207.
151	*outdoor sign*: Portis, *Delray's New Moon*, 207.
151	*life-size cardboard*: Portis, *Delray's New Moon*, 207.
151	**night club history:** Portis, *Delray's New Moon*, 233.
151	**very smart supper:** Portis, *Delray's New Moon*, 232.
151	**My vision is national:** Portis, *Delray's New Moon*, 233.
151	**highly select guests:** Portis, *Delray's New Moon*, 233.
152	**where diners could sit:** David Hill, *The Vapors: A Southern Family, the New York Mob, and the Rise and Fall of Hot Springs, America's Forgotten Capital of Vice* (New York: Farrar, Straus and Giroux, 2020), 231.
152	**hydraulic stage:** Hill, *The Vapors*, 231. Hot Springs gambling tycoon Dane Harris's plan for the Vapors (opened in 1960) was every bit as "national" as Delray's—he envisioned Hot Springs as a southern Las Vegas. Hill's book is a deeply researched survey of the whole scene.
152	**love child:** Portis, *Delray's New Moon*, 256.
152	**Receiving and:** Portis, *Delray's New Moon*, 255.
152	**Special Value Package:** Portis, *Delray's New Moon*, 221.

152	**There's always room:** Portis, *Delray's New Moon*, 229.
152	**No waiting list:** Portis, *Delray's New Moon*, 229.
152	**That won't do me:** Portis, *Delray's New Moon*, 220.
152	**the radiant Miss:** Portis, *Delray's New Moon*, 213.
153	**Police Detective:** Portis, *Delray's New Moon*, 205.
153	**four or five morons:** Portis, *Delray's New Moon*, 241.
154	**hang a placard:** Portis, *Delray's New Moon*, 246.
154	**They sometimes wake:** Portis, *Delray's New Moon*, 246.
154	**New Concept:** Portis, *Delray's New Moon*, 244.
154	**I wonder how:** Portis, *Delray's New Moon*, 245.
154	**One flat fee up front:** Portis, *Delray's New Moon*, 221.
154	**Fast turnaround:** Portis, *Delray's New Moon*, 245.
154	**Who would do:** Portis, *Delray's New Moon*, 245.
154	**A foul lump:** Portis, *Delray's New Moon*, 245.
154	**likes to have:** Portis, *Delray's New Moon*, 255.
154	**The great advantages:** Portis, *Delray's New Moon*, 255.
154	**Don't you have:** Portis, *Delray's New Moon*, 218.
154	**See?:** Portis, *Delray's New Moon*, 244.
154	***Stunned:*** Portis, *Delray's New Moon*, 274.
155	**Poor old Blanche:** Portis, *Delray's New Moon*, 274.
155	**She was all wore:** Portis, *Delray's New Moon*, 274.
155	***shipping tags:*** Portis, *Delray's New Moon*, 264.
155	**People don't know:** Portis, *Delray's New Moon*, 264.
155	**veterans' hospital:** Portis, *Delray's New Moon*, 264.
155	**bathrobe vapors:** Portis, *Delray's New Moon*, 264.
155	**Bus station air:** Portis, *Delray's New Moon*, 266.
155	**the air in your:** Portis, *Delray's New Moon*, 266.
155	**stagnant:** Portis, *Delray's New Moon*, 266.
155	**never parted:** Portis, *Delray's New Moon*, 266.
155	**over there in:** Portis, *Delray's New Moon*, 229.
156	**He's got Delray:** Portis, *Delray's New Moon*, 277.
156	**This must be Garland:** Portis, *Delray's New Moon*, 277.
156	**I don't know about this:** Portis, *Delray's New Moon*, 277.
156	**Garland will do:** Portis, *Delray's New Moon*, 277.
156	**Tell him I'd rather:** Portis, *Delray's New Moon*, 282.
156	**She's with Mr. Ramp:** Portis, *Delray's New Moon*, 278.
156–57	**y'all will laugh:** Portis, *Delray's New Moon*, 278.
157	**Tell Eula:** Portis, *Delray's New Moon*, 279.

NOTES

157	**You have my promise:**	Portis, *Delray's New Moon*, 279.
157	**wonderful companion:**	Portis, *Delray's New Moon*, 279.
157	**The dance floor isn't:**	Portis, *Delray's New Moon*, 280.
157	**Tell her I accept:**	Portis, *Delray's New Moon*, 281.
157	**I relinquish all:**	Portis, *Delray's New Moon*, 281.
157	**It's the miracle:**	Portis, *Delray's New Moon*, 281.
157	**I don't know about that:**	Portis, *Delray's New Moon*, 281.
157	**Executive clemency:**	Portis, *Delray's New Moon*, 281.
157	**He's up!:**	Portis, *Delray's New Moon*, 282.
158	**Now she's taken:**	Portis, *Delray's New Moon*, 282.
158	**Is she radiant?:**	Portis, *Delray's New Moon*, 282.
158	**Her cheeks are rosy:**	Portis, *Delray's New Moon*, 282.
158	**Already they're:**	Portis, *Delray's New Moon*, 282.
158	**Here they come:**	Portis, *Delray's New Moon*, 282.
158	**his red vinegar:**	Portis, *Delray's New Moon*, 230.
158	**Avedon photographs:**	Richard Avedon and James Baldwin, *Nothing Personal* (New York: Atheneum, 1964).
158–59	**We'll just be sitting:**	Portis, *Delray's New Moon*, 247–48.
159	**an old 'tourist court':**	Portis, "Motel Life, Lower Reaches," 134.
159	**sharp practice:**	Portis, "Motel Life, Lower Reaches," 134.
159	**unprecedented gesture:**	Portis, "Motel Life, Lower Reaches," 136.
159	**We did have:**	Portis, *Delray's New Moon*, 247.
159	**go for price:**	Portis, "Motel Life, Lower Reaches," 134.
159	**frills:**	Portis, "Motel Life, Lower Reaches," 134.
160	**How could you reckon:**	Portis, "Motel Life, Lower Reaches," 134.
160	**every square inch:**	Portis, *Dog of the South*, 20.
160	**very persuasive:**	Portis, *Dog of the South*, 115.
160	**a Satanic note:**	Portis, *Dog of the South*, 116.
160	**I couldn't work it:**	Portis, *Dog of the South*, 115.
160	**I could see myself:**	Portis, "Combinations of Jacksons," 200.
160	**delight value:**	Portis, "Motel Life, Lower Reaches," 134.
160	**little announcement:**	Charles Portis, "The Wind Bloweth Where It Listeth," in *Escape Velocity*, 177.
160	**pick of the litter:**	Portis, "Wind Bloweth," 176.
161	**Something further:**	Melville, *The Confidence-Man*, 251.
161	**We may have:**	Portis, "Wind Bloweth," 177.
161	**indulgent:**	Portis, *Gringos*, 305.
161	**They'll put you in:**	Portis, *Norwood*, 85.

161	**There it is:** "There it is" sticks in the head as just one of *Dispatches'* summary takeaways. Another "haunted man's report." See Michael Herr, *Dispatches* (New York: Avon, 1978), 254.
161	**I could find no:** Portis, "Motel Life," 148.
161	**Things disappear:** Portis, "Motel Life," 148.
161	**clean, new, modern:** Portis, "Motel Life," 148.
161	**of sly or rat-like:** Portis, "Motel Life," 148.
161	**genuine felons:** Portis, "Motel Life," 142.
161	**pretty close to that ideal:** Portis, "Motel Life," 148.
161	**Something felt wrong:** Portis, "Motel Life," 148.
161–62	**the very *carpet*:** Portis, "Motel Life," 148.
162	**I didn't get it:** Portis, "Motel Life," 148.
162	**I cleared out:** Portis, "Motel Life," 148.
162	**I had to get on with:** Portis, *Dog of the South*, 11.
162	**Hard worker. Solitary:** Portis, *Gringos*, 126.
162	**film version:** *I Don't Talk Service No More*, directed by Katrina Whalen, posted August 25, 2013, Vimeo video, 9:52, https://main.oxfordamerican.org/item/882-bold-talk.
163	**Blood was roaring:** Portis, *Gringos*, 30.
163	**narrow plot:** Dante, *Paradiso*, 22:151; my translation.

SUGGESTED ARTICLES, PROFILES, REVIEWS

Boyle, Brian. "*Masters of Atlantis* Is Essential Reading for the QAnon Age." *Slate*, December 31, 2020. https://slate.com/culture/2020/12/masters-of-atlantis-qanon-conspiracy-theories-comedians.html.

Brazzel, Kyle. "Appreciating Charles Portis." *Awl*, May 18, 2016. https://www.theawl.com/2016/05/appreciating-charles-portis/.

Brummett, John. "A Worthy Hero." *Arkansas Democrat-Gazette*, February 20, 2020. https://www.nwaonline.com/news/2020/feb/20/a-worthy-hero-20200220/.

Cep, Casey. "Oddballs and Odysseys." *New Yorker*, April 17, 2023.

Cline, Julie. "A Portis Reader." *Los Angeles Review of Books*, September 2, 2011. https://lareviewofbooks.org/article/a-portis-reader/.

Daigrepont, Lloyd M. "The Protestant Ethic and the Spirit of Capitalism in *True Grit*: The Lovelorn Character of Mattie Ross." *Western Literature* 50, no. 2 (Summer 2015): 105–17.

Dumas, Ernie. "The Jell-o Rule." *Oxford American*, February 28, 2020. https://oxfordamerican.org/web-only/the-jell-o-rule.

Gilbreath, Aaron. "A String of Maybes: Speculating the Elusive Charles Portis." *Gettysburg Review* 24, no. 2 (Summer 2011): 315–28.

Gold, Glen David. "The Lure of the Oeuthre: On Charles Portis and Flannery O'Connor." *Los Angeles Review of Books*, November 18, 2012. https://lareviewofbooks.org/article/the-lure-of-the-oeuthre-on-charles-portis-and-flannery-oconnor/.

Greenbaum, Abigail. "A Comedy of Extinction: 'True Grit,' 'Gringos,' and 'Masters of Atlantis' by Charles Portis." *Southern Literary Review*, June 6, 2011. https://southernlitreview.com/reviews/charles-portis-collection-ideal-fathers-day-gift.htm.

Heard, Alex. "Portishead: The Literary Genius of Charles Portis." *New Republic*, October 7, 2012. https://newrepublic.com/article/108232/charles-portis-escape-velocity-true-grit.

Horton, Kaleb. "The American Anthropology of Charles Portis." *Slate*, February 20, 2020. https://slate.com/culture/2020/02/charles-portis-obit-true-grit-norwood-masters-atlantis-gringos.html.

Jennings, Jay. "Charles Portis, a Journalist with True Grit." *Daily Beast*, September 25, 2012. Last modified July 14, 2017. https://www.thedailybeast.com/charles-portis-a-journalist-with-true-grit.

———. "On the Trail of 'True Grit': A Tale Comes to Life." *New York Times*, July 20, 2014. https://www.nytimes.com/2014/07/20/travel/on-the-trail-of-true-grit-a-tale-comes-to-life.html.

Lyster, Rosa. "On the Alert for Omens: Rereading Charles Portis." *Paris Review*, December 1, 2021. https://www.theparisreview.org/blog/2021/12/01/on-the-alert-for-omens-reading-charles-portis/.

McGrath, Charles. "True Grit, Odd Wit: And Fame? No, Thanks." *New York Times*, December 20, 2010. https://www.nytimes.com/2010/12/20/books/20portis.html.

Nelson, Elizabeth. "Pure Nitro: 40 Years of Charles Portis's Comic Masterpiece 'The Dog of the South.'" *Ringer*, February 1, 2019. https://www.theringer.com/2019/2/1/18206096/charles-portis-bill-hader-dog-of-the-south-novel.

Park, Ed. "Like Cormac McCarthy, But Funny." *Believer*, March 1, 2003. https://www.thebeliever.net/like-cormac-mccarthy-but-funny/.

Phillips, Brian. "Charles Portis's Celebration of the Absurd." *Ringer*, April 28, 2020. https://www.theringer.com/2020/4/28/21239287/ringer-reads-charles-portis-norwood-true-grit.

Rosenbaum, Ron. "Of Gnats and Men: A New Reading of Portis." *Observer*, May 24, 1999. https://observer.com/1999/05/of-gnats-and-men-a-new-reading-of-portis/.

———. "Our Least-Known Great Novelist." *Esquire*, January 1998.

Rosenberg, Jacob. "Nothing Makes Sense Except Charles Portis." *Mother Jones*, February 21, 2020. https://www.motherjones.com/media/2020/02/nothing-makes-sense-except-charles-portis/.

Stephenson, Will. "Signs and Wonders: Charles Portis and the Art of Getting Out in Time." *Harper's*, April 2023.

Tartt, Donna. "Donna Tartt on the Singular Voice, and Pungent Humor, of Charles Portis." *New York Times*, June 9, 2020. https://www.nytimes.com/2020/06/09/books/charles-portis-true-grit-dog-of-the-south-gringos-masters-of-atlantis.html.

Tower, Wells. "What Charles Portis Taught Us." *New Yorker*, February 20, 2020. https://www.newyorker.com/culture/postscript/what-charles-portis-taught-us.

Watson, Cary. "Masters of Atlantis (1983) by Charles Portis." *Jettison Cocoon* (blog), April 30, 2013. http://www.jettisoncocoon.ca/2013/04/masters-of-atlantis-1983-by-charles.html.

Wolfe, Tom. *The New Journalism* (New York: Harper and Row, 1973).

INDEX

Page locators in *italics* refer to figures.

A

accommodation. *See* charity/consideration
Acheron, 155
Acuff, Roy, 148
Adler, Lou, 8
Adonis myth, 136
Aeneas, 96
agápē, 33–34. *See also* charity/consideration
Agrippa, Heinrich Cornelius, 113
airplane travel, 7, 9–10, 18, 69, 145
Albany Movement, 9–10, 19
Allen, Ralph Waldo, 19–20
Allied Expeditionary Force, 56
American Expeditionary Forces, 95
American Legion, 56, 149, 162
Anderson, David, 6
animals: alligators, 73, 116; bats, 71, 107; Cape buffalo, 129, 138; cockfighting, 4, 9; horses/mules, viii, 46–50, 54, 60, 68, 76, 92, 130; insects, 84, 104, 106, 129; lions/tigers/jaguars, 5–6, 18, 129; livestock, *32*, 34, 80, 92, 141, 143; macaws, 112; monkeys, *114*, 159; performing chickens, 31–36, *32*, 41–43, 61, 92, 100, 116, 152; snakes, 53, 71, 133; talking blue jay, 92, 108, 140. *See also Dusicyon australis*
April Fools' Day, 31

Archimedes, 113
Argosy (magazine), 71
Ariosto, Ludovico, 108
Aristotle, 101
Arkansas Gazette, 4–5, 7–8, 10, 20–21, 39, 72
Arkansas Traveler, 1–3, 36
Atlantean myth, 114–15, 117. *See also Masters of Atlantis*
Atlantic Monthly, 147
Atlantis: The Antediluvian World (Donnelly), 114
Auschwitz, 154
"Auto Odyssey through Darkest Baja, An" (Portis), 39, 126–27
Avedon, Richard, 158
Azazel, 141
Aztec Empire, 93, 111

B

"back-to-Africa" movement, 7, 9
Bakker, Tammy Faye, 74
Banks, Nathaniel P., 3, 38
"Because" (song), 134
Beckett, Samuel, x, xii, 66, 117–19, 148
Benga, Ota, *114*, 116
Berryman, John, xi
bildungsroman, 36, 84
biography genre, x–xi, 111–12, 145–46, 160–61
"Bird Brain" exhibits, 33

"Birmingham Bargaining Before Watchful World" (Portis), 11, 14
"Birmingham Peace: An Omen" (Portis), 14
Birmingham riots, 9, 11–14, 16
Blake, Eugene Carson, 17
Blake, William, 103–4, 107–8, 118
Blavatsky, Helena, 113
Blood Meridian (McCarthy), 92
Blount, Roy, Jr., vii–viii
Boat, The (film), 149
bodily secretions/slime, 2, 72–73, 92, 102
Bonar, Kent, xiii
Bowery Boys (series), 31
Bragg, Braxton, 73
Brando, Marlon, 17
Bread Loaf (retreat), 79
Brecht, Bertolt, 67, 113
Breland, Keller and Marian, *32*, 33
British Museum, 110
Bronx Zoo, 116
Brown, Dee, 195
Browne, Thomas, 103–7, *105*, 108, 113
Bunyan, John, 108
Burroughs, Edgar Rice, 81
bus travel: in *Delray's New Moon*, 152, 155; in *The Dog of the South*, 23, 77, 87, 101, 106; in *Masters of Atlantis*, 121; in *Norwood*, 22–25, 29–30, 33–35, 43, 134

C –

Cagliostro, Alessandro, 113
"Call for a White Boycott Menaces Racial Accord" (Portis), 13
Camp Lejeune, 29–30, 33, 55
Camp Pendleton, 13

Camus, Albert, 20
Candide (Voltaire), 122–23
Captain Ahab, 60
Cassady, Neal, 77
Cervantes, Miguel de, vii
charity/consideration: in *Gringos*, 39, 64, 123, 127, 131, 133, 136–38, 142–45; vs. grit, 61–62, 163; in *Masters of Atlantis*, 10, 95, 121–23; in *Norwood*, 10, 31, 33–36, 39, 43, 61, 64, 123, 136, 145
Charon, 155
Chaucer, Geoffrey, 73, 75
Cherokee Nation, 47, 49, 54
Choctaw Nation, 49
cholera, 52
churches/Christian precepts: church burnings, 19; Communism and, 3; evangelical hucksters, 74–76, 98–99; miracles and, 157; missionary work, 80–83, 102; Puritan self-reliance, 60; tent meetings, 72, 91; Westminster Confession of Faith, 80–81. *See also* charity/consideration; effectual calling; scripture
Churchill, Randolph, 21
Churchward, James, 115
circuses, 22, 30–31, 38, 52, 73, 116
Cirque d'Hiver Bouglione, 30, 38
Civil Rights Act (1957), 19
civil rights movement: Albany Movement, 9–10, 19; Birmingham riots, 9, 11–14, 16; Ku Klux Klan activities, 5, 13–14, 16–18; March on Washington, 17–18; Medgar Evers assassination/Jackson violence, 5, 9, 15–18, 31,

145–46; Tuscaloosa integration efforts, 9, 14–15; voter registration, 19–20
Civil War, ix, 3, 38–39, 52, 55–57, 66, 68, 73–74
Cleveland, Grover, 3
Coen brothers, 45
Cole, James "Catfish," 14
Coleridge, Samuel Taylor, 108
colonialism/neocolonialism: Indigenous peoples and, 115, 138–40, *139*, 142; Portis's subplots and, 84, 90, 93, 115–16, 131, 162; religion/effectual calling and, 80–83, 92–93, 116, 142; symbols/signals of, 91, 102. *See also* conquistadors; *Dusicyon australis*; racism/bigotry
"Combinations of Jacksons" (Portis), 35, 39, 68, 127, 159–60
Commedia (Dante), 53–54, 101, 103, 106
Communism, 2–3, 113
Confidence-Man, The (Melville), 31, 73–74, 161
con men. *See* reprobates
Connor, Eugene "Bull," 11–13, 15
conquistadors, 69, 83, 89, 92–93, 102, 106, 140, 142. *See also* colonialism/neocolonialism
Conrad, Joseph, 84
Cooper, James Fenimore, 60
Cops (film), 103, 106
Cortés, Hernán, 89, 92–93, 140
country music, 41, 147–48
Creek Indians, 52
Critias (Plato), 114
Croesus, 38
Cromwell, Oliver, 37
Crowley, Aleister, 113
Cuyahoga River fire, viii, 102

D

"Damn!" (Portis), 21–23, 116
dancing, 57, 66, 88–89, 142, 151–52, *153*, 157
Dante Alighieri, 53–54, 70, 96, 101, 103, 106, 117–19, 163
Darwin, Charles, 91, 106, 113
Davis, Jefferson, 73–74
Debtor to the Law, A (film), 54
De La Beckwith, Byron, 5
DeLillo, Don, vii, 160
Delray's New Moon (Portis): "brief reprieve" in, 156–58, 160–62; food in, 29, 152, 155, 159; nadir in, 71, 154–55; setting/characters of, 150–53; threatened protagonist in, 152, 154–56, 158–59; vehicle maintenance/wrecks in, 14, 152; villainous character in, 102, 152, 154, 158–59; women's presence in, 154, 156, 159
Dembo, Joe, 8
Democritus, 77, 101
De Soto, Hernando, 69
Díaz del Castillo, Bernal, 89
Díaz Romero, Belisario, 115
Dickens, Charles, 73
Dies Committee, 113
direct address, 145
Dog of the South, The (Portis): authorial impishness in, 25, 55–56, 116; Browne as epigraph to, 104–7, 113; charity/consideration in, 10, 39; Civil War references in, 3, 38, 55–56, 66, 68, 73–74; class hierarchies in, 74, 79–80, 126–27;

Dog of the South, The (Portis) (*continued*)
colonialism critiqued in, 80–84, 90–93, 102, 116, 139; Dix's salesman manual in, 23, 73, 76–78, 101, 137, 160; *Dusicyon australis* in, 90–93, *90*, 100, 102, 112, 138; "FLORR"/nadir in, 70–72, 74–75, 77–78, 88–90, 117; food in, 29, 69–71, 74, 80, 84–86, 88; "gringo of goodwill" in, 82, 116, 127; hapless/bookish protagonist in, 45, 55, 65–68, 84–90, 101, 116–17, 123, 162; happy domestic setting in, 83–84, 86; highbrow citations in, 107–8, 117; "horde control" in, 79–80, 92, 158; humor/gags in, vii–viii, xi, 64, 67–68, 100; vs. other Portis novels, 65–67, 89, 93, 100, 116–17, 131; out-and-back journey in, 49, 64, 69–70, 89–90; plot/subplot in, 64, 84, 90, 93, 140–41; Polton/writers in, 48, 73, 76–77, 79–80, 100, 111–12, 116; "ranchettes" in, vii–viii, 27, 60, 67, 149; "Skraelings" in, 80, 91–92, 100–102, 106, 112, 127; statics vs. dynamics in, 88–90, 103–6; "strange birds" in, 84, 92–93; Symes as reprobate in, 25, 37, 64, 71–76, 82, 100, 106–7, 110–11, 149–50, 154, 158; vehicle maintenance/wrecks in, 14, 65, 67, 70–71, 74–75, 83, 87, 126; "weekly embraces" in, viii, 87–88, 134

Donald Duck, 28
Donnelly, Ignatius, 114
draft dodging, 25, 79, 110

"Dream Song" (Berryman), xi
Dumas, Ernest, 8
Durango Kid, 27
Dusicyon australis (Falkland Islands wolf), 90–93, *90*, 100, 102, 112, 115, 134, 138, 140. *See also* colonialism/neocolonialism
dystopian visions, 80, 102, 116, 131, 154

E –

Early, Jubal Anderson, 56
East Louisiana State Mental Hospital, 158
Eaves, Duncan, 108
effectual calling (election), 46, 80–83, 92–93, 116, 127, 142
Eliot, T. S., 48
Elks, 17
Elvas account of De Soto, 69
Empedocles, 101
Entwicklungsroman, 36
environmental disasters, viii, 102, *103*
Ephron, Nora, vii
Erik the Red's Saga, 102
Escape Velocity (Portis), ix, xi, 5–6
Esther Greenwood, 134
Euclid, 95
Euripides, 113
Euro-American entrada, 116, 138–41
Evers, Medgar, 5, 9, 15–16, 146
Evers-Williams, Myrlie, 15

F –

"Fall of the House of Usher, The" (Poe), 108
Faubus, Orval, 18
Federalist Papers, The, 17
"Figs" (Lawrence), 134

"Fingal" (Beckett), 118–19
"Fires of Hate in Jackson" (Portis), 16–18, 31
"First Fig" (Millay), 134
Flanagan, Hallie, 113
Fludd, Robert, 113
flu epidemic (1918), 52
food: bacon, 62; berries/melons, 27, 69–70, 74, 80, 134; fish fry, 34, 37, 61, 123; green figs/pomegranates, *132*, 133–36, 144; pizza/sandwiches/tortillas, 30, 84, 86, 155; shrimp, 88, 143; sweets, 85, 137, 142–44, 152, 159; vegetables, 29, 34, 110, 122
"Forgotten River, The" (Portis), 68–69, 158, 161
Forrest, Nathan Bedford, 56
Fort Chaffee, 36
Fort Smith, 39, 49–50, 52
forty-niners, 142
Fox Company (US Marines), 147–49
Freeman, Douglas Southall, x
Freemasons, 96
Frizzell, William Orville "Lefty," 48
"From West Point to Far East—Taps" (Portis), 18–19
Fucci, Vanni, 53
funerals/graves, 4, 18–19, 136, 144, 146, 150, *151*, 162
Fu-Sang theory, 115, 117, 130, 140

G –

Gallesio, Giorgio, *132*
García Márquez, Gabriel, vii
Garden of Cyrus, The (Browne), 104–7, *105*, 113
Garvey, Marcus, 7, 9
Gibran, Kahlil, 29

"gnomon"/"gnomic," 96–97. *See also Masters of Atlantis*
Gogol, Nikolai, vii
Goldman, Peter, 8
Gould, Jay, 50
Grace Abounding to the Chief of Sinners (Bunyan), 108
Grant, Ulysses S., 38
Great Depression, 99, 107, 109, 117, 151
Great Newspaper Strike, 18
Gringos (Portis): affable/self-sufficient protagonist in, 46, 101, 103, 125, 127–28, 137, 140, 142–45, 159, 162; antiquities theft in, 125–28, 135, 142; authorial impishness in, 25, 56, 67, 144; charity/consideration in, 39, 64, 123, 127, 131, 133, 136–38, 142–45; colonialism critiqued in, 138–41; Dan as reprobate in, 26, 72, 102, 131, 138–41, 159, 163; domestic accord in, 42, 134–36, 142, 144, 160–62; epistemological questions in, 64, 101, 115, 126, 128–30, 140, 145; figs/pomegranates in, *132*, 133–36, 144; "haunted man" in, 145–46, 149; highbrow citations in, 101, 108; lawyer in, xiii, 112, 127, 137, 140; military service talk in, 38, 56–57, 125–26, 128, 133, 144–46, 149; vs. other Portis texts, 60, 73, 93, 104, 107, 125–26, 131, 140; sales defended in, 126, 136–38; scholars critiqued in, xiii, 112, 126, 130, 143; upbeat ending of, 142–44, 150; vehicle maintenance/wrecks in, 125, 143;

Gringos (Portis) (*continued*)
  women's presence in, 97, 127, 133–36, 142–44, 156
grit (character trait), 43, 49–50, 57–62, 118, 163
Grit (newspaper), 31
Guthridge, Amis, 11
Gwaltney, Francis Irby, 5

H
Hakluyt, Richard, 69
Haley, William J., 12
Hamlet (Shakespeare), 48–49, 69
Handbook of Texas, 22
hangings and hangmen, 13, 50–52, *51*, 58, 61–62
happy interludes/domestic settings, 35, 42–43, 83–84, 86, 134–36, 142, 149, 156–57
Hayes, Rutherford B., 50, 78
Heart of Darkness (Conrad), 84
Heifetz, Jascha, xi
Helen, 67
Heraclitus, 101, 119
Hermes Trismegistus, 113–14
Hermetic Order of the Golden Dawn, 98
hippies, 71, 83, 102, 117, 125–26, 137, 139, 162
Hitler, Adolf, 25, 78
Homer and Jethro, 5
homophobia, 83
Hood, James A., 14–15
"How the Night Exploded into Terror" (Portis), 11–14, 17
Huck Finn, 60
Humbert Humbert, 26
Humboldt, Alexander von, 91

Hustead, Ted, 151
Huxley, Aldous, 80

I
Iago, 25
Ibsen, Henrik, 140
Icelandic sagas, 91, 102, 106, 138
"I Don't Talk Service No More" (Portis), 38, 56, 102, 119, 147–50, 162
"Imaginary Poll Divulges Opinions on Integration" (Portis), 2
Indigenous peoples: colonial enterprise and, 115, 138–39, *139*, 140, 142; in *Masters of Atlantis*, 115–17, 121; in *True Grit*, 47, 49, 52, 54. *See also* "Skraelings"
Inferno (Dante), 53–54, 101
In the American Grain (Williams), 60, 93
IQ Zoo, 31–33, *32*, 152
Ishi (Yahi Indian), 116
Island in the Moon, An (Blake), 107, 118

J
Jackson, Thomas Jonathan "Stonewall," 3, 38, 73
Jackson civil rights violence, 9, 15–18, 31, 146
Jackson *Clarion-Ledger*, 5
James, Frank, 52, 58
Jarrell, Randall, 99–100
Jefferson, Thomas, x
Jennings, Jay, ix, 195
Johnston, Albert Sidney, 73
journalistic writings (Portis): on Alabama civil rights efforts, 9, 11–16; on Albany Movement

INDEX   217

(Georgia), 9–10, 19; college features/early sketches, 1–6, 36, 39, 131, 162; at *Herald Tribune*, 4–6, 10, 18, 21, 91; on Klan rally, 13–14, 16–18; on Medgar Evers assassination, 5, 9, 15–18, 31, 145–46; Our Town column, 4–5, 10, 21, 39; personal component in, 18–20; salary for, 45; on women's peace march, 5–7, 9
"Journey of the Magi" (Eliot), 48
Joyce, James, x, 35, 112
jurisprudence/legal system, 54, 59, 63–64, 112

K –

Katzenbach, Nicholas, 15
Keaton, Buster, ix, 60, 103, 106, 149
Keats, John, 195–96
Keeley, Leslie E., 74, *75*
Kennedy, John F., 6, 13
kēryx (herald), 157
Kesey, Ken, 84
Kimpel, Ben, 108
King, Martin Luther, Jr., 11, 13, 18
King James Bible, 54
Kiss, Edmund, 115
"Klan Rally—Just Talk" (Portis), 13–14, 16–18
Korean War, 13, 24, 55–57, 126, 145, 150, *151*, 162
Krapp's Last Tape (Beckett), 118, 148
Kroeber, Alfred, 116
Ku Klux Klan, 5, 13–14, 16–18

L –

Ladies Garment Workers, 17
La Vita Nuova (Dante), 103

Lawrence, D. H., 60, 134
Law West of Fort Smith (Shirley), 50, 52–54
Leatherstocking Tales (Cooper), 60
Lee, Robert E., ix, x, 73
Legion Hut, 89
Leibniz, Gottfried Wilhelm, 113
Leopold Bloom, 35
Let's Find Out (radio program), 7–9, 17
Library of America, ix–x, 16
Life (magazine), 2, 14, 146
Life of Nelson (Southey), 116
Lincoln, Abraham, 20
Lingo, Al, 11–12
literary criticism, xi, 23, 59, 141
Little, Malcolm. *See* X, Malcolm
Lolita, 25
longshoreman/lion story, 5–6, 18
Lopez, Barry, 91
Lost Cause, The (Pollard), 56
Lost Continent of Mu, The (Churchward), 115
Louisiana Hayride (radio/TV show), 42
Luce, Clare Boothe, 2, 131
Luce, Henry, 1–2, 6, 131
Luftwaffe, 109

M –

MacLeish, Archibald, 19
Madison, James, 69
Mahone, William, ix
Malcolm X, 7–10, 17
Malcolm, Janet, x, 112
Maledon, George, 50–52, *51*
Malone, Dumas, x
Malone, Vivian Juanita, 14–15

Malraux, André, 20
Malvolio, 162
Manifest Destiny, 92
Mann Act (1910), 27
Man's Fate (Malraux), 20
Manson, Charles, 26, 125
"Marchers: Blueprint for Protest, The" (Portis), 17–18
March on Washington, 17–18
Marlboro Man, viii
Marlowe, Christopher, 113
Marshall, George C., 109–10
Massachusetts Bay Colony, 138, *139*
Masters of Atlantis (Portis): ancient text in, 77, 95–99, 114; Atlantean myth in, 114–15, 117; authorial impishness in, 24–25, 99–100, 107, 113, 116; charity/consideration in, 10, 95, 121–23; colonialism critiqued in, 93, 115–16, 123, 162; credulous/bookish protagonist in, 23, 45, 77, 95–97, 113, 117, 123, 125, 128, 131; epistemological questions in, 76, 78, 96–97, 99, 104, 110, 115; female caregiver in, 97–98, 109, 117, 121, 156; food in, 110, 122; Gnomon Society/"Masters" in, xii, xiii, 56, 95–101, 108–11, 114, 118–22; highbrow citations in, 107–8, 113–15, 117–19; lawyers in, 3, 64, 111–12, 126; military service talk in, 56, 95, 109, 111; occult in, 104, 109, 113–15, 117, 120; "odd birds" in, xii, 98, 101, 109, 113, 130; vs. other Portis texts, 73, 100, 104, 116–17; plot/subplot in, 140–41; Popper as reprobate in, 25, 108–13; talking blue jay in, 92, 108, 140; "Those Who Know" in, 96, 100–101, 106, 119; upbeat ending of, 117, 119–23, 125, 150

Mather, Cotton, 80
Mauretania (ship), 21
Mayan ruins, 83–84, 125, 127–30, 135, 142
Mayflower, 140
McCarthy, Cormac, ix, 92
Mead, Margaret, 8, 10
medical quackery, vii, 22, 25, 72–74, *75*, 110, 149, 158
Melville, Herman, vii, 31, 60, 73–74, 100, 146, 161
Memphis *Commercial Appeal*, 4
Mencken, H. L., 1
Menelaus, 67
Mennonites, 137
Meriwether, Jack, 72
Merriam-Webster, 140
Metro-Goldwyn-Mayer (MGM), 31
Mexican-American War, 92
Mexican Revolution, 92–93
Midsummer Night's Dream, A (Shakespeare), 134
military "talk service": in *Gringos*, 38, 56–57, 125–26, 128, 133, 144–46, 149; in "I Don't Talk Service No More," 38, 56, 102, 119, 147–50, 162; in *Masters of Atlantis*, 56, 95, 109, 111; in *Norwood*, 55, 57, 125–26, 149; Portis as "haunted man," 145–46, 160–63; Portis's Marine background, 5, 13, 19–20, 56–57, 126, 150, *151*, 162; in *True Grit*, 55–56, 149
Millay, Edna St. Vincent, 134
Milton, John, 25, 70

Missouri, Kansas and Texas Railway Company, 49–50
Montezuma II, 93, 140
Moore, Jamie, 12
More Pricks Than Kicks (Beckett), 118–19
Morton, Thomas, 162
Moscow State Circus, 30, 38
Moses, 96
"Motel Life, Lower Reaches" (Portis), 56, 159, 161–62
Mr. Peanut, 28, 41
Mrs. Grundy, 162
Muhammad, Elijah, 9
"Murder in Mississippi" (Portis), 15
museums, 90–91, *90*, 110, *114*, 115–16

N–

Nabokov, Vladimir, 26
nadir/underworld: in *Delray's New Moon*, 71, 154–55; in *The Dog of the South*, 70–72, 74–75, 77–78, 88–90, 117; environmental disaster and, 102–3; in *Norwood*, 28–29, 71, 102; in Portis's short texts, 149–50, 161–62; in *True Grit*, 53–54, 71
Nation of Islam, 7–8, 116
Natty Bumppo, 60
Natural History Museum (London), 91
Nazism, 17–18, 25, 115, 154
"New Englander on Mission in Georgia" (Portis), 19–20
New Journalism, 5, 8
Newton, Isaac, 113
New Yorker, 33
New York Herald Tribune, 4–6, 10, 13, 17–18, 21, 91, 162

New York Telephone Company boiler explosion, 6, 18, 146
New York Times, 6, 45
"Nights Can Turn Cool in Viborra" (Portis), 158
Noah's Ark, 140
Northwest Arkansas Times, 2–4
Norton Anthology of English Literature, 104
Norwood (Portis): authorial impishness in, xi, 36–37, 64; bus-ride courtship in, 29–30, 33, 37, 42–43, 134, 136, 156; charity/consideration in, 10, 31, 33–36, 39, 43, 61, 64, 123, 136, 145; food in, 29–30, 34, 37, 61, 123; Fring as reprobate in, 25–26, 31, 36–38, 41–42; happy interlude in, 34–35, 83, 119, 123, 162; historical/cultural citations in, 3, 25, 28, 31, 38, 78, 81, 161; homecoming narrative in, 34–36, 41–43, 49, 61, 89, *95*; Joann the Wonder Hen in, 30–31, 33–36, 41–43, 61, 92, 100, 116, 152; jobs/money in, 23, 25, 28, 35, 41–42, 131; military service talk in, 55, 57, 125–26, 149; nadir/underworld in, 28–29, 71, 102; narrative oddities/arc of, 22–25, 50; vs. other Portis novels, 60–62, 64–65, 67, 83, 89, 93; outbound journey in, 26–29, 49; protagonist's self-consciousness in, 46–48, 123; publication of, 21, 45, 104; racial/ethnic tags in, 27–28, 40–41, 52; triple rescues in, 29–34; vehicle maintenance/wrecks in, 23, 27–28, 34, 41

Nostradamus, 113
Noveltoons cartoons, 31
Nugget (magazine), 22
N-word, 2, 13, 40, 52, 72, 80, 84, 135

O –
Obregón, Álvaro, 93
occult, 104, 109, 113–15, 117, 120
Odysseus, 34, 42
"Of *TIME* and the River and Greasy Creek, Etc." (Portis), 1–2
Of Wolves and Men (Lopez), 91
"Old Time Religion" (song), 46–47
Ole Miss, 66, 68
Ominato, 56–57, 161–62
One Flew Over the Cuckoo's Nest (Kesey), 84
Orlando, Tony, 69
Orlando Furioso (Ariosto), 108
Otago Museum, *90*, 91
Otto Olaf bboggs, 66
outlaws. *See* reprobates

P –
Paley, Grace, 22
Pappus, 95
Paradiso (Dante), 106, 117
Pardoner, 73, 75
Park, Ed, viii–ix, 92
Parker, Isaac C., 50, 53–54, 59, 63
Pauline charity. *See* charity/consideration
Peace Corps, 83
peanuts/Jell-O/cookies, 70
Pearl Harbor, 109
Penelope, 34
Plath, Sylvia, 134
Plato, 114

Playboy, 22
Poe, Edgar Allan, 108
Pollard, Edward Alfred, 56
Pol Pot, 100
Pomona Italiana (Gallesio), *132*
Popol Vuh, 121
Portis, Charles McColl: author's graduate seminar on, xi–xii, *xii*, 87, 146; author's pull toward, xi–xiii; aversion to biography, x–xi, 111–12, 145–46, 160–61; calls for recognition of, vii–x; character sketches of, 7, 68, 72, 131, 137–38; comedic staples of, 2–3, 68, 159–60; deadpan tone of, 7, 138; gravestone of, 150, *151*; haunted "report" of, 145–46, 160–63; "impishness" of, 24–25; as "laconic cutup," 8–9, 14, 36–39, 55–57, 79, 90–91, 99–100, 106–7, 149–50, 153; military service of, 5, 13, 19–20, 56–57, 126, 150, *151*, 162; "Olmec aesthetic" of, 100–108, 119–20, 136, 163, 195; as omnivorous reader, 31, 69, 91, 100–101, 107–8, 113, 134; plots/subplots of, 93, 101–2, 115–16, 131, 136, 140–41, 146, 149–50, 158–63; treatment of race by, 2, 40–41, 52, 59. *See also* journalistic writings; *individual texts*
Posnansky, Arthur, 115
Prescott, William H., 89
Presley, Elvis, x, 4, 162
Price, Sterling, 55
Prophet, The (Gibran), 29
Proverbs, 54
Ptolemy, 95

Puritanism, 60
Pynchon, Thomas, vii
Pythagoras, 113–14, 119, 121, 130

R –

racism/bigotry, 25, 56–57, 59; "Asiatic," 158; "half-breed," 52, 59; human exhibitions, *114*, 115–16; "peckerwood," 27–28, 41; "redbone," 40–41; white supremacy, 80–84, 92, 115–16, 138–39, *139*, 142. *See also* civil rights movement; colonialism/neocolonialism; N-word; "Skraelings"
radical movement, 78–80, 116
Raines, J. G., 19
Randolph, Vance, 195
Ranjel, Rodrigo, 69
"Rare Specimen" (Portis), 4–5
Red River Arsenal, 36
Reed, Roy, 2–4, 7–8, 21
Religio Medici (Browne), 104
reprobates (con men/scam artists/outlaws): in *The Dog of the South*, vii, 25, 37, 64, 71–76, 82, 100, 106–7, 110–11, 149–50, 154, 158; in *Gringos*, 26, 72, 102, 131, 138–41, 159, 163; historical figures, 54, 58, 74–75, *75*, 92; in *Masters of Atlantis*, 25, 108–13; in *Norwood*, 25–26, 31, 36–38, 41–42; in *True Grit*, 48–49, 52–54, 58–59, 62–63
Reynolds, Debbie, 17
Rime of the Ancient Mariner, The (Coleridge), 108
Ripley's Believe It or Not! Odditorium, 28

Road Runner Show, The, 31, 100
Robinson, Marilynne, vii
Rockwell, George Lincoln, 17–18
Rockwell, Norman, 7
Roosevelt, Franklin D., 109–10
rootlessness/rootedness, 22–23, 42–43, 77, 106, 122–23, 135, 160
Rosenbaum, Ron, vii–viii, 104
Roth, Philip, x
Rules (restaurant), 38

S –

Saga of the Greenlanders, The, 102, 138
"Sahara of the Bozart, The" (Mencken), 1
sales: Dix's manual on, 23, 73, 76–78, 101, 137, 160; *Gringos*' positive portrayal of, 126, 136–38
Salinger (film), 9–10
Salinger, J. D., 7, 9–10
Sartre, Jean-Paul, 20, 70
Satan, 25
Saturday Evening Post, 21, 45, 147
scam artists. *See* reprobates
Schaefer, Jack, 60
schoolboy humor, 76, 100, 107, 116, 133
scripture, 16, 31, 33, 42, 46–47, 50, 54, 140–41. *See also* churches/Christian precepts
"Second Fig" (Millay), 134
segregation/integration. *See* civil rights movement
Semmes, Raphael, 55
Sermon on the Mount, 16
sex/eroticism, 107, *132*, 133–35
Shakespeare, William, 25, 48–49, 69, 77, 108, 134, 162

Shakespeare's Sonnets, 108
Shaw, Irwin, 2
Shelby, Joseph Orville, 56
Shirley, Glenn, 50, 52–54
Shuttlesworth, Fred, 11
silent film comedy, ix, 60, 103, 106, 149
"Skraelings," 80, 91–92, 100–102, 106, 112, 115, 127, 139–40, 142
Slovik, Eddie, 56
Smith, Al, 78
Smith, Ledger, 17
Southern Presbyterianism, 46
Southey, Robert, 116
Sovine, Woodrow Wilson "Red," 67
Spencer, John, 53
spirit world, 128–30, 145
Stafansky, Abe, 7
Starnes, Joe, 113
Starr, Henry, 54, 58
Steamboat Bill, Jr. (film), 149
Steinbeck, John, 2
Stevens, Dana, 103
Stevens, Wallace, xi
St. Louis Post-Dispatch, 8
stop-smoking story, 5, 18
Stuart, J. E. B., 56
Student Nonviolent Coordinating Committee (SNCC), 19–20
surnames, 7, 100, 116, 118, 123
Swaggart, Jimmy, 74
Swamp Fire (film), 81

T–

Tamerlane, 114
tape recorders, 68, 118, 148
Tartt, Donna, ix, 3, 45, 59–60, 103

Tarzan, 31, 81, 92, 100
Tarzan's New York Adventure (film), 31
Taylor, Zachary, 86
Telemachus, 42
Telluric Currents, xii–xiii, 98, 120, 122, 130, 146, 163
Thales, 119
"That New Sound from Nashville" (Portis), 147–48
Theosophical Society, 98
Thomas, Oldfield, 91
Thompson, Allen, 16
Tihuanacu, the Cradle of American Man (Posnansky), 115
Timaeus (Plato), 114
Time (magazine), 1–2, 131
Tisquantum/Squanto, 140
Tiwanaku/Tihuanacu, 115, 117
Tōjō, Hideki, 78
Train, William F., III, 18–20, 162
train travel, 24, 27, 49–50, 62
Trillin, Calvin, 33
True Grit (Portis): animal welfare in, 92, 130; audiobook/publication of, ix, 45, 59, 104; blood vengeance in, 48–50, 60, 126; "bullet department" in, 13, 55, 126; charity/consideration in, 39, 61–62; Civil War references in, 3, 38–39, 55; forceful protagonist of, 45–48, 57–62, 73, 128, 131; "grit" in, 43, 49–50, 57–62, 118; jurisprudence in, 54, 59, 63–64, 112; Mattie's voice/rhetoric in, 46–48, 63, 103, 111, 125; military service talk in, 55–56, 149; nadir/underworld in, 53–54, 71;

vs. other Portis novels, 49–50, 60–62, 64, 66, 93; outlaw/reprobate characters in, 26, 37, 53, 58–59, 61–63; scholarship on, xi, 36, 59; scrupulous historical research for, 24–25, 50–54, 78; truth questioned in, 63–64, 97, 128

truth/knowledge/wisdom questioned, 63–64, 73, 76–78, 95–97, 104, 110, 128–30

Twain, Mark, vii, 60, 73, 146

U –

Un-American Activities Committee, 113

United States v. Raines, 19

University of Alabama, 14–15

University of Arkansas, xi–xii, *xii*, 1, 66, 108, 145

US Marines: camps/bases, 22, 29–30, 33, 55, 79; Portis's past in, 5, 13, 19, 145, 150, *151*; Portis's writings about, 20, 22–23, 128, 147–50

US Military Academy (West Point), 18–20

US Navy, 57

USS *Panamint*, 57

US Supreme Court, 19, 54

Ute Indians, 115, 117

V –

Vapors (nightclub), 152, *153*

vehicle maintenance/wrecks: in *Delray's New Moon*, 14, 152; in *The Dog of the South*, 14, 65, 67, 70–71, 74–75, 83, 87, 102,
126; in *Gringos*, 125, 143; in *Norwood*, 23, 27–28, 34, 41; in Portis's short texts, 148, 160

Veterans Administration, 144

Veterans of Foreign Wars, 89

Vietnam War, 5, 18–19, 57

Villa, Pancho, 93

Vinland Sagas, 91, 102, 106, 138

Virgil, 96

Voltaire, 122–23

Voyage of the Beagle, The (Darwin), 91

W –

Wagner, Robert F., Jr., 17, 28, 78

Waiting for Godot (Beckett), 118–19

Wallace, George, 9, 15

Wall Drug, 151

Walter Draffin, 66

Wayne, John, 79

WCBS radio show, 7–9, 17

Weissmuller, Johnny, 31, 81

Welk, Lawrence, 162

Western Union, 38

Westminster Confession of Faith, 80–81

West Point (US Military Academy), 18–20

white phosphorus, 38, 133

"Who, What, When, Where" (Portis), 2

"Wild West" show, 61

Wilkins, Roy, 17

Williams, William Carlos, 60, 93

"Wind Bloweth Where It Listeth, The" (Portis), 158, 160–61

Wolfe, Tom, 2, 8–9, 36, 55

women's peace march, 5–7, 9

"words must fail" trope, 16–17

Wordsworth, William, 107–8
"World Is Too Much with Us, The" (Wordsworth), 107–8
World Wars I and II, 56–57, 99, 108–9, 112, 117, 119

X –
X, Malcolm, 7–10, 17

Y –
Yaddo (retreat), 79
"Young Dead Soldiers Do Not Speak, The" (MacLeish), 19
"Your Action Line" (Portis), 158

Z –
Zeno, 113